Tiny Worlds

Creative Macro Photography Skills

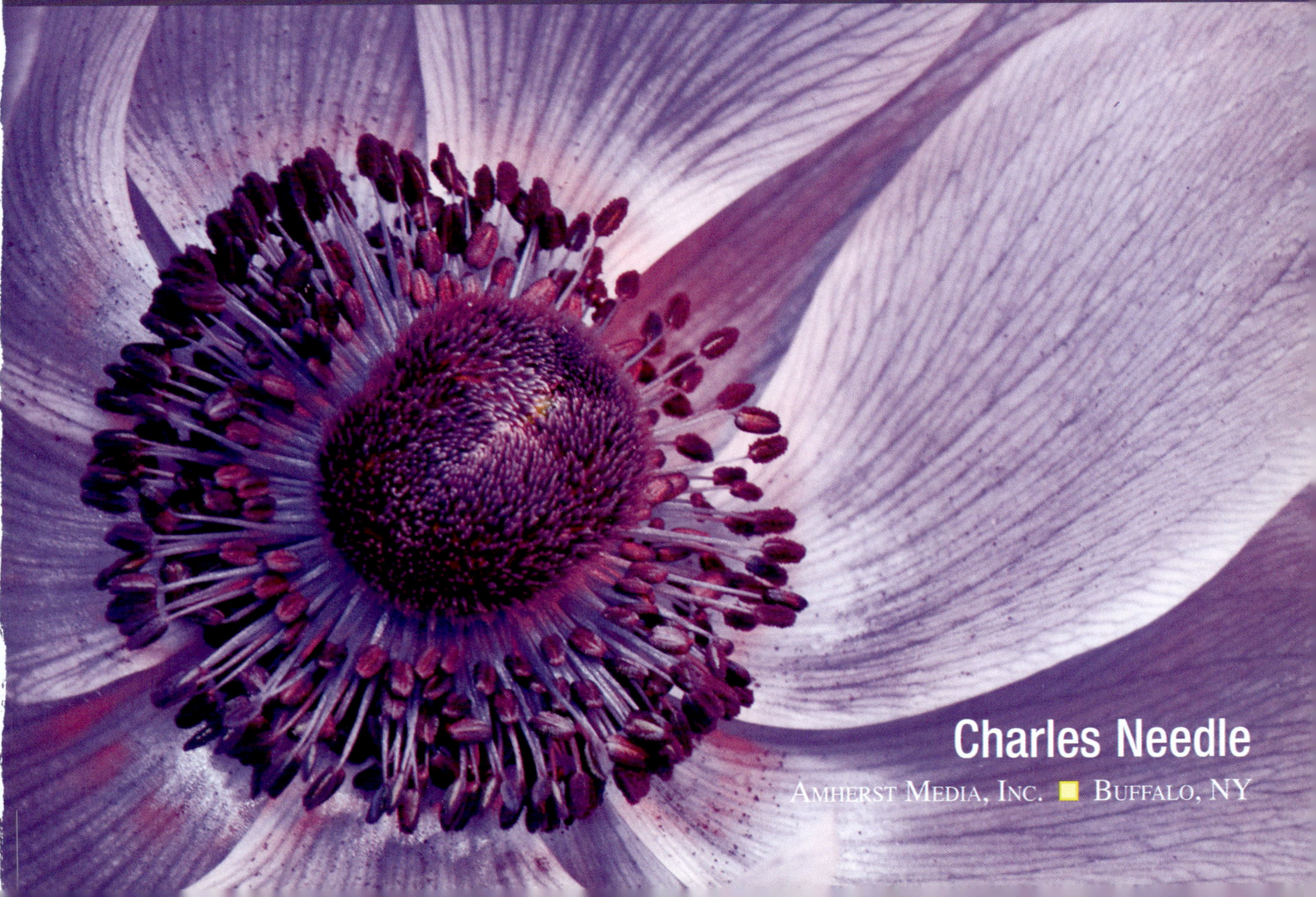

Charles Needle

AMHERST MEDIA, INC. ■ BUFFALO, NY

About the Author

Charles Needle is an award-winning, Seattle-based fine art nature photographer, author, and workshop leader with a unique eye for design and artistic interpretation. His popular "Art of Nature" creative macro photography workshops have attracted students nationwide. A FujiFilm USA Talent Team member and North American Nature Photography Association (NANPA) Showcase Award winner, Charles teaches over a dozen location workshops per year, including international destinations such as Canada, Holland, Great Britain, and Giverny, France with private access to Monet's Garden. Charles' photographs have been published in *Nature's Best* and *Outdoor Photographer* magazines and are in private and public collections nationwide and abroad. For a complete schedule of upcoming workshops and information on ordering fine art prints, visit www.charlesneedlephoto.com.

Charles Needle Photography
211 Kirkland Ave.
Suite 503
Kirkland, WA 98033-6408
425.968.2884
www.charlesneedlephoto.com

Published by:
Amherst Media, Inc.
P.O. Box 586
Buffalo, N.Y. 14226
Fax: 716-874-4508
www.AmherstMedia.com

Publisher: Craig Alesse
Senior Editor/Production Manager: Michelle Perkins
Editors: Barbara A. Lynch-Johnt, Harvey Goldstein, Beth Alesse
Editorial Assistance from: Carey A. Miller, Sally Jarzab, John S. Loder
Associate Publisher: Kate Neaverth
Business Manager: Adam Richards
Warehouse and Fulfillment Manager: Roger Singo

ISBN-13: 978-1-60895-763-7
Library of Congress Control Number: 2014933302
10 9 8 7 6 5 4 3 2 1

Check out Amherst Media's blogs at: http://portrait-photographer.blogspot.com/
http://weddingphotographer-amherstmedia.blogspot.com/

Contents

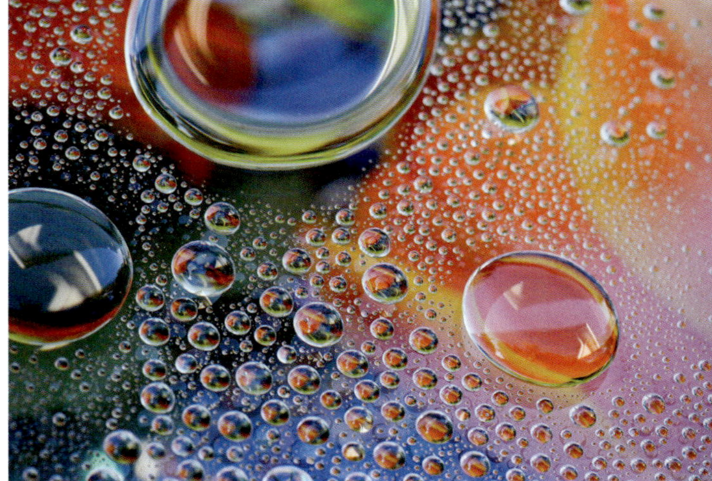

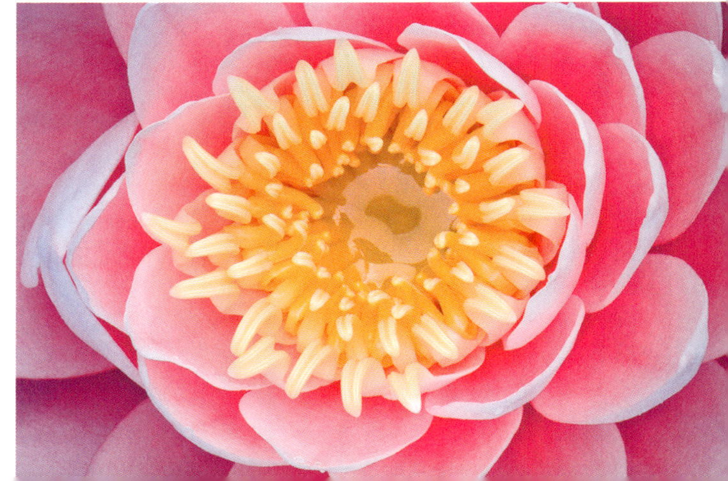

Resources

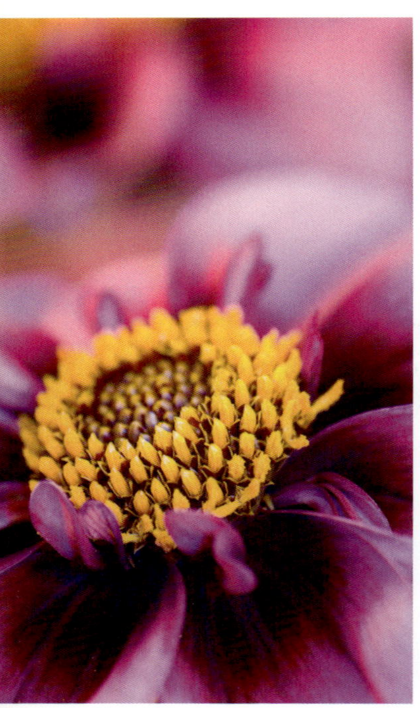

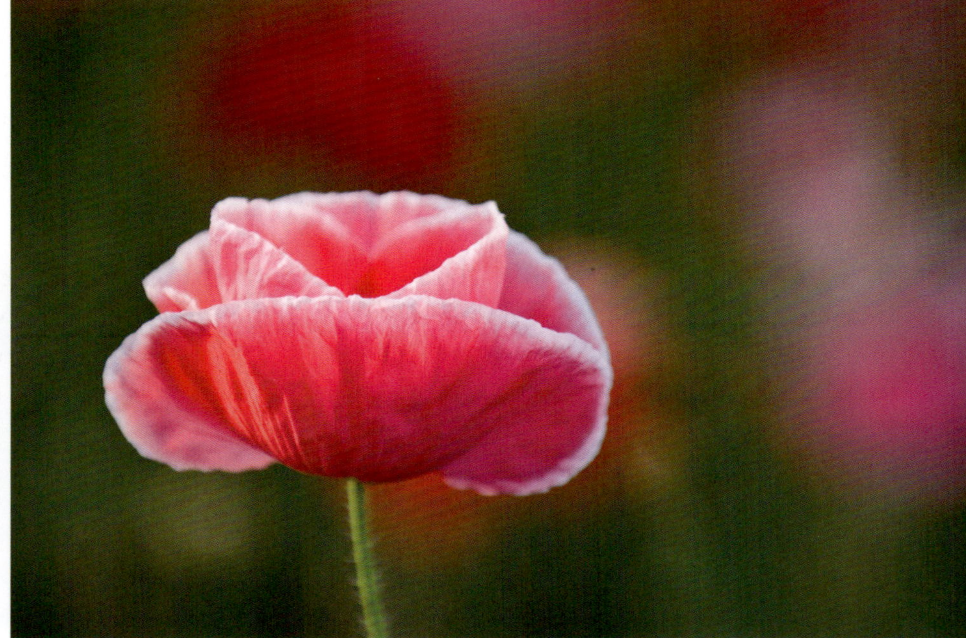

Acknowledgments

Producing a book requires much talent and discipline. This particular project could not have become a reality without assistance and inspiration from several individuals.

With deepest gratitude, I wish to thank the collaborative efforts of: the late Nancy Rotenberg for her contagious creative spirit and for giving me a profound appreciation for the beauty in tiny worlds; Freeman Patterson for teaching me the fundamentals of visual design and for reminding me to doh-si-doh with my camera; Phyllis Hlavac for her expert help with many of the illustration photos; Phyllis Burchett for her keen eye and excellent image-processing skills; Stacy Riley for helping me stay organized, focused, and productive, and for her efficient help with several aspects of this book's production; Ethan Riley, Sydney Riley, Allison Riley, and Samantha Riley for all their help with illustration photos and book production; Mark S. Johnson for helping to ignite the passion within and for his expert Photoshop instruction; Pat Fiorello for her positive encouragement and sound business advice; George Bradfield for his creative eye, dry humor, and abstract view of the world; Carole Sigmon for always believing in me with unconditional love, and for reminding me to keep my camera back parallel to the subject; Mom and Dad for providing opportunities that gave me a deep appreciation of nature and for fostering a creative, loving home environment; and finally, all of my workshop students who continue to inspire me to expand the boundaries of creativity and venture into the unknown with confidence and faith.

t takes bravery to climb mountains, to explore canyons, to wander jungles inhabited by snakes, but nothing is as brave as the journey inward. Like Dorothy in *The Wizard of Oz*, Charles Needle got caught in a twister. His physical condition, caused by Chronic Fatigue Syndrome, sent him into a downward swirl of body, mind and spirit.

While some might have chosen to define themselves in a woundology sort of way, Charles chose to connect with his vulnerability and to journey along his yellow brick road, discovering his creativity, his true Self, his home.

Viktor Frankl, in his riveting memoir, *Man's Search for Meaning* (Beacon Press, 2006), describes life in a Nazi death camp and its lessons for spiritual survival. Frankl's experiences were dramatically beyond one's control—so traumatic as to cause anyone to lose all hope. It would have been so easy just to give up on life altogether. Frankl argues that everything you possess can be taken away—except for one thing—your freedom to choose how you will respond to a given situation.

Charles chose how he would respond. *Tiny Worlds* is about that and more. Through a personal account of his choices and with professional photographic tips and techniques, Charles shows us that choosing to care about beauty and the power of little things can become a rapturous union of embracing and cultivating our inner spark. Through developing a capacity for responding to magic and miracles, there is a possible healing and a wonderfully, transformative journey.

Real art is our essence revealed and expressed.

Charles shares ideas on how to connect to subjects in unique, imaginative ways. He will inspire you to go beyond the handshake, beyond so-called limitations, into interpretive worlds of mystery and imagination. Photography should be just that—emanating from your heart and soul—bold, sensual, unapologetic.

Real art is our essence revealed and expressed. Through his words and images, Charles demonstrates how to open the door to yourself, letting your inner light be your compass, while developing a deeper appreciation for the joy and passion in photography and in life.

Nancy Rotenberg
Aliquippa, PA
January 2008

Preface

My journey into the captivating world of close-up photography began as a quest for meaning in my life almost two decades ago.

In November of 1989, I was diagnosed with Chronic Fatigue Syndrome, and the world as I had known it changed forever. For almost an entire year, I was completely housebound and felt like every ounce of energy had been sucked from my body, mind, and spirit.

Feeling lifeless, I had no choice but to leave a stable job as a magazine editor in Knoxville, TN, and return home to live with my parents in Atlanta, GA. During all the uncertainty surrounding that period in my life, I discovered how the camera could become a powerful therapeutic tool and a catalyst for healing.

With child-like curiosity, I began photographing close-up . . .

Before I was strong enough to venture outdoors during that fateful year, I would surround myself with as much natural beauty as I could find—fresh-cut flowers at my bedside, a soothing indoor fountain, or coffee-table books containing awe-inspiring nature photographs.

To pass the time, I would position myself by a window and stare outdoors for hours in deep thought, studying the nuances of the "scene" before me. I watched sunlight dance across trees, windswept blades of grass, and listened to the blissful song of birds. This was my little world, which, metaphorically, became a window to my soul.

I imagined the window in my room as my own giant "camera," where I could record these images in my mind's eye, store them, and take them into each and every cell of my body. The longer I focused through the "lens" of this window, the more I began to appreciate beauty and the happier I became.

Gradually, as I became stronger, I ventured outdoors, literally crawling on my hands and knees at times because I felt such profound exhaustion. Soon, I invested in a pair of knee pads and dug my camera out of the closet, along with my tripod. How would a flower in the garden appear through the lens? What could I discover in these tiny universes?

With child-like curiosity, I began photographing close-up and became entranced and uplifted. I saw a world that had perfect order and noticed the small miracles contained within very minute details. What a revelation—a true awakening of all my senses! I soon realized I had to literally journey home to come home to myself. The images I was capturing became forever embedded in my heart, mind, and soul. And I discovered the "still point" where eye, mind, and heart merged as one.

No longer did I have to lament the fact that I could not physically travel to exotic locations and photograph. I began to accept what was here and now, what was right in front of me, with all its so-called limitations. And what incredible limitations those were, for there were gifts to be discovered through my lens right in my own backyard!

I view macro photography as a profound form of meditation.

Today, some twenty years later, completely healed from my illness, I view macro photography as a profound form of meditation. As an art form, it teaches the photographer and the viewer to remember to embrace the gift of present moments, which we are blessed with each and every day. In particular, artistic abstract close-up photography is a metaphor for taking us beyond literal understandings because it allows us to see familiar subjects in unfamiliar ways and visually express inner feelings. As a photographer, you can convey a personal expression, rather than just a record of the scene.

Developing an "inner eye" for beauty requires patience, time, and being open and mindful. You must stay focused but also surrender and accept whatever circumstances, lighting, weather, or subject matter you are presented with in the present moment.

If you learn to surrender, "let go," and just be open and present, allow the mystery and serendipity to envelope you, take it all in fully like a deep breath, and engage all your senses, then miracles beyond your wildest expectations will occur. Subjects literally begin to reveal themselves to you, rather than the other way around. And you begin to see real magic in one profound instant with the click of a shutter—the moment when creative vision merges with the subject's "essence," and intangible but powerful emotions are forever translated into pixels.

It is my sincere hope that the tips and techniques presented in this book not only will educate and inspire you to make great images but also give you a much deeper and richer appreciation for beauty in the world.

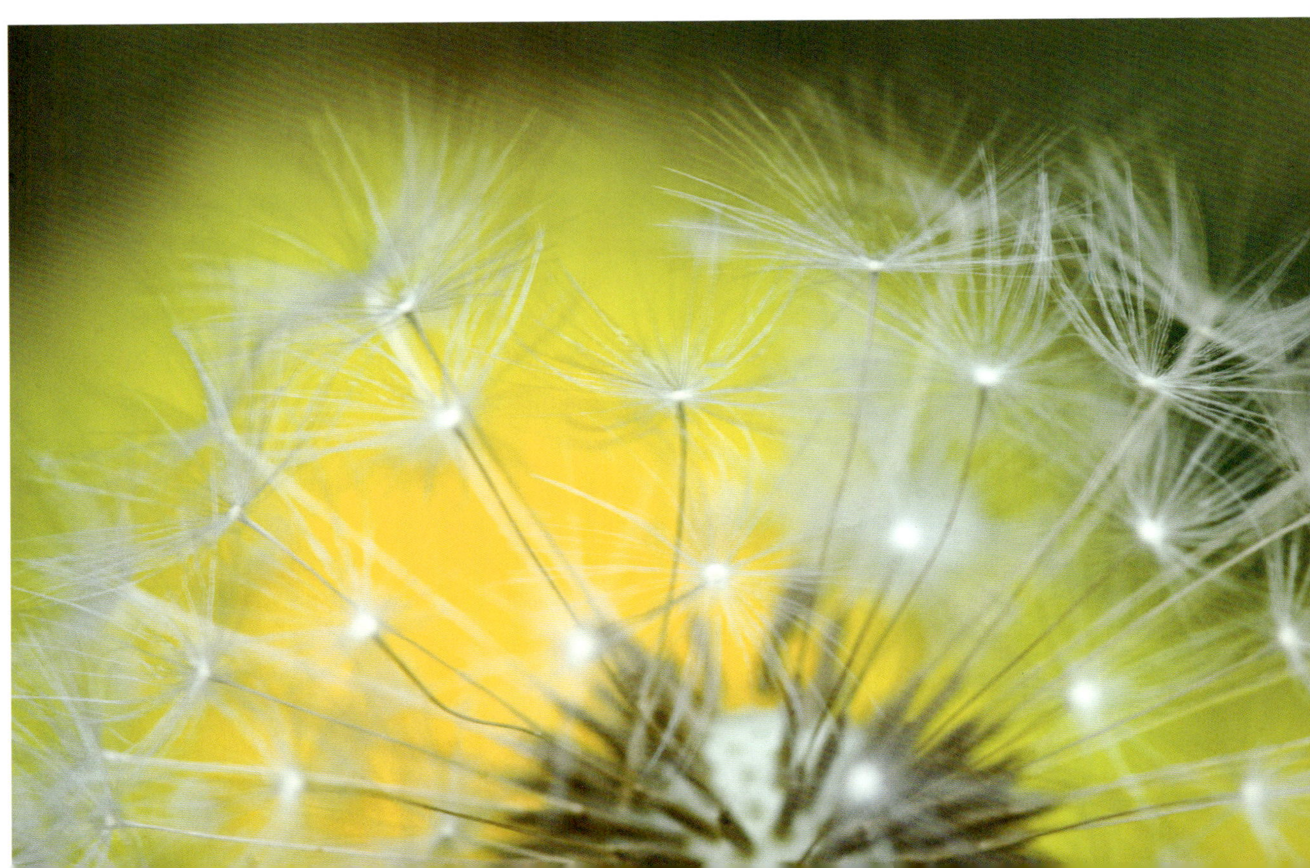

1. Mindful Photography

In my workshops, I often ask students if they understand the difference between "looking" and "seeing." Some look at me with puzzled looks on their faces, while others seem to know exactly what I mean.

During the course of any given day, you (and your eyes!) are looking at thousands of people, places, and things. But how often are you really seeing what's before you? Are you fully present and "awake" to the richness each moment potentially offers?

For me, photography provides just the right vehicle for helping us slow down and pay attention to present moments. Best-selling author Veronique Vienne once said, "A camera is a mousetrap for the here and now." You may not have thought about your camera in this way, but truly it offers a mechanism for you to focus on the "here and now," eliminate all distractions from the "viewfinder" of your life, and see beauty in its purest form.

"A camera is a mousetrap for the here and now."

Essentially, there are three levels of awareness in life and in photography. As we go about our busy lives day-by-day, at any given moment, our eyes are doing the looking, observing, and seeing. Our mind often forms opinions about what we're seeing and interprets the scene before us. And finally, if we're perceiving on an even deeper level, then our emotions become activated and attuned. Images that go beyond the documentary level almost always involve a synthesis of all three levels of awareness. The eye, mind, and emotions (or heart) all become aligned, and image making becomes a blissful, almost meditative experience.

It's this third level of awareness—emotions—that you, the photographer, need to pay close attention to when observing the world around you and capturing its essence in pixels. In doing so, you'll be able to engage your heart as you click the shutter. By shifting your level of perception—really paying attention and allowing the subject to speak to you and through you—you will elevate your work and attune your senses to what lies beneath the surface. You'll be able to capture the true essence of your subject and evoke feelings in yourself and the viewer of your work.

One of the greatest photographic "seers" of all time was Minor White, who often discussed the profound role that spirit plays in photography: "Be still with yourself until the object of your attention affirms your presence," he said. The underlying creative process is what truly makes an image. The camera is merely a mechanical device that serves to focus our attention to pressing the shutter at precisely the right moment when our inner and external experiences align.

More than any other type of nature photography, macro photography forces you to "find the poetry" in your subject, because you're much more intimate with your subject—physically, psychologically, and emotionally. Your job, as the photographer and artist, is to let go of any preconceived ideas, eliminate all distractions, go beyond thinking, and develop mindful awareness.

So what is "mindful awareness"? Put simply, it's nonjudgmental seeing in its purest form. It's about paying attention to what is before you, including any feelings or sensations that may arise, and acknowledging and accepting those feelings and sensations as they are.

Mindful seeing involves paying attention to present moments, noticing small and subtle details—how the light is falling on a subject, for example. When you observe on a deeper level, your photography begins to improve. You begin to see and appreciate things you weren't even aware existed before.

That's what is so wonderful about the world of macro photography. For me, macro opens up a world of infinite possibilities. Unlike other forms of photography, when you are making close-up images, you must slow down and be patient. By slowing down, you allow the essence of your subject to speak to you, and in doing so, you allow that essence to flow through you, the creator/artist and image-maker, translating your own unique vision.

So, when reading this book and attempting to apply some of the tips and techniques described herein, I challenge you to open your heart, absorb the feeling and the sensory feast before you without judgment, and delight in making images that would not have existed before without your heightened awareness and mindful way of seeing.

Paradise Found

Impressionist master Claude Monet once said, "To see, we must forget the name of the thing we are seeing." Monet was probably one of the first to recognize that art is not necessarily what you see, but rather what you as the artist make others see.

The same principle can certainly be applied to making photographs. Anyone can take a picture of a flower because that's what the camera records when you point your lens at the subject and press the shutter. However, it takes a true artist to use the image of the flower to show you something else about the flower, or something else entirely that has nothing to do with the flower per se.

Mindful seeing involves paying attention to present moments . . .

If we approach image making with mindfulness, the heart, mind, and eye all become perfectly aligned, and something magical happens. This certainly occurred for me one morning when I was photographing a bird-of-paradise that was in a tropical flower arrangement given to me as a fortieth birthday gift from my mother.

Mom and I were on vacation in Barbados, and she decided to sleep in one morning. While eating my breakfast, I began studying the beautiful flower arrangement in the center of the table. Immediately, I was taken with the flower, and it seemed to be beckoning me to photograph! What a perfect opportunity, I thought, with Mom still sound asleep.

So I set up my tripod and camera on the open-air hotel room patio, which overlooked a tropical courtyard. I wanted the flower to be positioned in sunlight in order to experiment with backlighting and rim lighting, so I put the flower arrangement on top of an ironing board, which was in the closet in the hotel room. (This required some ingenuity, but it was the next best thing to using a table! It also put the flower at just the right height so I wouldn't have to strain my back by having to bend over while photographing.)

I decided my 200mm Nikkor lens was the best choice since I wanted to get in close and explore the bird-of-paradise. As I poked my lens around various parts of the flower, I began noticing its exquisite perfection and appreciating—even celebrating—just how beautiful the flower was. In composing my images, I was certain to pay attention to all the elements of design: line, shape, color, tone, and texture. **Images 1-1** through **1-7** are the first in a series of images I made that morning. During the whole process, I was feeling an overwhelming sense of gratitude toward the flower itself and toward the universe as a whole. I began to feel a deep interconnectedness between my subject—the flower—and my soul. All my senses were heightened, and with each click of the shutter, my visual acuity became sharper and sharper. I was noticing the interplay of each flower part through my viewfinder— how my camera angle and f-stop impacted depth of field, how highlights and shadows were rendered on my LCD, how the point of focus would alter the overall result. It was truly a kind of "dance," and I was falling in love with my floral dance partner!

After about an hour had gone by (which I didn't realize until I looked at my watch because, after all, when you're in such a creative

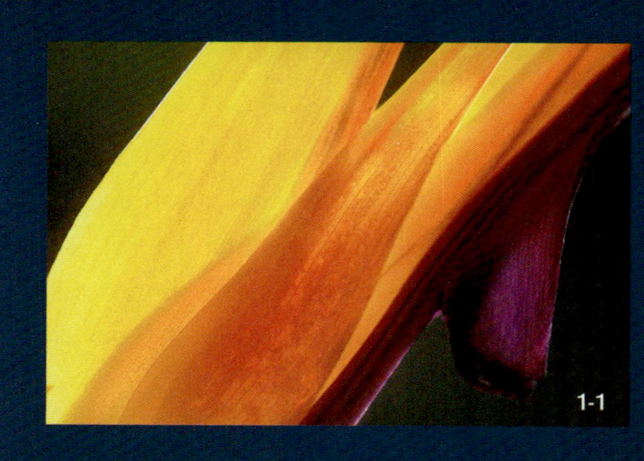

1-1

Images **1-1** through **1-7** were captured with my 200mm macro lens. Images **1-8** through **1-15** were captured with the 500D close-up lens in front of my 200mm macro lens.

"flow," the concept of time vanishes), I decided I had pushed the envelope enough with the 200mm alone. It was time to add a close-up lens to get closer, fill the frame more, and try to really capture the "inner essence" of the bird-of-paradise. **Images 1-8** through **1-13** were all taken with the 500D close-up lens in front of my 200mm macro lens. Still paying close attention to all the design elements, I was able to get even closer. These "mini landscapes" all spoke to me and conveyed the joy I was feeling. I became so enamored that I completely forgot I was photographing a bird-of-paradise. Visual design elements of line, shape, color, and texture took center stage. I was a happy camper!

However, it wasn't until I completely "let go" and surrendered to accept the "what is-ness" of the bird-of-paradise that its true essence began to emerge through the lens. I decided to see what would happen if I defocused the lens completely to abstract the flower. Keeping my lens wide open at f/4, I clicked the shutter and knew in an instant that I had successfully captured the essence. (See **images 1-14** and **1-15**.)

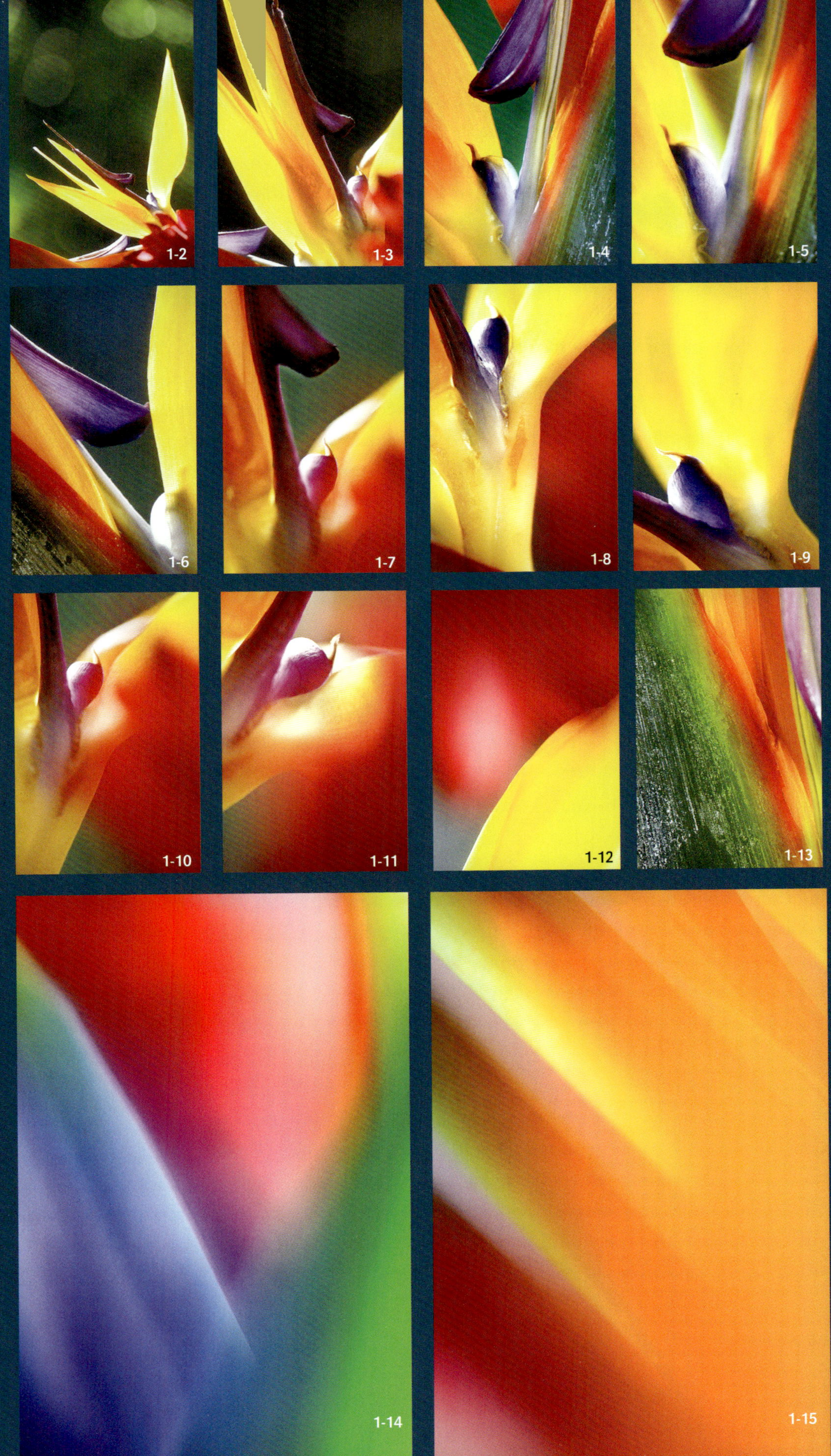

I found my own personal "paradise" within the visual poetry of the flower, and an inexplicable peace gently washed over me. The flower and I had become one. I began to reflect upon what it meant to turn forty and was captivated by what had transpired in just a couple of hours. Had I not stayed fully present with the flower and completely open to exploring it intimately, these images would not have ever been made.

Heartsong

A second, similar experience occurred three years later when photographing in the Oregon Dunes National Recreation Area on the central Oregon coast.

I arrived mid-morning, tired and uninspired, as I had been awake since 4:30AM to photograph a sunrise elsewhere along the coast. My body, mind, and spirit were all screaming, "Just sit awhile and rest," but I felt compelled to forge ahead and experience the dunes anyway, especially since I knew I wouldn't have a chance to return anytime soon.

So, with pack and tripod in-hand, I hiked to the top of the dunes, feeling my feet sink deep in the sand with each arduous step. Finally, after reaching the summit, with some reluctance I began photographing what I saw. What struck me at first was the fact that there was simply very little color. Since I was accustomed to shooting vibrant scenics and close-ups, I could sense my inner resistance. In my mind, I felt forced to compromise because I could not find much inspiration in the monochromatic landscape before me. Unlike the situation with the bird-of-paradise, where I felt completely in sync with what I was photographing and "at one" with my subject, this time nothing really spoke to me—or even whispered in my ear!

I made a conscious choice to just "go with the flow" and stop resisting. I would simply shoot for the sake of shooting what I saw, naming each thing in my mind as I went along. There were: patterns in the sand, shadows falling upon the sand, mounds of rocks protruding from beneath the sand, grasses blowing in the breeze, even single blades of grass criss-crossing one another. (See **images 1-16** through **1-23**.) My mind and eye were certainly engaged as I tried to find a creative camera angle or an unusual composition, but my heart was nowhere to be found.

Finally, after "getting it out of my system" and feeling even more physically exhausted, I decided to take a break and rest, which was what my intuition had tried to tell me about an hour earlier. I laid my pack down in the sand, took my shoes off so I could feel the sand between my toes, and rested awhile, closing my eyes and surrendering to the fatigue. Ironically, with my eyes closed, I discovered I could "see" better. My senses began to awaken. I became aware of the sweet smell of the morning air, I heard the rustle of the breeze that had gone unnoticed previously, and I paid close attention to how the warm sand felt between my toes. Gradually, feeling somewhat refreshed, I opened my eyes with a fresh, new perspective. I looked around me again and drank it all in, feeling gratitude for being able to witness such beauty, even though I had not made an award-winning photograph that morning. The experience became more important than the outcome, the journey more important than the destination.

Then, low and behold, I glanced over near where I was sitting and noticed a small strand of purple lupine growing in the sand. (See **images 1-24** and **1-25**.) It was a lovely, delicate

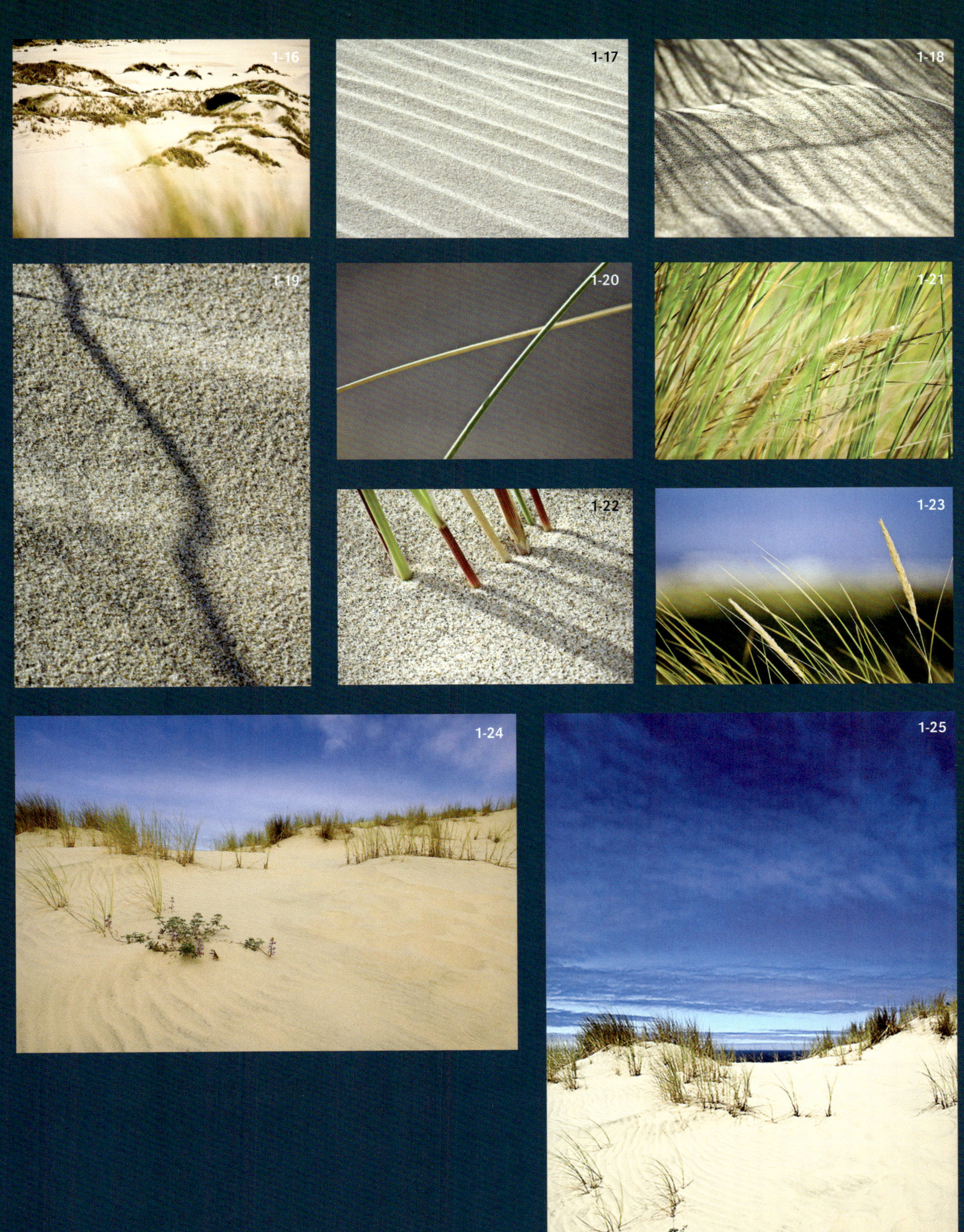
1-16
1-17
1-18
1-19
1-20
1-21
1-22
1-23
1-24
1-25

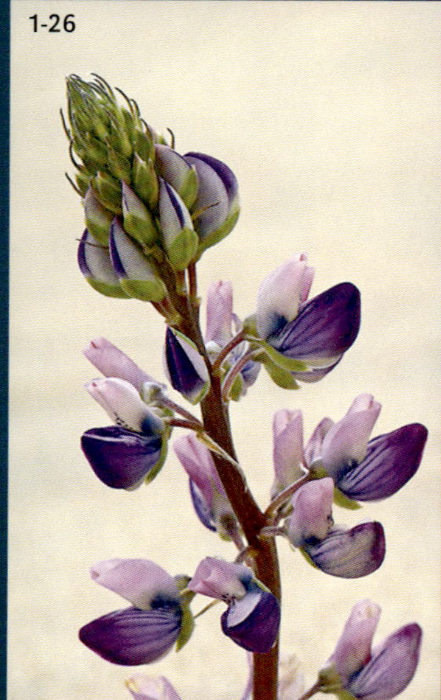

1-26

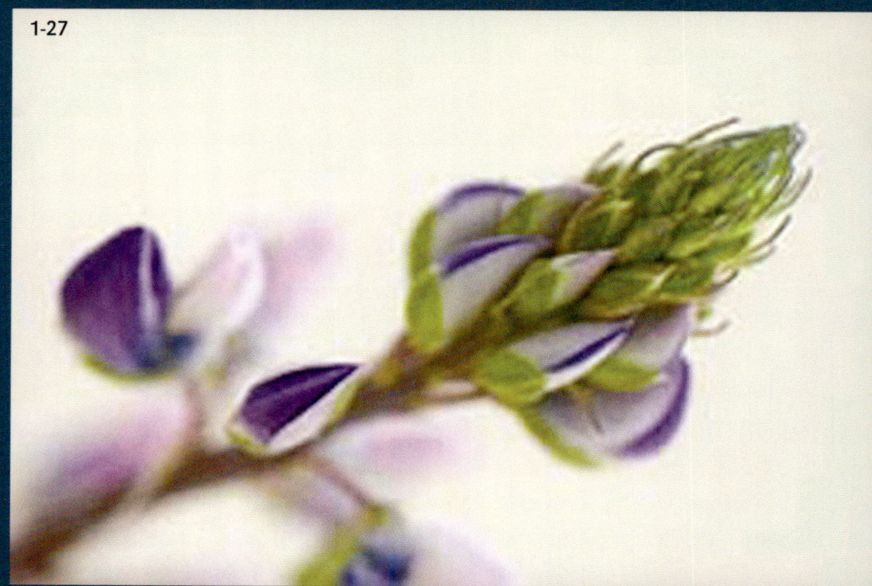

1-27

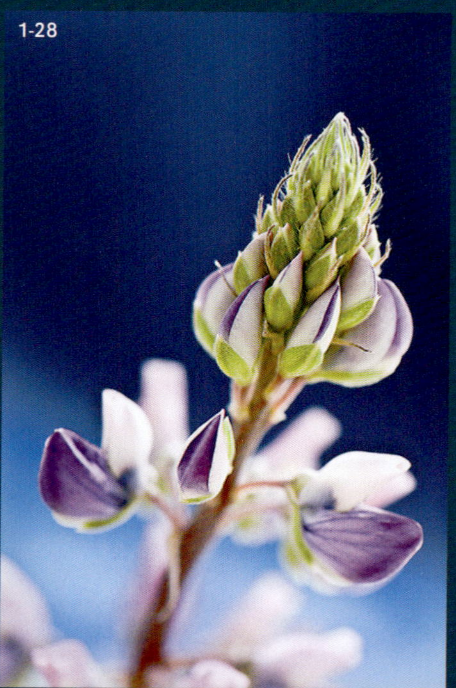

1-28

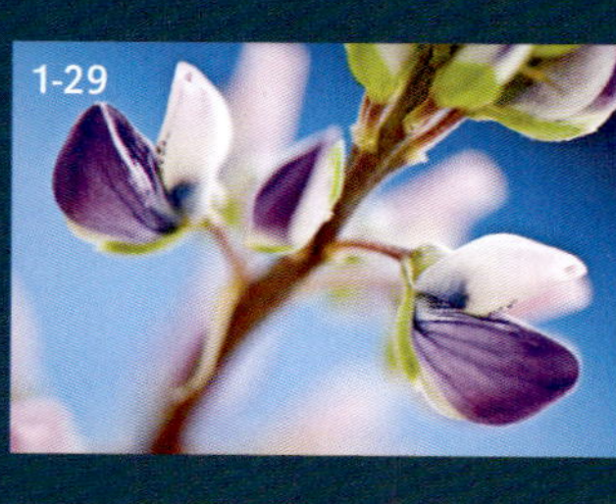

1-29

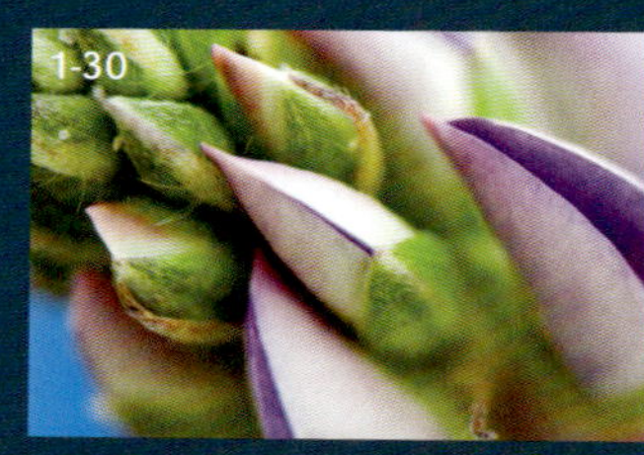

1-30

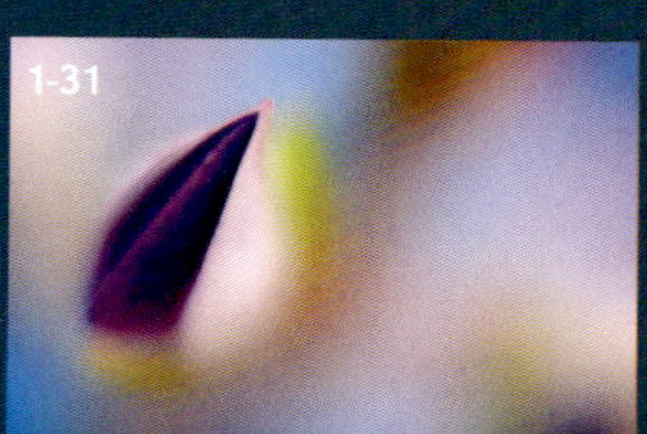

1-31

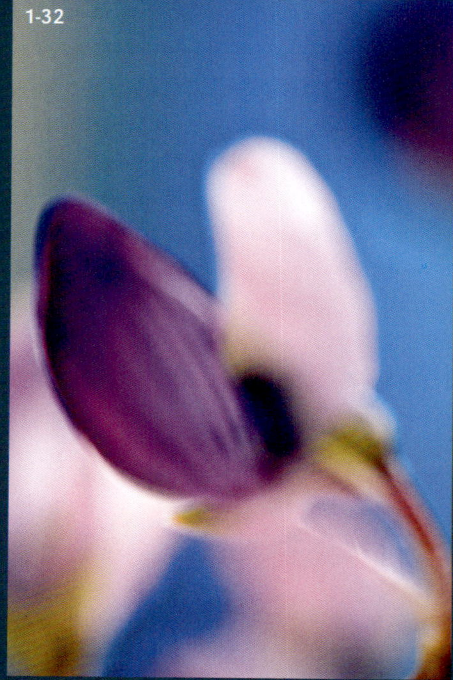

1-32

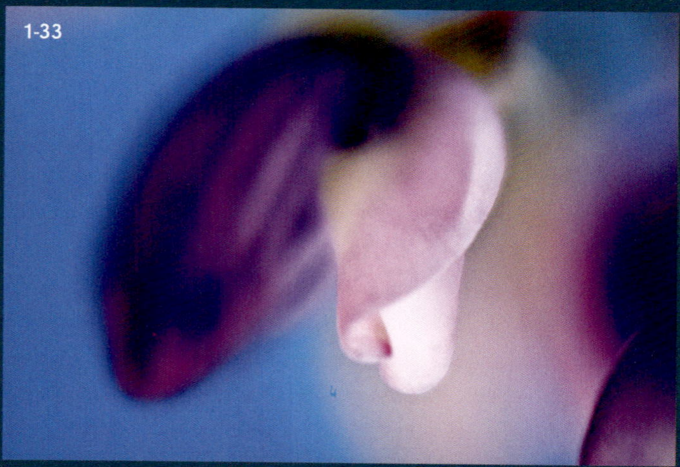

1-33

plant that had survived rather harsh weather conditions. Feeling reenergized, I decided to photograph this lupine using my 200mm Nikkor lens and tripod. As always, the tripod helped me to stay "grounded," literally and figuratively. I concentrated on one small bud and was able to isolate it against the background of the white sand. (See **images 1-26** and **1-27**.)

The image was nice . . . fairly documentary and not really all that exciting, but I stuck with it and could sense that my creative juices were finally beginning to flow. I asked myself, "What could I do to improve the image?" "Color" was the first word that popped into my head. Well, there really wasn't much color in the middle of the sand dunes! Inspiration struck, and I took off my blue sweatshirt, threw it behind the lupine to create a colored background, and continued to try to make an exciting close-up image. My heart was beginning to sing, and I found joy in the interplay of colors, experimenting with various compositions, camera angles, and depths of field. (See **images 1-28** through **1-30**.)

Then, after I felt as if I had exhausted all the creative possibilities, I asked myself the same question again, "What could I do to improve the image?" This time, the answer that came to me was "Move in closer." So, I placed the Canon 500D close-up lens on the end of my 200mm macro lens and began to explore the lupine with greater intimacy. (See **image 1-31**.) I remember pretending that I was a small bug crawling all over the flower, as I explored by moving the camera around on my somewhat loosened ballhead. At the same time, I began changing the focus on my lens as I moved around the tiny flower. Soon, all time seemed to stop. I was "in the creative flow," and enjoying

the visual feast before me. I noticed two petals touching each other, one pink and the other purple, and began to focus on that relationship. (See **image 1-32**.) As I was exploring that and changing my camera position, I noticed the pink bud, in particular, which had a nice graceful curve to its edges. So, I repositioned my lens once again and began to explore this curve in greater depth.

Out of this experience came one of the most magical moments of my photographic career thus far. I noticed that at the end of the pink petal, a heart shape was beginning to emerge. (See **image 1-33**.) My adrenaline was flowing, and at that instant, I felt an indescribable oneness with my subject. I shouted for joy and felt like getting up and doing whoopee dances around my tripod!

What started out as an uninspiring, dreary morning had suddenly become sheer bliss. It was as though the "heart" of the tiny lupine had found me. I wasn't looking for it, but because I was awake enough to see mindfully, and patient enough to stay with the tiny lupine bud, the subject seemed to mysteriously find me.

Now, for the first time all morning, my mind, eye, and heart were all fully aligned and engaged. I clicked the shutter umpteen times with umpteen different compositions, umpteen different depths of field, and umpteen different lighting conditions. I even experimented with using my small colored LED flashlight and a 12-inch gold reflector to alter the lighting in some of the images. (See **images 1-34** through **1-44**.)

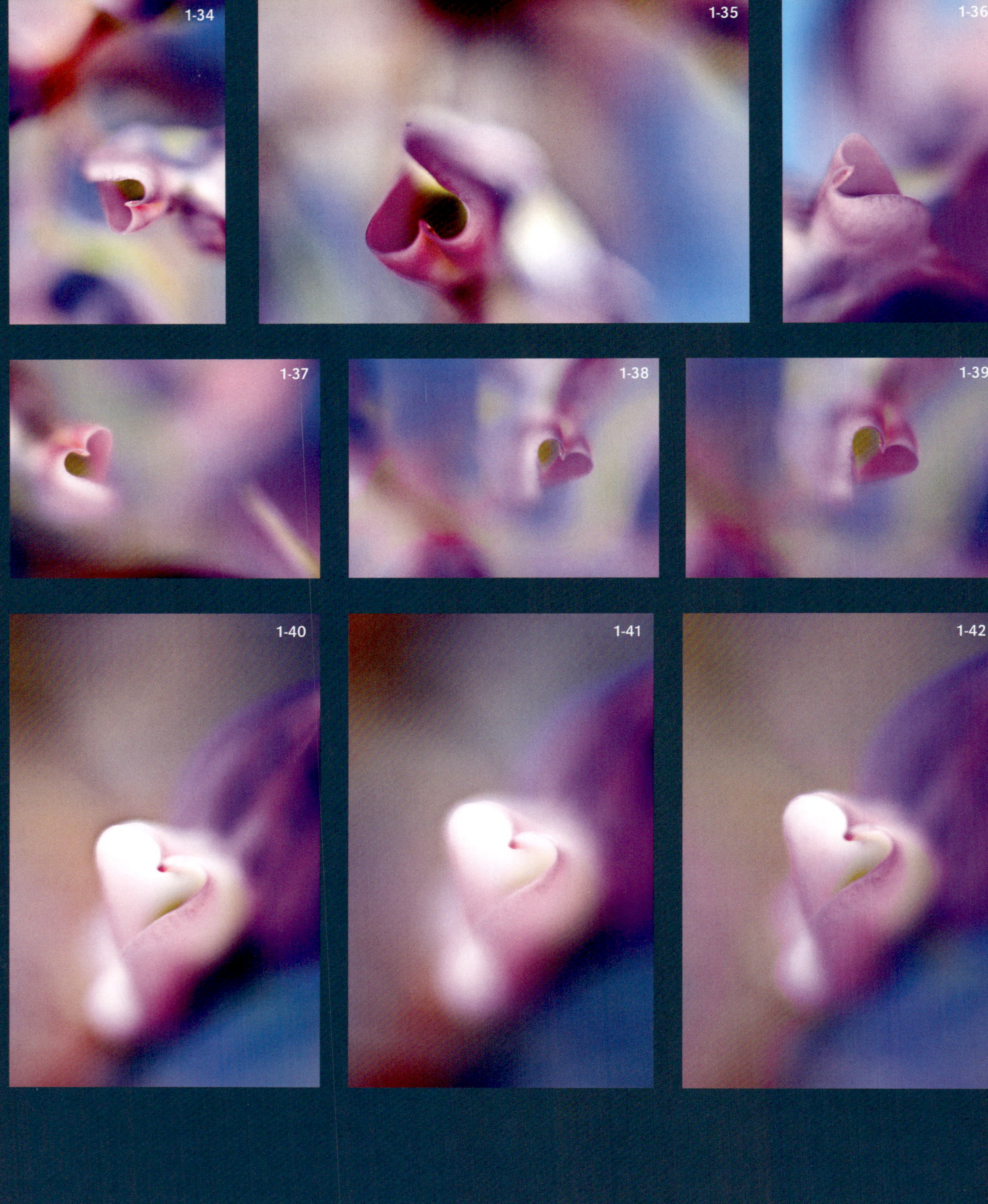

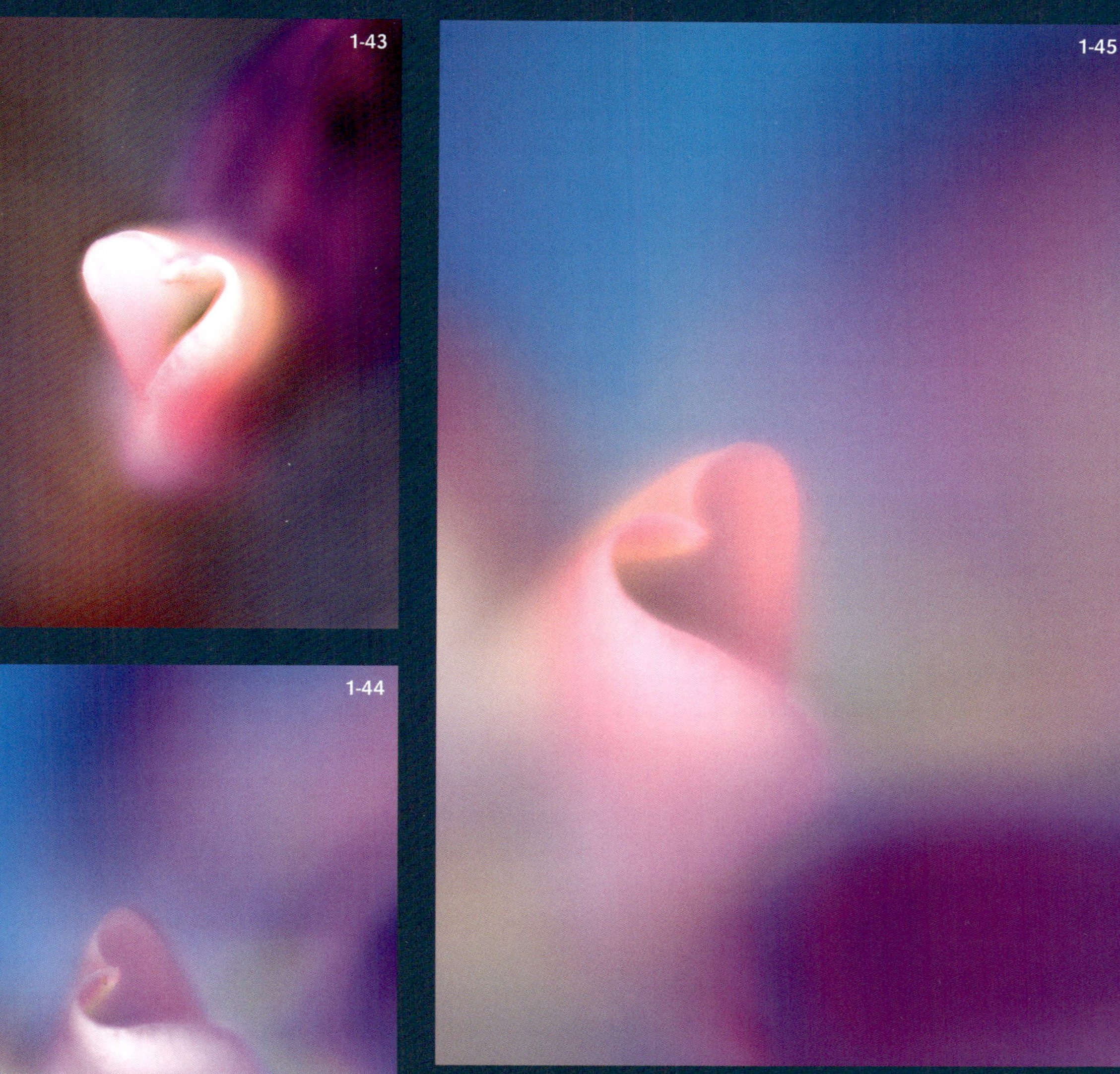

I continued to explore with childlike wonder, loving each moment and appreciating the beauty of what I was witnessing through my lens with deep gratitude and respect.

Eventually, after burning through several CompactFlash cards, I was pleased with image **1-45** because it most clearly expressed the feelings of love and joy I experienced that morning.

The magic of that morning never would have happened if I weren't open to infinite possibilities, fully awake and engaged with my subject in a state of utter bliss and gratitude. The small tip of the lupine flower, the graceful curl of its petals, all unfolded as a visual feast right before my eyes and touched me on a profound, personal level because it also came during a period in my life when I had been struggling with Chronic Fatigue Syndrome. At that one instant, before I even clicked the shutter, all pain and uncertainty vanished through the lens, and I fell in love again with who I was and why I was here. I remembered that true love involves surrendering your heart and opening yourself to vulnerability. Thus, the image itself—and the process of making the image—became a visual metaphor for something much larger and much more profound.

I fell in love again with who I was and why I was here.

You, too, can experience this same level of creativity by bringing mindful awareness to your image making. It is my sincere hope that the pages of this book will inspire you to make images that truly make your heart sing.

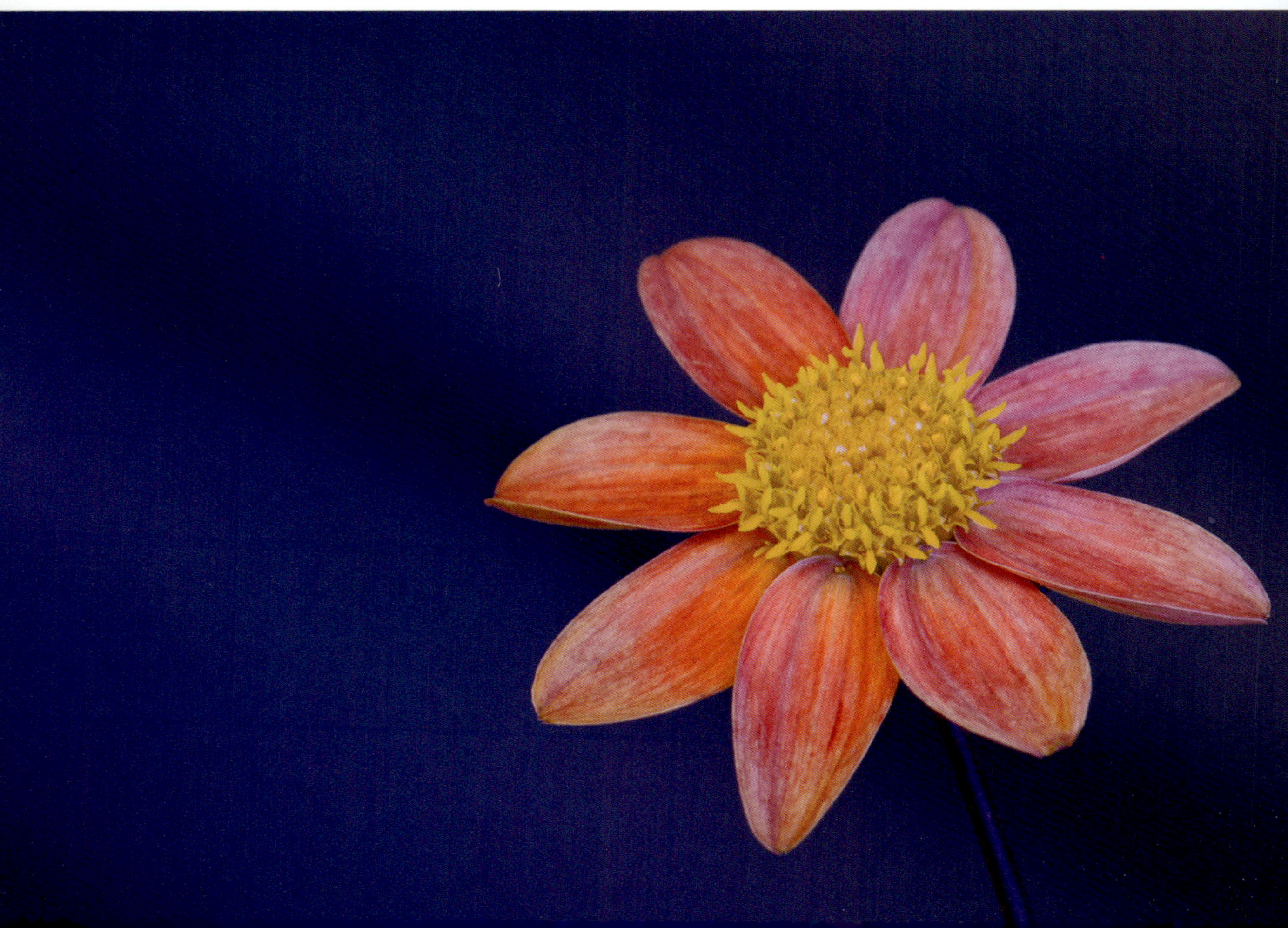

2. Macro Equipment Essentials

Great images do not necessarily come from the fanciest cameras. Case in point: my good friend and mentor, Freeman Patterson (www.freemanpatterson.com), who still makes award-winning fine-art images using a 35mm Minolta SLR film camera, basic tripod, and a couple of lenses!

Whether you're shooting macro and close-up photographs or otherwise, it's essential to remember that equipment is certainly important but is not the "be all, end all" of great photography. Equipment and fancy gadgetry can suppress creativity if you're not careful. The goal is to master the technical aspects of your equipment first (learning camera menu navigation, settings, aperture/shutter speed combinations, lighting, etc.), and then allow your creativity to take center stage.

Professional nature photographer John Shaw (www.johnshawphoto.com) once said, "Not once did my lenses ever go out to shoot." This is so true, for it's the photographer behind the camera that's making the picture, not the other way around. So often, we get caught up in mind-blowing megapixel mazes and forget that the camera and all its accessories are merely tools to enable us to translate our creative vision into pixels or onto film.

When it comes to macro photography, in particular, I've tried to offer some hints below, based on what I carry in my own camera bag. When I'm in the field, I try to carry as little equipment as possible (because of weight and also because I think if you have too many choices, you can't be nearly as creative). When I'm at home photographing in my own garden studio, of course, I have all of my tools at my disposal.

Camera System

Nikon and Canon seem to be the two biggest players these days when it comes to professional-level digital SLR cameras. Deciding which to buy is rather like trying to decide between a Mercedes or BMW. Both are reputable companies manufacturing high-quality cameras, and I highly recommend either one. Of course, there are other fine camera manufacturers (Olympus, Fujifilm, Leica, Pentax, Samsung, etc.), but Canon and Nikon are the two most popular among serious amateur and professional 35mm digital photographers.

One common misconception: Often, people who are new to digital photography think that choosing a camera with the largest number of megapixels will yield the highest-quality print. While megapixels do make a difference, it's equally important to consider the size and quality of the camera's image sensor.

When comparing various camera models, here are some of the most important features to look for when shooting macro and close-up imagery:

- **Mirror Lock-up Device.** Just prior to exposure, the mirror inside your camera automatically flips up to allow light from the scene to strike the digital image sensor. This abrupt mechanical action can sometimes create internal vibrations, which can result in a blurred image, especially when using long telephoto lenses and longer shutter speeds. Mirror lock-up allows you to manually raise the mirror and delay shutter activation until the vibrations have subsided. When shooting macro, I always use the mirror lock-up feature because sharpness is critical at higher magnifications. Please be aware, however, that you won't be able to see your subject through the viewfinder once you press the shutter.

Image 2-1. The depth-of-field preview feature on my Nikon D3 is the top button.

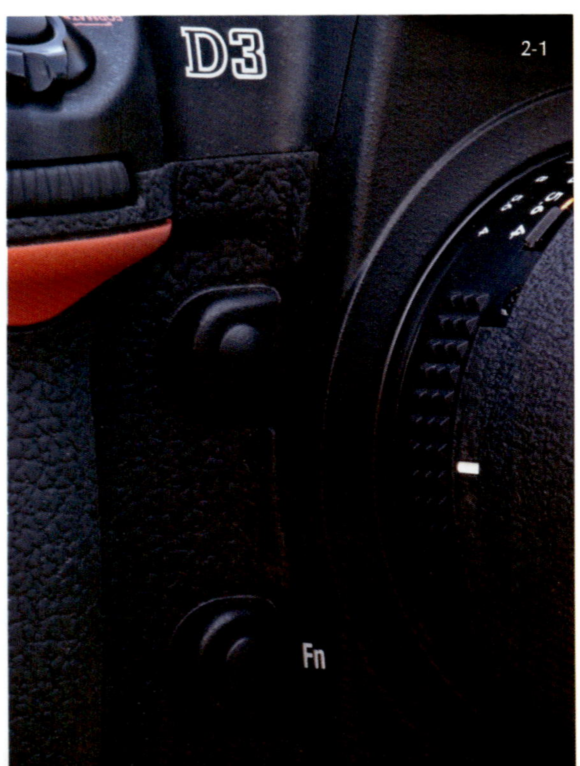

- **Manual Focusing.** Most modern-day digital SLR cameras have fancy auto-focus features. When photographing stationary macro subjects, however, I recommend you turn off auto focus and use manual-focus mode because of very narrow depth of field and the need to have precise sharpness. If your eyesight is not the greatest, consider adjusting the camera's diopter setting and/or use auto focus first to get your subject reasonably sharp, then switch to manual for any necessary fine-tuning. If you own a digital point-and-shoot camera, you may be stuck with auto focus, so it's important to make sure the camera you're about to purchase has manual focusing capability.
- **Depth-of-Field Preview.** One of the most important camera features when making macro images is depth-of-field preview. When you look through your viewfinder, you are viewing the scene at the widest lens aperture. Activating the depth-of-field preview feature allows you to preview the scene at the aperture that will be used during the exposure, which is often smaller, unless you are shooting at a wide aperture. (See **image 2-1.**) This is an important consideration, especially when shooting close-ups, because you can better evaluate sharpness in your image and see if you've eliminated distracting background elements at a given aperture. One tip when using a depth-of-field preview button is to press and hold the button while looking through your viewfinder and change apertures at the same time. This allows you to see how depth of field changes from one aperture to another.
- **Automatic TTL Flash Exposure.** Electronic flashes (strobe lights, speedlights) are often

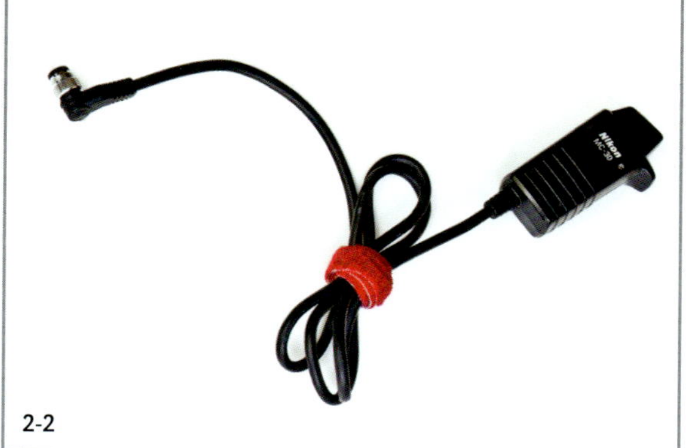

2-2

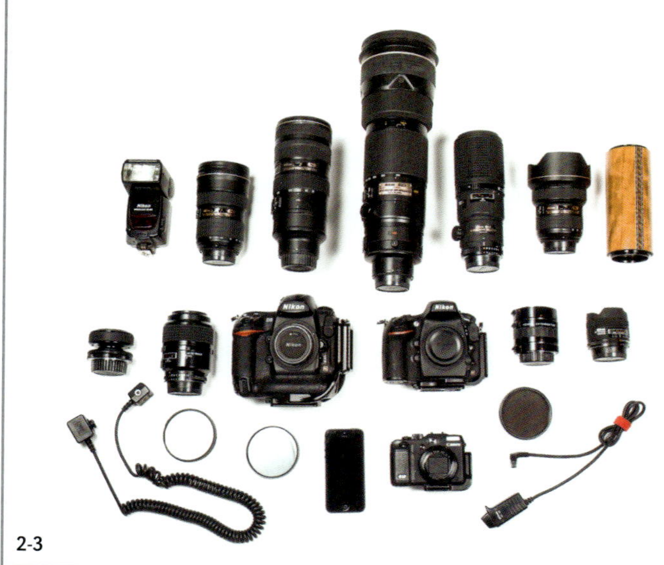

2-3

Image 2-2. Cable release. **Image 2-3** (Clockwise, L-R). Nikon SB-800, Nikon 24–70mm, Nikon 70–200mm, Nikon 200–400mm, Nikon 200mm macro, Nikon 14–24mm, taleidoscope lens, Lensbaby Composer Pro, Nikon 105mm macro, Nikon D3, Nikon D800, extension tubes, Nikon 16mm fisheye, flash-sync cord, Canon 500D close-up filter, circular polarizer, iPhone 5, Canon G12, Singh-Ray Vari-ND filter, and cable release.

used in close-up photography. By setting your flash to "TTL" (or "through-the-lens") mode, the camera automatically controls flash exposure based on the amount of ambient or available light in the scene, even when close-up accessories and multiple flash units are used. (For more detailed information about the use of flash and fill flash when shooting close-ups, see chapter 3.)

- **Remote Flash Capability.** To add depth and drama to your macro images, you'll want to be sure you can remove the flash from the camera's hotshoe and activate it either wirelessly or using a sync cord, which allows the camera to talk to the flash, as if it were mounted to the hot shoe. Some SLRs have built-in flash capability; however, be sure you have the ability to deactivate this flash whenever desired because often it produces flat, harsh lighting when shooting close-ups. Ideally, you'll want to use an external flash unit mounted to a macro flash bracket. (We'll get to this later in the chapter.)
- **Remote Shutter Release.** To avoid camera shake during the exposure (even when

shooting on a tripod) and achieve maximum image sharpness, you'll want to purchase a remote shutter release (or "cable release"). I'd stick with the simple, flexible electric cable variety and avoid using wireless and infrared transmitters, which are easily lost and must be aimed precisely at the camera's receptor (usually from the front). A cable release that can be locked is a good choice for those times you might wish to shoot long exposures in "bulb" mode. *Tip:* To shorten the length of your cable release (and make it easy to spot when sitting inside your camera bag), tie a small red Velcro strap around the folded cable. (See **image 2-2**.)

Lenses and Accessories

Once you start with one camera system, it's a good idea to stick with that camera manufacturer because of lens compatibilities, etc. Since I shoot professionally and make my living through photography, I am a firm believer in choosing brand-name lenses, since they are made from the highest-quality glass optics. (See **image 2-3**.) That's not to say that you won't find excellent quality lenses that are not name-brand. DP Review (www.dpreview.com)

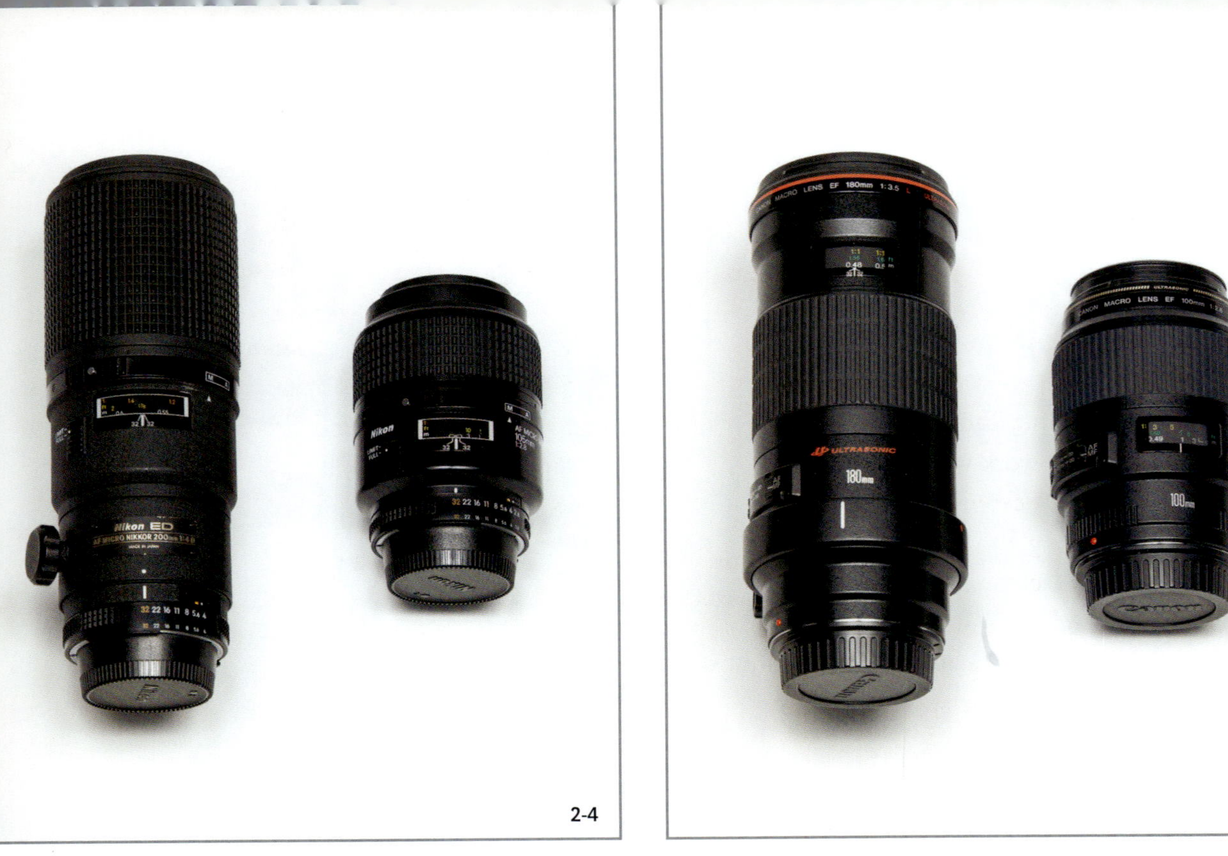

Image 2-4 (L-R). Nikon 200mm and 105mm macro lenses. **Image 2-5** (L-R). Canon 180mm and 100mm macro lenses.

is a useful website to consider when evaluating which lens/lenses to purchase. Visiting the site will also help you keep up with the latest digital photography and imaging news.

A "true" macro lens is one that captures the subject at life size.

- **True Macro Lenses.** Macro lenses allow you to fill your photograph with a subject that is physically small. The longer the focal length of the macro lens, the greater the working distance, which is important with subjects such as live insects. A "true" macro lens is one that captures the subject at life size, at a 1:1 ratio at a fixed focal length. So, for example, if I were to take a frame-filling

photo of something that is 24x36mm (1x1.5 inches) in size, the same dimensions as the sensor on a full-frame digital camera body, then the subject would be rendered at life size.

If you're in the market for a macro lens and don't mind working at a moderately close distance from your subject, I'd suggest a lens in the 90–105mm range. Canon makes a 100mm macro, and Nikon's equivalent is the 105mm micro. (See **images 2-4** and **2-5**.)

If money is no object and you think you'll be shooting a lot of insects and small animals, then you may want to consider a longer focal-length macro lens, such as the Canon 180mm or Nikon 200mm. One real advantage to using both of these lenses is that they come with a built-in lens collar, which allows you to easily alternate between horizontal and vertical compositions, and anything in between, for even more dynamic impact. (See **images 2-6** and **2-7**.)

- **Macro-Zoom Lenses.** These lenses will focus reasonably close, but they're not a substitute for a true macro lens because it's difficult to obtain true 1:1 magnification. Like fixed focal-length lenses, they can be adapted for extreme close-up work with screw-on supplementary lenses, extension tubes, and bellows. I prefer using a fixed focal-length "true" macro lens because it yields a higher-image quality.
- **Tilt-Shift Lenses.** Traditionally, tilt-shift lenses are used to correct perspective and eliminate distortion, or for making panoramic photos. With this type of optic, you can tilt and shift the front lens elements to align the sensor plane with the subject without changing the angle of view. This maximizes the effectiveness of the depth of field by positioning it most advantageously in the scene. If you're photographing a meadow of wildflowers on a windy day, using a tilt-shift lens will enable you to achieve maximum sharpness without sacrificing depth of field.

Among the most popular tilt-shift lenses used for close-up photography are the Canon TS-E 90 (90mm f/2.8) and the PC Micro-Nikkor (85mm f/2.8). Both of these lenses focus closely and are further enhanced when you add extension tubes, teleconverters, and close-up supplementary lenses.

- **Close-up Supplementary Lenses.** These lenses, which are available in various "strengths" (e.g., +1, +2, +3, etc.), screw onto the front of a prime or telephoto lens like a filter and are sometimes referred to as "diopters." One-element close-up supplementary lenses are less expensive and are a reasonable alternative to purchasing a dedicated macro lens, especially if you are new to macro photography; however, they do not produce high-quality results. One real advantage in using close-up supplementary lenses is there is no light loss, which allows you to work under low-level ambient lighting conditions.

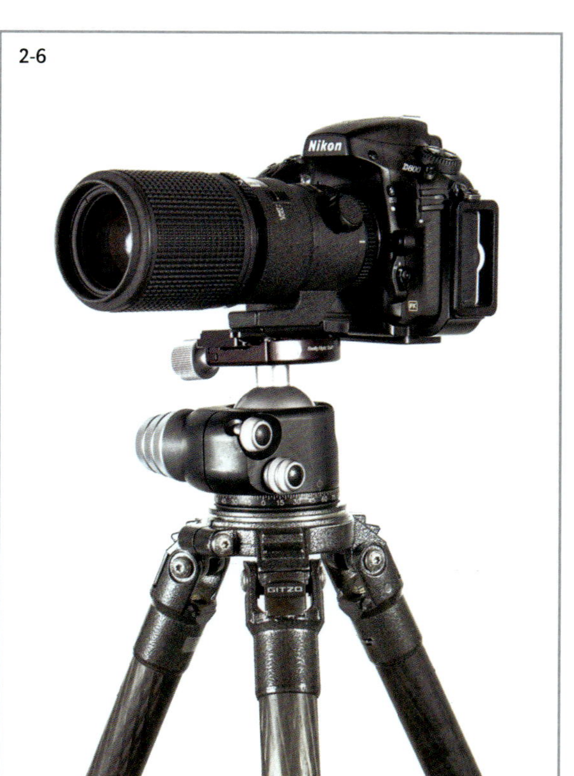

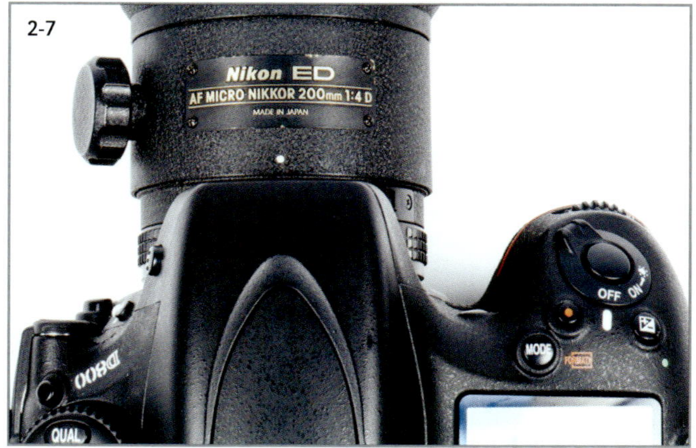

Image 2-6. Nikon 200mm macro lens mounted on Really Right Stuff BH-55 ballhead. **Image 2-7.** Nikon 200mm macro lens comes with a built-in lens collar, which allows you to change from horizontal to vertical compositions (and anything in between) easily and quickly by turning the knob (at left) on the side of the lens.

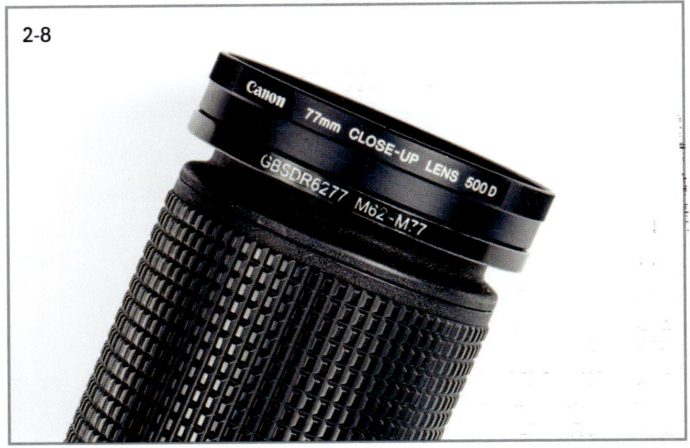

I prefer using a two-element diopter, specifically the Canon 500D close-up filter. (See **image 2-8**.) These are optically designed for lenses with focal lengths between 80mm and 200mm and yield very good results. Putting a two-element diopter on a true macro lens or a macro-zoom lens can produce some amazingly beautiful images, especially when you're going for a dreamy effect with shallow depth of field and selective focus. (See chapter 4 for image examples and instructions on how to use a dual-element close-up filter, such as the 500D.)

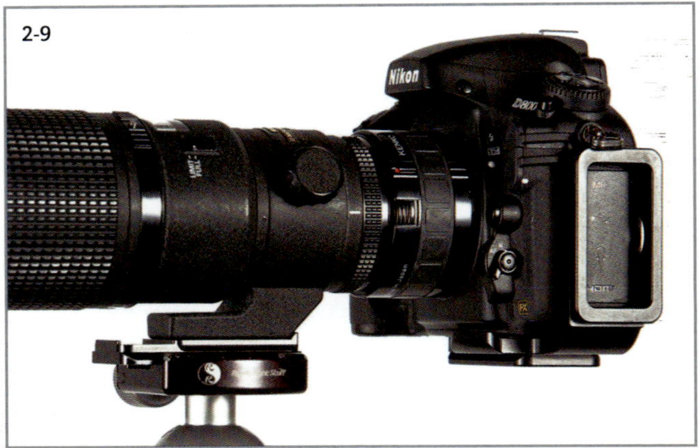

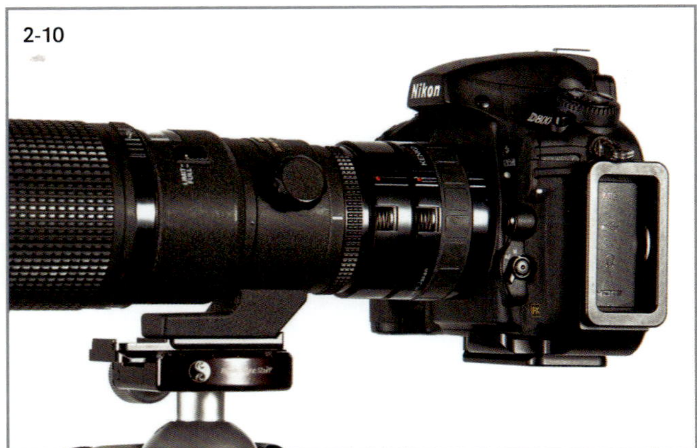

- **Telephoto Zoom Lenses.** Medium-to-long telephoto zoom lenses (70–400mm range) can be used for macro and close-up photography, especially when combined with supplementary close-up lenses, teleconverters, and extension tubes. I enjoy the creative technique of "shooting through" (explained in chapter 4) using my Nikon 70–200mm lens with the lens set at the widest aperture. Often, these types of zoom lenses come equipped with a lens collar, which can be loosened, allowing you more compositional creativity by rotating the lens.
- **Wide-Angle Lenses.** Believe it or not, wide-angle lenses make for great macro photography when combined with a short extension tube (12–15mm). At close range, you get the same feeling of expanded perspective as you would when using a wide-angle lens shooting a landscape. A more advanced way of working with wide-angle lenses is to reverse the lens (accomplished by screwing an adapter to the front of the lens) and add extension tubes or bellows. In this

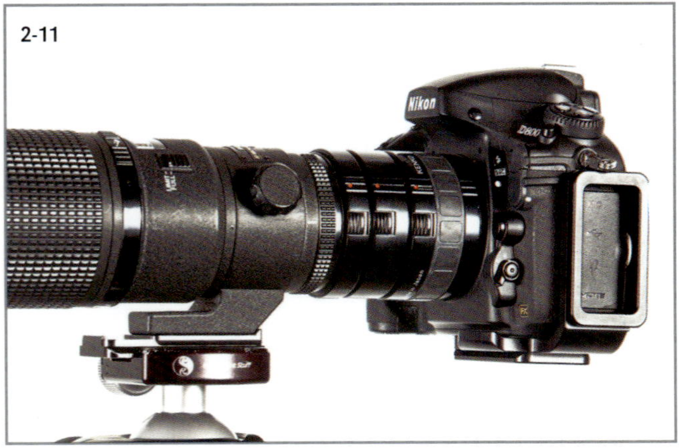

Image 2-8. Canon 500D close-up filter mounted on the end of my Nikon 200mm macro lens using a 62–77mm step-up ring. **Image 2-9.** Nikon 200mm macro lens with 36mm extension tube. **Image 2-10.** Nikon 200mm macro lens with 20mm extension tube. **Image 2-11.** Nikon 200mm macro lens with a 12mm extension tube added.

scenario, your subject is rendered greater than life-size.

- **Extension Tubes.** These hollow metal tubes fit between the lens and the camera body to extend the close-focusing range of the lens. Getting closer has the effect of magnifying your subject, making it appear larger in the viewfinder, as well as in the final image. One disadvantage of using extension tubes is that there is some loss of light, depending on how many tubes you use, which usually means you'll need a slower shutter speed to obtain the same amount of depth of field.

  I recommend a set of three tubes made by Kenko (12mm, 20mm, and 36mm; www.thkphoto.com), which can be used individually or in any combination to obtain the desired magnification. (See **images 2-9** through **2-11**.) Kenko's tubes are ideal because they're designed to maintain the camera's auto-focus and TTL auto exposure capability with most lenses. When purchasing, be sure you're getting the tube set designed for your particular camera system.

- **Extension Bellows.** Similar to extension tubes, extension bellows are also placed between the lens and the camera body for close focusing. Unlike extension tubes, however, they are adjustable in length, which allows for variable magnification.

- **Teleconverters.** These auxiliary lenses, when placed between the lens and the camera, multiply the focal length of the lens while retaining its close-focusing distance, thus allowing increased magnification. The two most common "powers" are 2X, which doubles the focal length of the lens and reduces the maximum aperture by two stops, and 1.4X, which increases the focal length of the lens by 1.4X and reduces the maximum aperture by one stop.

- **Lensbaby.** One of the coolest digital SLR accessories on the market today is the Lensbaby, a selective-focus lens that mounts directly to your camera body and allows you to creatively control a sweet spot of sharp focus, surrounded by graduated blur. Available in three distinctly different styles— Composer Pro, Muse, and Scout—the Lensbaby is guaranteed to take your macro photography to a whole new level with a little previsualization and practice.

  If you're just starting out and do not currently own a Lensbaby, I suggest you purchase the Composer Pro with Sweet 35 Optic. (See **image 2-12**, page 26.) The Sweet 35 features a twelve-bladed adjustable aperture, which gives you a smooth transition for shooting in all lighting conditions. You can also swap the Sweet 35 with a Double Glass Optic, but the disadvantage is that you'll need to use drop-in aperture rings with the Double Glass Optic, which can be more tedious and not as fluid when shooting.

One of the coolest DSLR accessories on the market today is the Lensbaby.

To achieve optimal results when shooting close-ups with a Lensbaby, I recommend you purchase either the Macro Kit or the Macro Converters, depending on which Optic you're using. You'll want a Macro Kit if you purchase or already own a Composer Pro with a Double Optic. The Macro Kit allows you to use selective focus on a very small scale. The kit includes one +4 filter and

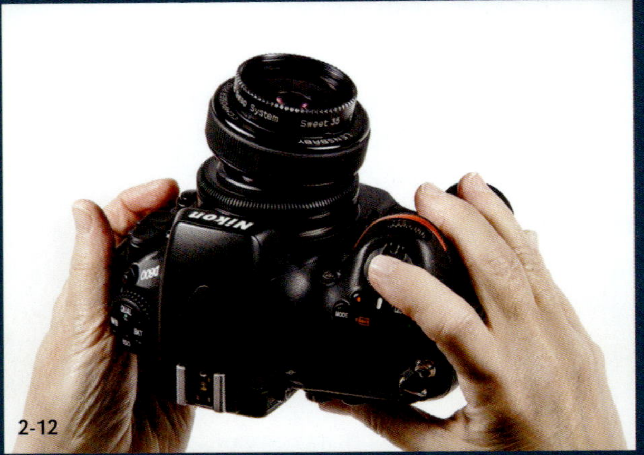 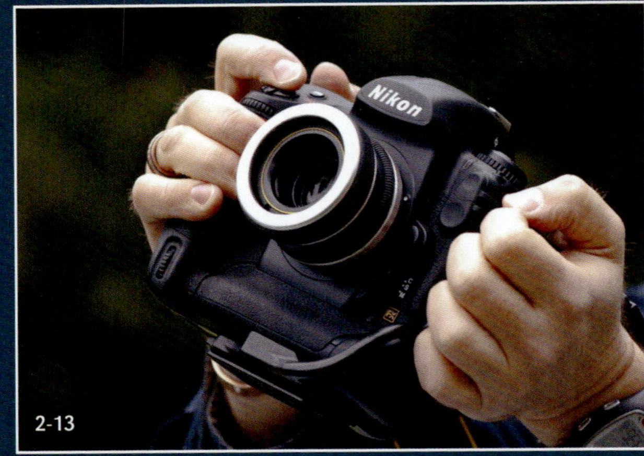

Image 2-12. Lensbaby Composer Pro with Sweet 35 Optic. **Image 2-13.** Lensbaby Composer Pro with Double Optic Glass.

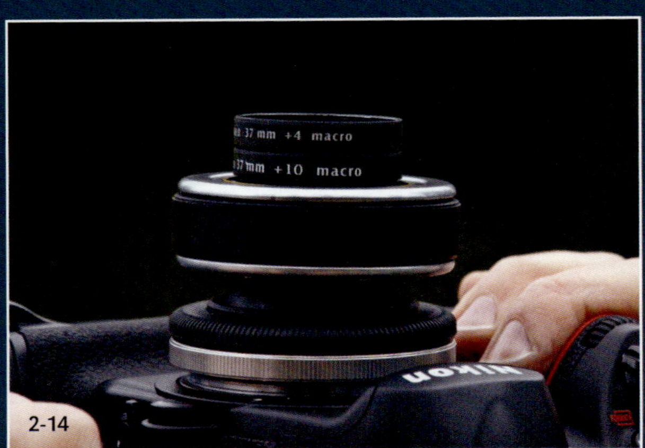 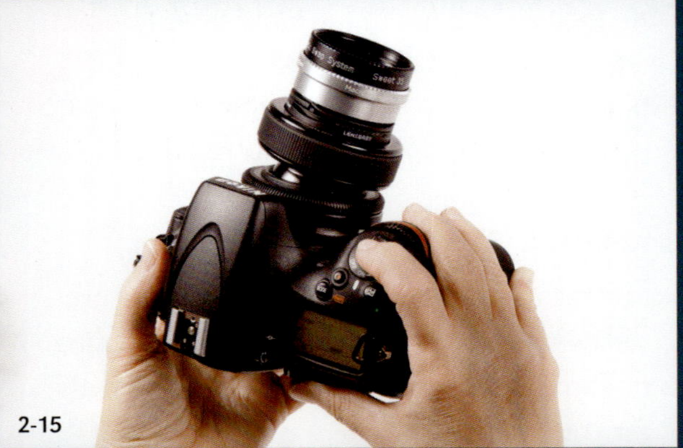

Image 2-14. Lensbaby Composer Pro with Double Optic Glass, +4 and +10 macro filters. **Image 2-15.** Lensbaby Composer Pro with Sweet 35 Optic and two macro converters.

one +10 filter, which are screwed onto the front of the Lensbaby (separately or stacked together), enabling you to focus from 2 to 13 inches away.

If you purchase or already own a Composer Pro with the Sweet 35 Optic, then you'll want to consider adding a set of Macro Converters (8mm and 16mm, sold as a set) to allow you to focus from 1.63 to 5 inches away. (See **images 2-13** through **2-15**.)

Another Optic you might wish to consider purchasing for your Lensbaby macro photography is the 0.42x Super Wide Angle lens attachment, which converts your Lensbaby's focal length from 50mm to 21mm, allowing you to focus as close as 2¾ inches from the front of the lens. (See **image 2-13**.) I've been experimenting with this lens attachment and am extremely excited by the results, especially when combined with the

500D Canon close-up lens for an even more unusual perspective.

You will learn more about rule-bending Lensbaby creative techniques in chapter 4.

- **Taleidoscope Lens.** This exclusively designed, specialized lens allows you to create a kaleidoscopic effect when photographing close-up subjects. This handmade optic contains three internal mirrors and comes with a 62mm thread size. It can be mounted either flush to a macro or medium-telephoto lens, or held 6–12 inches in front of the lens. Flowers and other macro subjects with strong graphic lines work best with a taleidoscopic lens. (See **image 2-17**.)
- **Right-Angle Viewfinder.** These devices help you get creative low-angle shots without having to bend your neck and back in awkward, often painful positions. They're also useful when you're trying to get a shot with limited space behind the camera (e.g., near a large tree). I like the Professional Right Angle Viewfinder made by Hoodman Corporation (www.hoodmanusa.com) because it comes with four universal mounting attachments (to fit all Canon, Nikon, and Fuji digital SLR cameras), built-in 2.5X magnification capability, and an eyepiece that rotates 360 degrees. (See **image 2-18**.)
- **Polarizer.** With the advent of digital photography, I've found I'm using fewer and fewer filters in front of the lens, since I can make corrections post-capture. However, one tried-and-true choice I'm consistently reaching for is my 77mm circular polarizing filter (77mm because that's the largest filter thread size on my largest lens). Polarizers are commonly used for landscape photography,

but there are plenty of uses when shooting macro. I've used mine to eliminate blown-out highlights on shiny foliage as well as unwanted reflections on glass and glass objects. Another creative way to use a

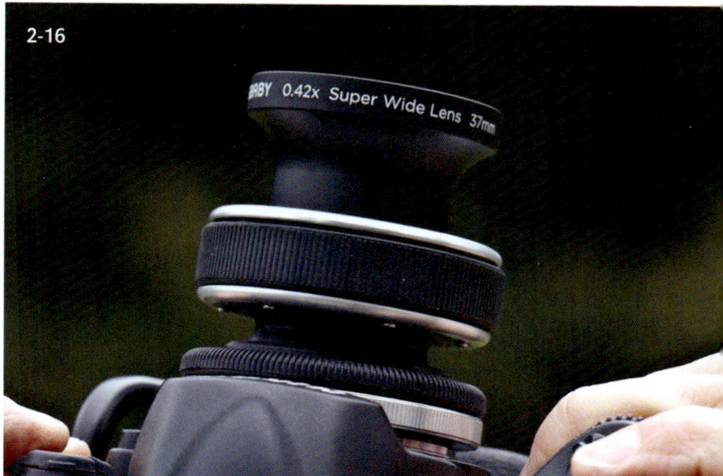

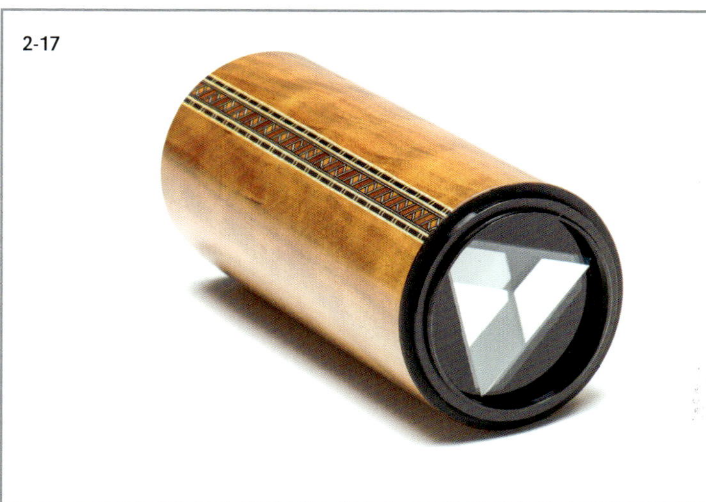

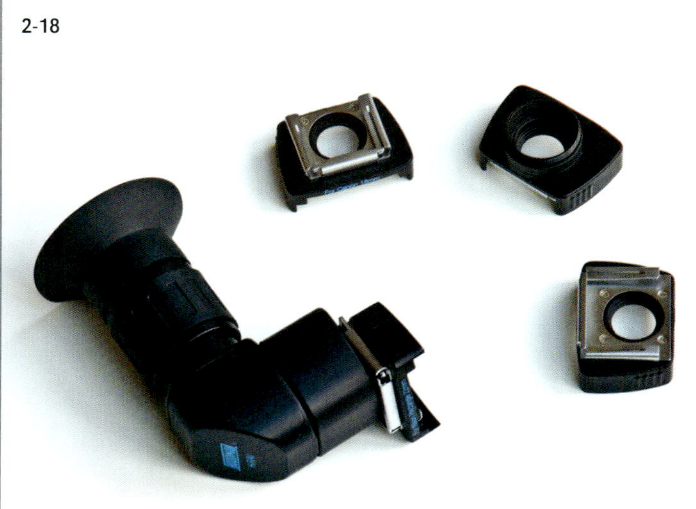

Image 2-16. Lensbaby Composer Pro with double optic glass and .42X super-wide-angle lens. **Image 2-17.** Taleidoscope lens (with 62mm thread size). **Image 2-18.** Hoodman right-angle viewer with interchangeable viewfinder adapters.

polarizer when shooting macro is to combine its use with polarizing paper, a technique called "cross-polarization." (See chapter 5 for more on cross-polarization.)

- **Variable ND Filter.** The variable neutral-density filter from Singh-Ray Filters (www.singh-ray.com/varind.html) greatly expands your creative possibilities when it comes to motion blur, selective focus, and longer exposure time. (See **image 2-19**.) It also provides better close-up flash control by reducing the quantity of ambient (available) light in the scene. The variable ND filter is available only from Singh-Ray and allows you to continuously control the amount of light passing through your lens from 2 to 8 exposure stops with no loss of color fidelity or sharpness. I've experimented with this filter with a variety of creative camera techniques, including slap-zooms, panning, rotating, and even in-camera multiple exposures.

Camera Supports

Macro photography necessitates the use of a sturdy, stable camera support because even the smallest amount of camera shake at high magnification can cause image blur. Here are some of the options:

- **Tripod.** One of the most important purchases you'll ever make for macro photography is a good, sturdy tripod. I use a tripod 99 percent of the time because it helps me refine my compositions, have greater control over depth of field, and make sharper images. When shopping for tripods for close-up/macro work, keep in mind it's best to buy one in which all three legs move

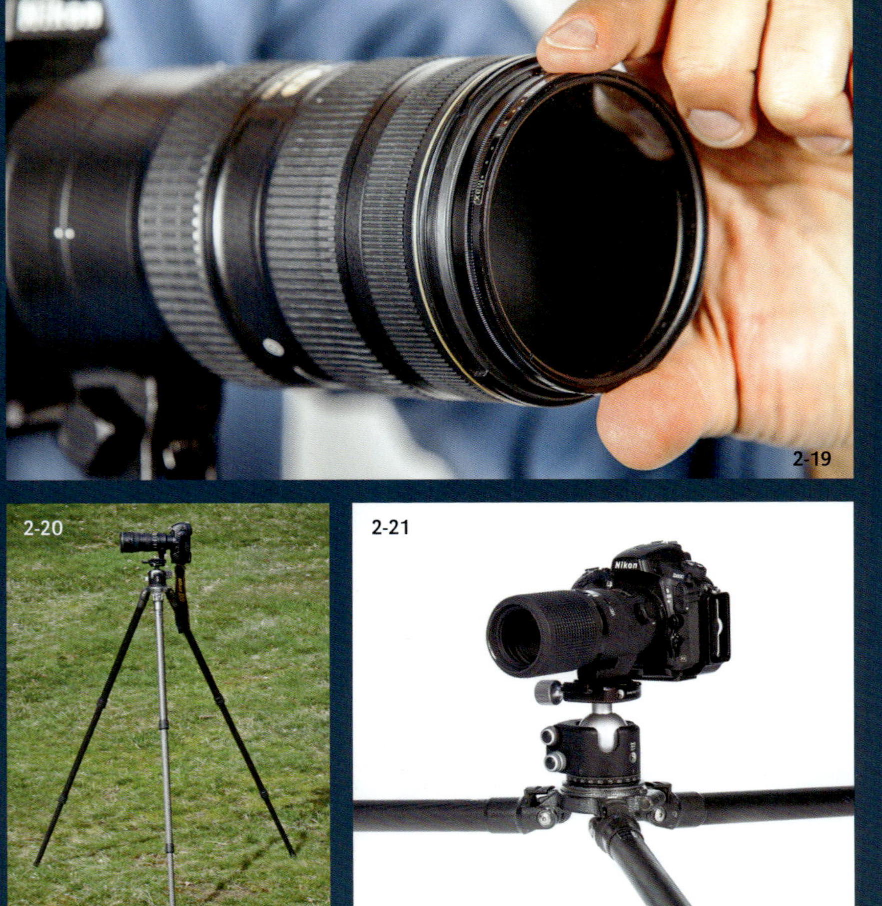

Image **2-19.** The Singh-Ray variable neutral-density (ND) filter can prevent up to 8 stops of light from entering the lens with no loss of color fidelity or sharpness. **Image 2-20.** Gitzo 3532LS carbon-fiber tripod. **Image 2-21.** Gitzo tripod with legs fully collapsible to within 6 inches from the ground. **Image 2-22.** Joby GorillaPod SLR-Zoom model.

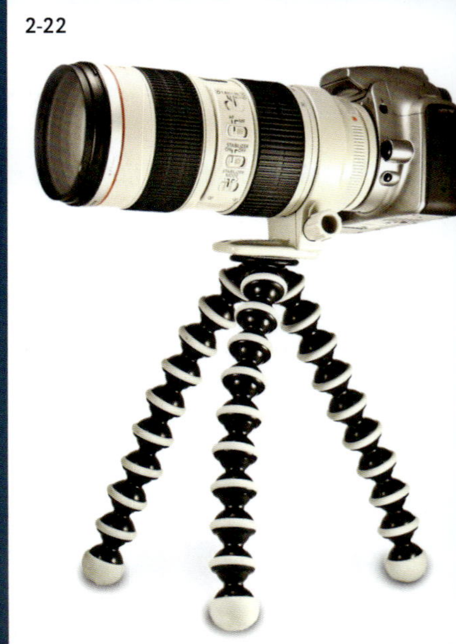

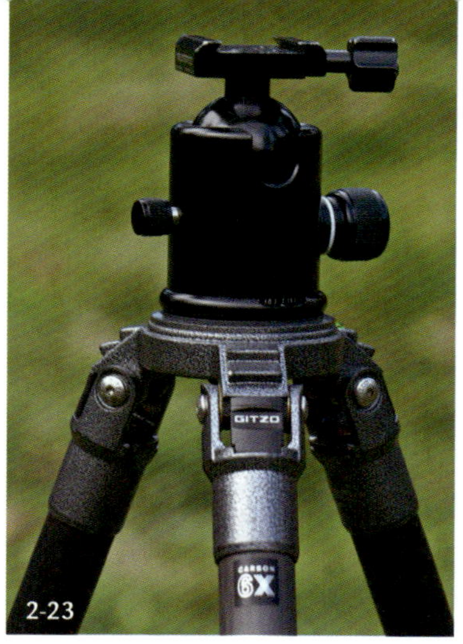

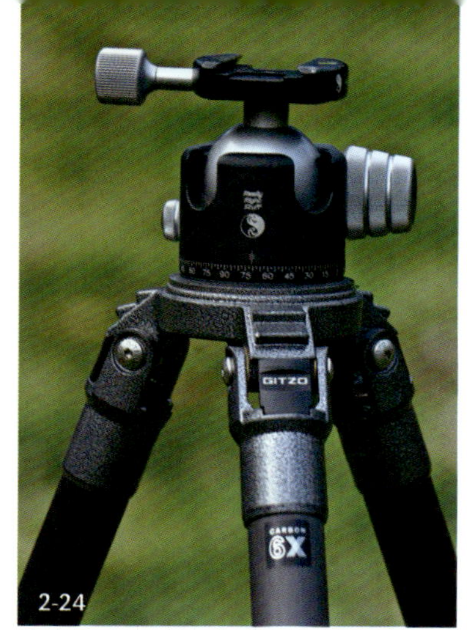

Image 2-23. BH-1 ballhead with quick-release plate (manufactured by Kirk Enterprises). **Image 2-24.** BH-55 ballhead with quick-release plate (manufactured by Really Right Stuff).

independently from one another. (Often, video tripods and less-expensive consumer models are designed so that all three legs move together simultaneously, thus hindering tripod leg positioning if you're shooting on uneven terrain.) Equally important is the ability to lower the legs to within 6 inches of the ground, especially when working with tiny macro subjects in the field, such as wildflowers and mushrooms. This means finding a tripod without a center column or at least with a removable one.

My tripod of choice is the Gitzo GT3532LS (see **images 2-20** and **2-21**) because it's sturdy, lightweight (four pounds), and collapses down to within 4 inches of the ground. This professional-level tripod is designed for digital SLRs with 300–500mm lenses (with a maximum supported weight of 40 pounds). If you can't afford a Gitzo, I'd consider going with either Manfrotto or Bogen brand tripods.

Another useful tripod for tabletop macro photography is the Joby GorillaPod, which is flexible and can wrap around almost any surface. Be sure to get the SLR-Zoom version or the Focus model, because these two can support 6–11 pounds. (See **image 2-22**.)

- **Tripod Head.** Tripod heads come in all shapes, sizes, and configurations and are usually sold separately from the tripod. I prefer ballheads because they're more user-friendly (with one main knob to loosen and tighten and another for panning). Other types include: pistol-grip style and three-way pan/tilt heads. I've found the latter two to be much more cumbersome and less stable. Regardless of which head you choose, I'd recommend getting a quick-release plate (a flat metal plate on top of the head, which sometimes comes standard). This allows you to quickly remove and replace the camera atop the ballhead—very helpful when composing close-up shots, since often you want to establish working distance and minimum focus quickly without having to lift the entire tripod. In my mind, two ballheads, in particular, stand out: the BH-1 (or smaller BH-3) by Kirk Enterprises and the BH-55 (or smaller BH-40) by Really Right Stuff. (See **images 2-23** and **2-24**.) Both of these companies produce high-quality products that will last a lifetime.

Note: Purchasing this type of ballhead with a quick-release plate requires that you also buy a metal camera body plate—or an

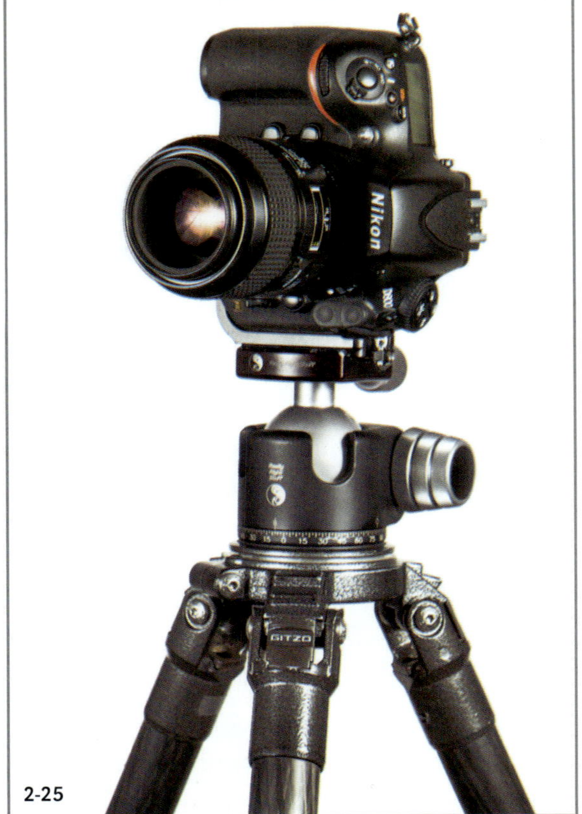

2-25

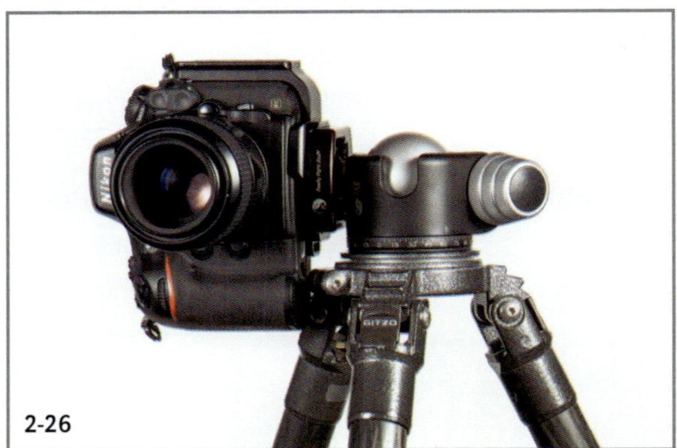

2-26

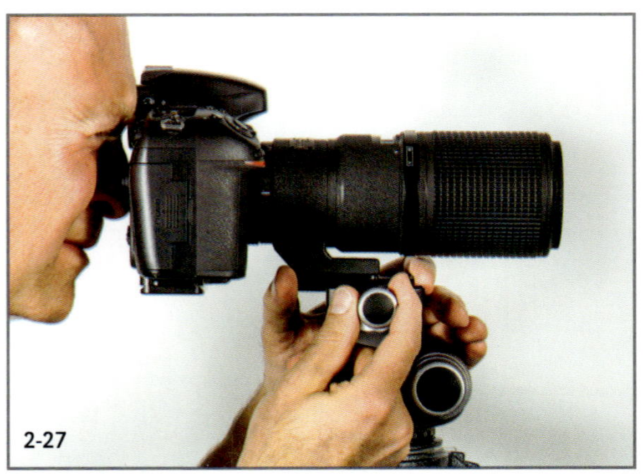

2-27

L bracket, if you prefer. (See **images 2-25 and 2-26**.) Ask Kirk or Really Right Stuff to recommend the right camera body plate for your particular camera. If you own a longer-focal length lens that mounts via a lens foot, you'll also need to purchase the appropriate lens plate.

I highly recommend you consider purchasing a flash bracket.

- **Focusing Rail.** This support accessory is attached between the tripod head and the camera or lens collar and allows for fine-tuning camera-to-subject distance in minute increments, resulting in super-fine focus. Personally, I have not yet purchased a focusing rail because I use the 200mm macro lens primarily and am able to adjust camera positioning by manually loosening the jaw grip on the quick-release plate and sliding the camera back and forth along the lens plate, which is mounted permanently to the foot of my 200mm macro lens. (See image **2-27**.)
- **Macro Flash Bracket.** In order to facilitate using your external flash off-camera—especially important when shooting macro—I highly recommend you consider purchasing a flash bracket. One of the most versatile, easy-to-use and durable macro flash brackets

Images 2-25 and 2-26. The advantage of installing an L bracket is that you can place the camera in a vertical position without having to alter the composition. (Image 2-26 illustrates what happens when you want to change to a vertical position without an L bracket installed.) **Image 2-27.** If you don't own a focusing rail and want to fine-tune your focus, you can loosen the knob on the quick-release plate and slide the camera back and forth in small increments. Of course, this is only possible when using longer focal-length macro lenses, such as Canon's 180mm and Nikon's 200mm macro lenses.

I've found is the F-2 Macro Bracket made by Wimberley. Unlike many other flash brackets currently on the market, this one is designed specifically for macro photography and is comprised of two double-ball-and-socket links that lock into a great range of flash positions. It is lightweight and very portable as well. The bracket attaches quickly to your lens or camera body plate with a narrow Arca-Swiss style quick release and can be used in a dual-flash setup, if desired. (I use only one F-2 for most of my close-up work.) If you're mounting the F-2 to your camera body plate (not a lens plate), you will need to purchase the Module 8 (M-8) Perpendicular Plate.

When using Wimberley's macro flash bracket, I recommend adding the Wimberley Module 3 (M-3 Tilt Arm) to your flash bracket. This arm gives your flash extra reach and can also serve as a grip when holding the camera while composing. Keep in mind you will need to purchase a sync cord for your flash, which is mounted between the flash unit and the camera's hot shoe, or use a wireless flash system. (See **images 2-28** through **2-31**.)

- **Beanbag.** For those situations when you need to position your camera very low, don't want to use a tripod, or when tripods are not allowed, I've found that a beanbag works well. You can make one yourself using strong

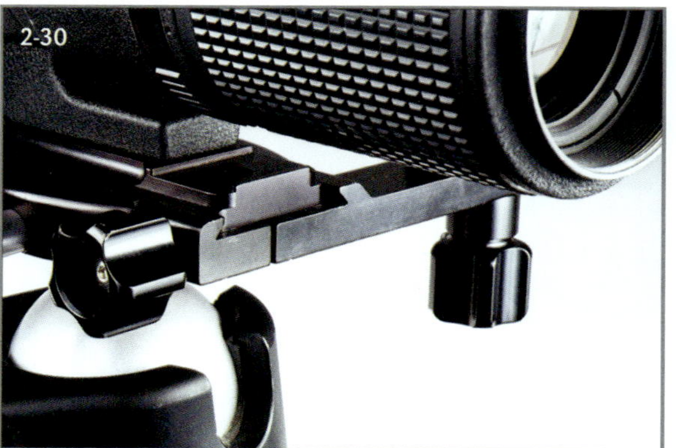

2-28

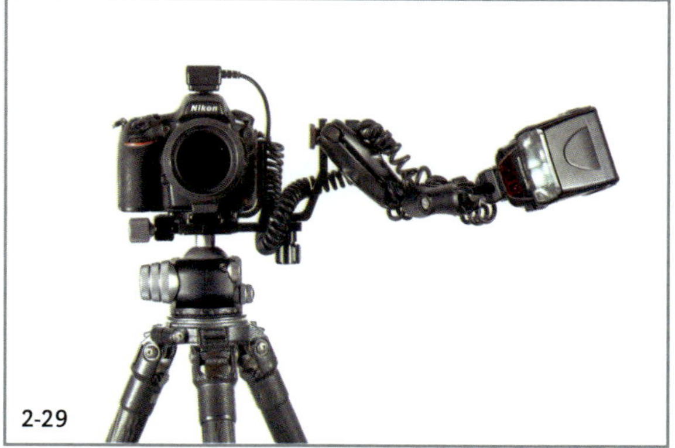

2-29

Images 2-28 through 2-31. Wimberley's F-2 Macro Bracket, when combined with the M-3 Tilt Arm, gives your flash extra reach and allows the flash to quickly and easily be repositioned, as illustrated in image 2-29. The bracket attaches to the end of the lens plate, as illustrated in images 2-30 and 2-31.

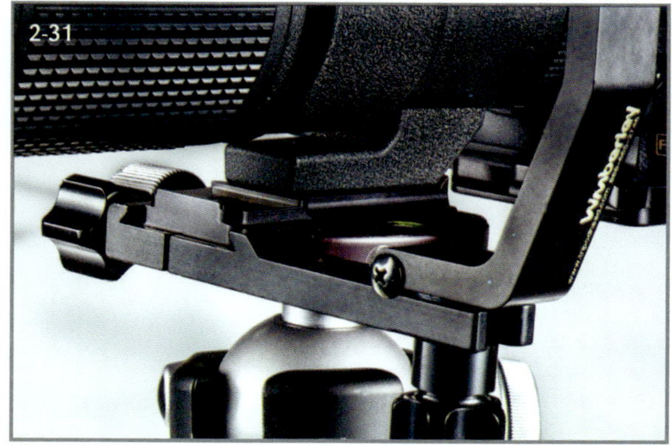

2-30

2-31

nylon material and fill the pouch with beans or sand, or you can purchase one, such as the Gura Gear Sabi Sack.

Other Cool, Useful Gadgets and Props

- **Plamp.** This easily positionable, flexible arm clamps to a tripod (or any other stationary object, if you're working in a home studio) and is useful in stabilizing plants, flowers, and other items. (See **images 2-33 and 2-34**.) I've used a Plamp for everything from removing distracting elements from backgrounds, to holding tools such as a small reflector, to holding a piece of colored paper to create a more pleasing background. I like adding a 12-inch "Plamp extension" to my Plamp for a longer reach, especially when I'm shooting with my 200mm macro lens. In my opinion, no serious macro photographer should be

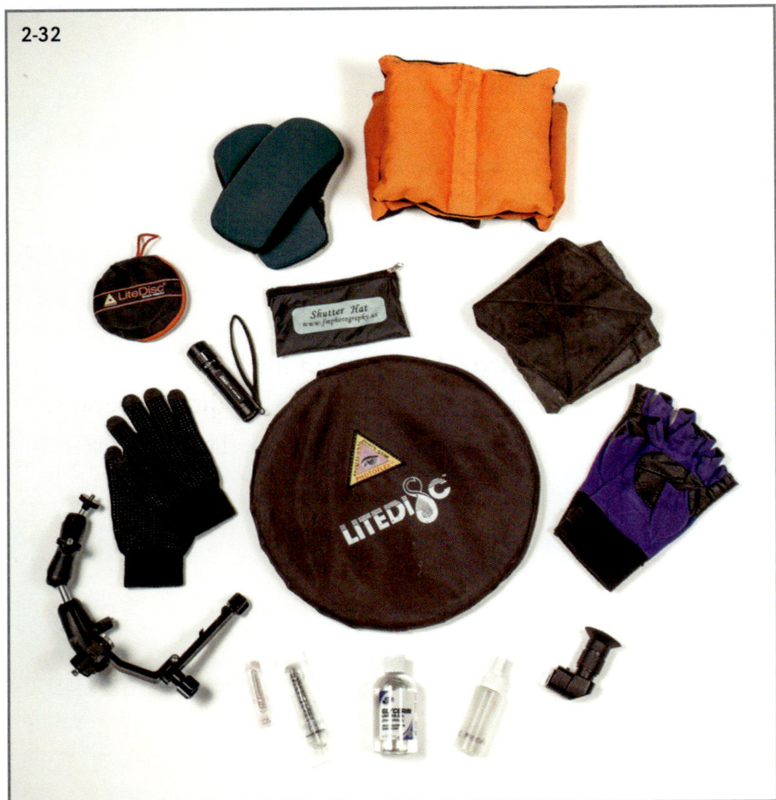

Image 2-32. I find these accessories helpful when shooting close-ups. (Clockwise L-R): 12-inch gold/silver reflector, macro knee pads, Shutter Hat, GroundHog beanbag (no longer available from manufacturer), macro ground cloth, fingerless gloves, right-angle viewer, small spray bottle, glycerin, syringe, macro flash bracket, tech gloves (to operate your smart phone and/or tablet in cold weather), multi-color LED flashlight, and 42-inch diffuser.

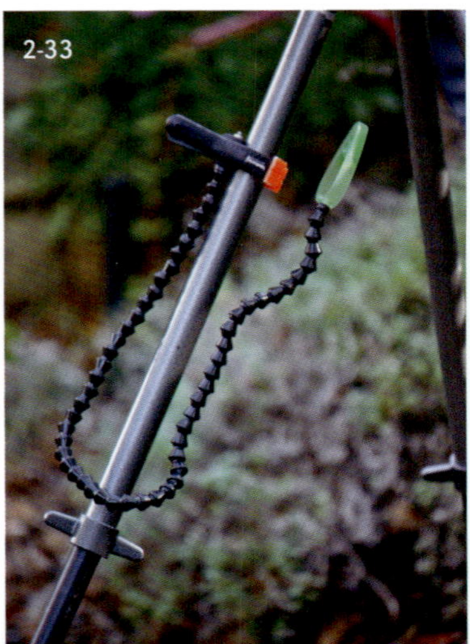

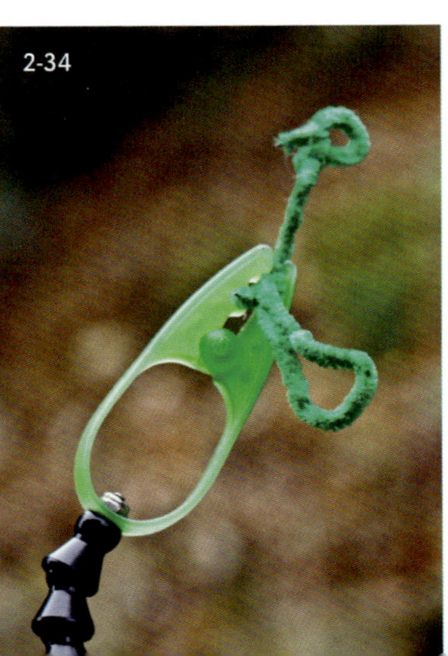

Image 2-33. The Plamp easily clamps to a tripod leg. Image 2-34. Use a pipe cleaner at the end of the Plamp to help stabilize delicate flower stems.

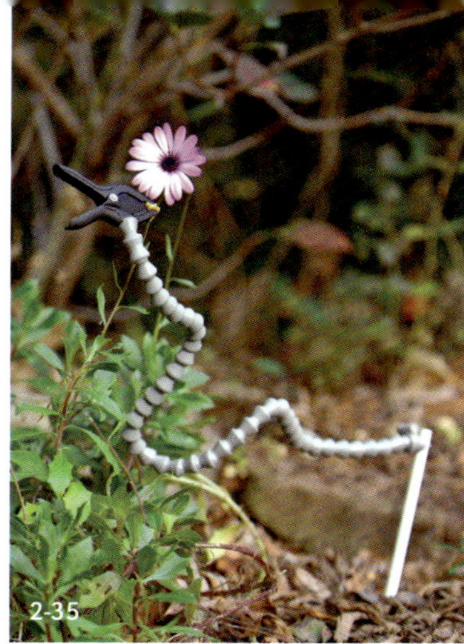

Image 2-35. The McClamp stick clamp can be anchored into the ground.

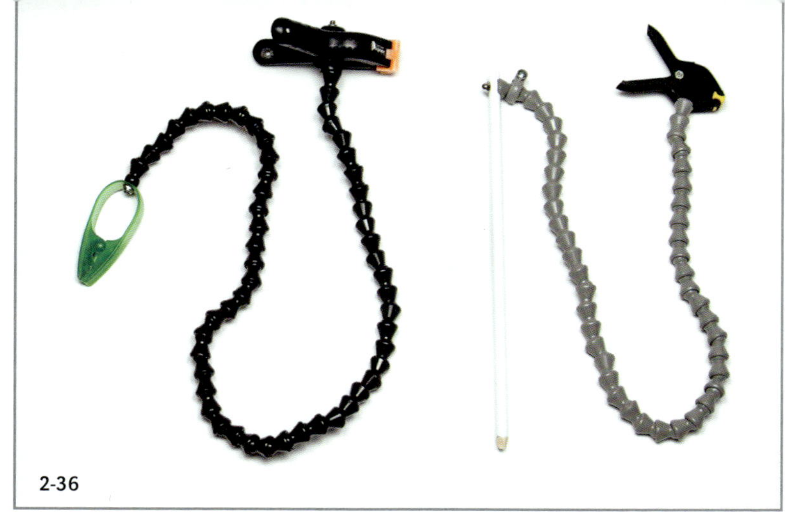

Image 2-36 (L–R). Plamp with "R" Plamp extension and McClamp stick clamp.

without at least one Plamp in his/her camera bag.

Tip: To avoid harming the stem on delicate flowers, attach a pipe cleaner to the clamp and then wrap it around the flower stem. (See **image 2-34**.)

- **McClamp Stick Clamp.** Not to be confused with the Plamp, the McClamp is a similar device hinged to a stick but can be anchored into the soil, allowing you to move your tripod without disturbing the subject and fine-tune your composition. It's also great for holding a diffuser or reflector in place when you don't have an extra arm. (See **images 2-35** and **2-36**.)

- **Flexible Knee Pads.** If you're going to shoot a lot of close-ups close to the ground, then I'd purchase a pair of knee pads. These can come in handy especially when you're down on your knees for long periods of time on concrete walkways in public gardens, or even just at home in your backyard "macro studio" on a deck or patio. I have tried several different types of knee pads over the years and prefer ones that are flexible, as opposed to ones made of hard plastic. These are more compact (making them easier to carry in your camera bag) and more comfortable, as they bend with your knees. Gardening supply stores usually sell the flexible variety, but I also sell them in my workshops.

- **Shutter Hat.** One of the best times to shoot macro photos is during a light rain because colors are more saturated. The Shutter Hat is a device that helps keep your camera dry while shooting under these weather conditions. It's made from lightweight, coated nylon and folds into a tiny pouch about the size of a deck of cards (weighing just a couple ounces). A couple of Velcro tabs hold the front sleeve on the lens barrel, and unlike similar products currently on the market, this one allows for unobstructed access to the rear of your camera body. (See **images 2-37** and **2-38** on page 34.)

- **Macro Ground Cloth.** This 60x26-inch waterproof, heavy-duty nylon ground cloth is perfect for keeping yourself clean and dry when shooting macro subjects in the field. It rolls up to size $6\frac{1}{2}$x$2\frac{1}{2}$ inches, small

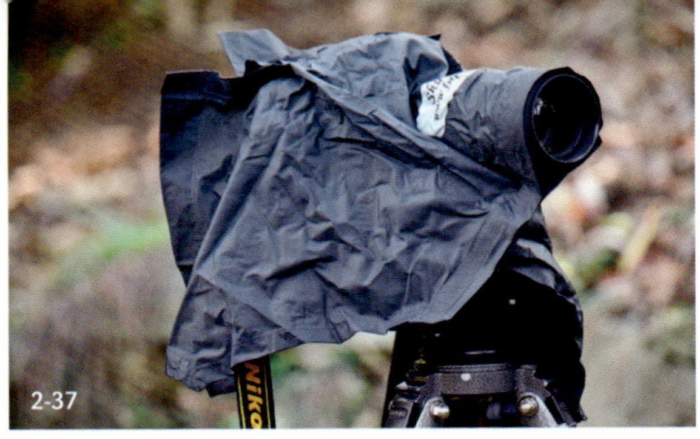

enough to fit in your camera vest pocket. The ground cloth is available from A. Laird Photo Accessories.

- **Rocket-Air Blower.** I carry a medium-sized Rocket-Air Blower in my camera bag at all times for blowing dust and dirt off my camera body and lenses. This is a much better solution than compressed air because you don't risk damaging expensive equipment by expelling liquid.

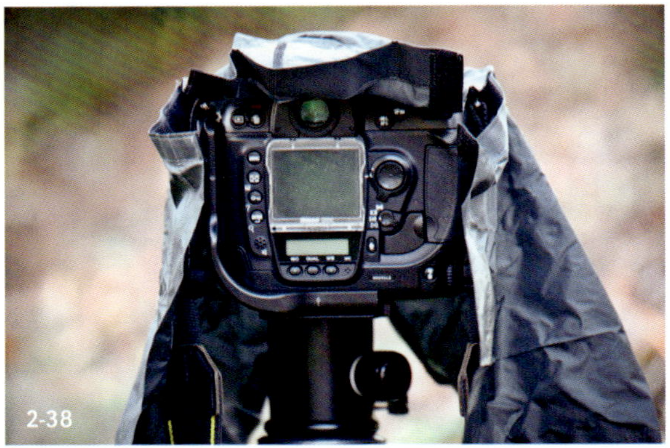

A Hoodloupe allows you to review your shot on the camera's LCD without glare.

- **LCD Viewer (HoodLoupe).** This device allows you to review your shot on the camera's LCD without glare, which can be a problem on bright, sunny days. I prefer the HoodLoupe 3.0 for digital SLR cameras from Hoodman Corporation, which features an adjustable diopter and 1:1 ratio magnification of the LCD screen. (See **image 2-39**.)

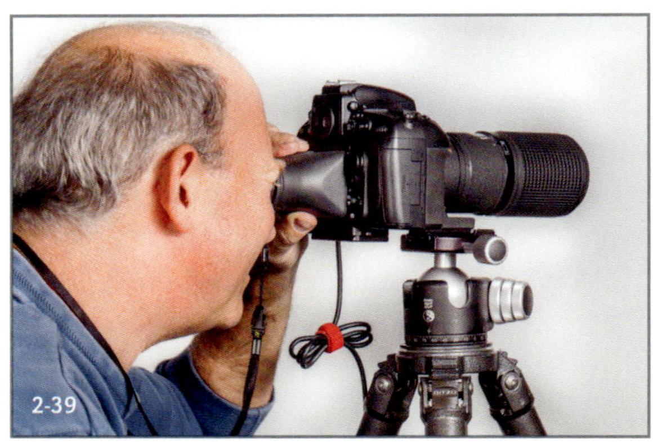

- **Reflector.** To extend tonal range in shadow areas and add a sense of warmth to your macro images, I recommend using a small collapsible 12-inch gold/silver reflector, since it's small enough to hold close to flowers and other macro subjects without getting in the way of your shot or damaging the flower. I use the gold side almost always, since it simulates the warm glow of natural sunlight. (See **image 2-40**.) For more tips on using a reflector to enhance your macro photography, see the "Lighting" section in chapter 3.
- **Diffuser.** Collapsible diffuser discs are made of translucent material—similar to that of a

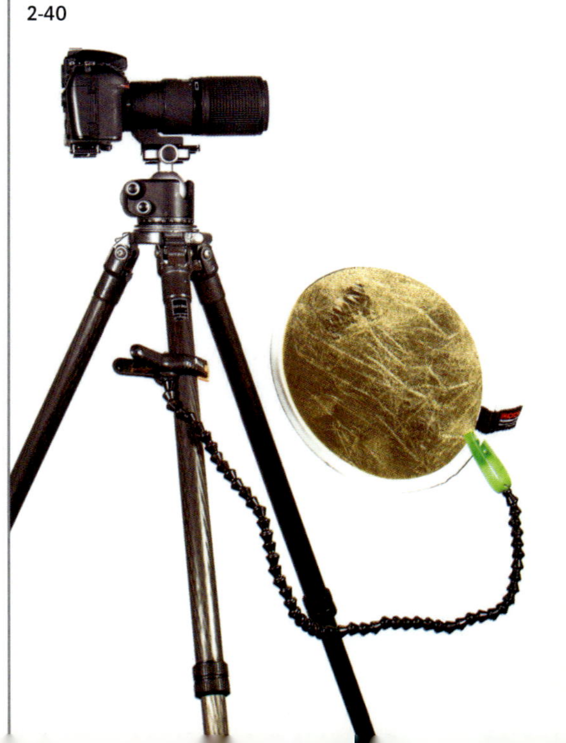

Image 2-37. The Shutter Hat can be attached to a longer macro lens to allow for shooting under misty, drizzling weather conditions. **Image 2-38.** The Shutter Hat keeps your camera dry during a light rain and still allows access to the camera controls from the rear. **Image 2-39.** An LCD viewer (HoodLoupe) can be especially helpful on a bright, sunny day because it blocks incoming light and magnifies the image. **Image 2-40.** The 12-inch gold reflector disc can be easily held using a Plamp.

fabric shower curtain liner—and they help soften and spread the light to significantly reduce or eliminate shadows and glare from sunlight. They allow you to create soft light instantly and achieve greater control over your light source, yielding very pleasing results. I recommend the 42-inch translucent LiteDisc made by Photoflex because it covers a broad area, which is often necessary when working in the field under sunny skies and you wish to eliminate harsh shadows in both the foreground and background. (See **image 2-41**.)

- **Multi-Colored Flashlight.** This cool macro tool allows you to selectively illuminate a portion of the subject or background. Typically used for first responders, military, policemen, or hunting enthusiasts, these flashlights come in many shapes and sizes. I highly recommend the Browning Black Ice Xenon/LED Flashlight or the Coleman Multi-Color LED Flashlight, which both feature built-in colored LED lights—red and blue and white. (See **image 2-42**.)

If you'd prefer a flashlight that has different levels of output, then you could go with the Fenix L1D flashlight, available from LightHound. You can even purchase various diffuser attachments (Surefire FM34 or Surefire F04 diffuser) as an accessory that clamps onto the front of a flashlight at www.opticsplanet.com.

For more on the creative use of colored flashlights, see chapter 3.

- **Toolbox.** For those times when you need something unusual to aid in getting the perfect shot, it's a good idea to create your own macro toolbox. (See **image 2-43**.) Mine has evolved over the years and consists of pipe cleaners, clothespins, Blu-Tack reusable

Image 2-41. The 42-inch diffuser disc softens harsh sunlight and covers a wide area. **Image 2-42.** Coleman Multi-Color LED flashlight allows you to shine red, blue, or white beams of light onto your close-up subject, which can create a subtle, pleasing lighting effect. **Image 2-43.** My macro toolbox.

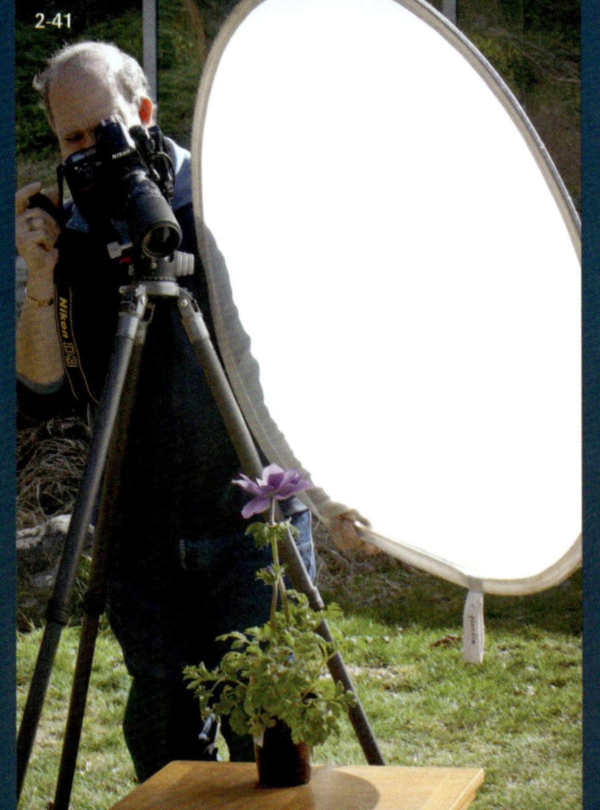

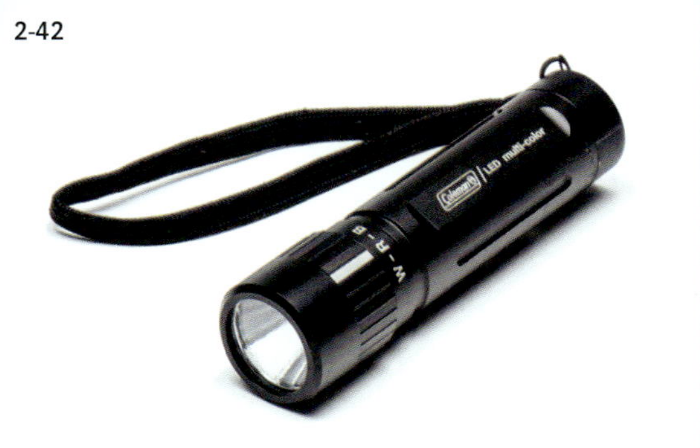

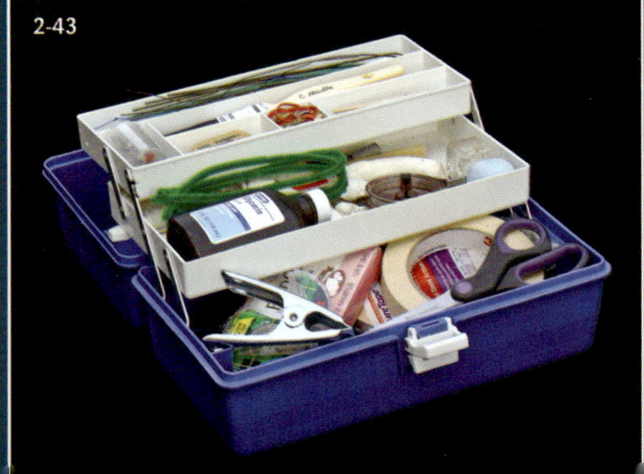

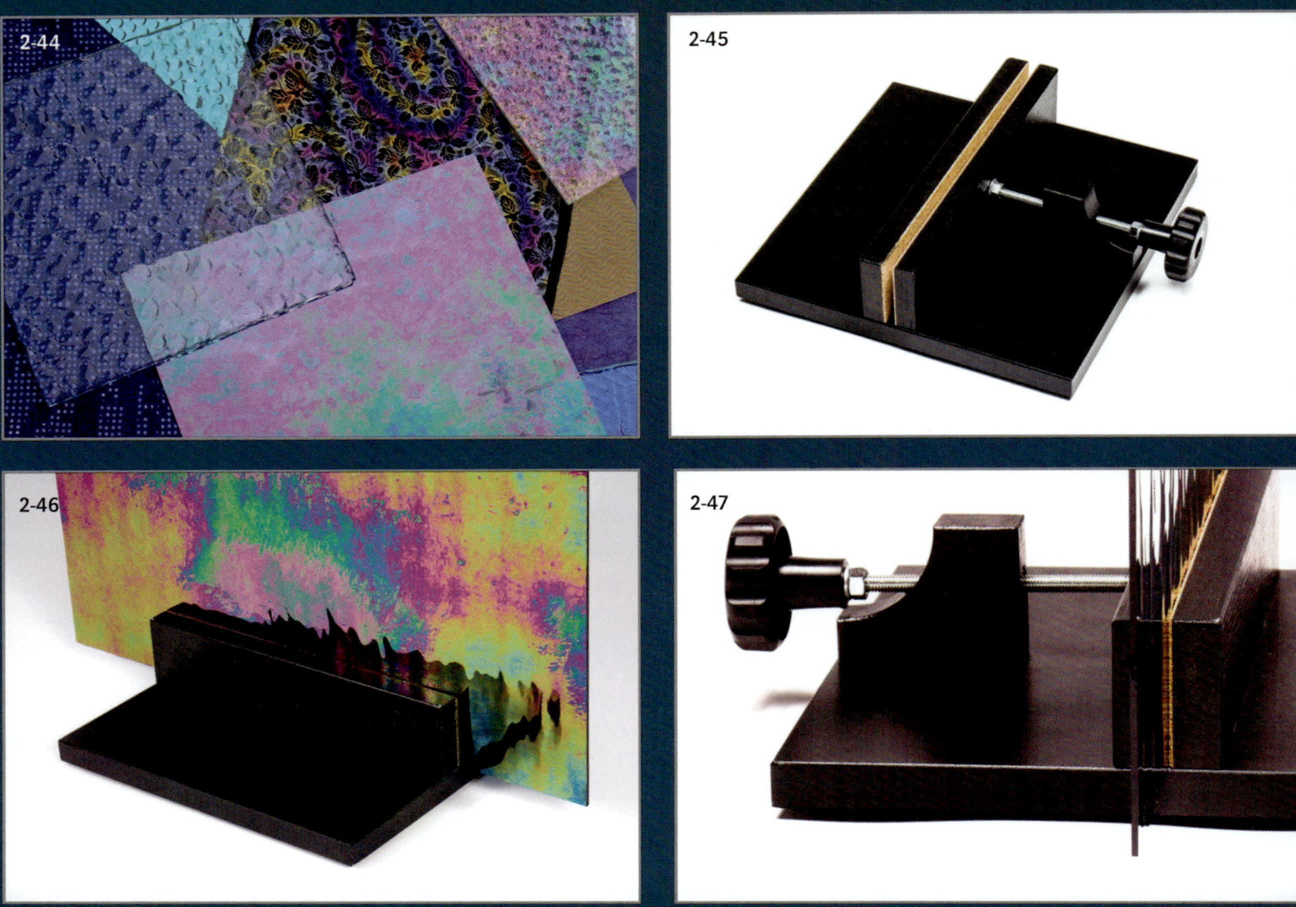

Image 2-44. Iridescent glass, clear textured glass, colorful fabric, and background materials. **Images 2-45 through 2-47.** This exclusively designed glass stand keeps glass in an upright, vertical position and adjusts to various glass widths. It also features small rubber feet on the bottom to prevent slippage.

adhesive putty, scissors, tweezers, floral wire, tin foil, glycerin, small clamps, drinking straws, masking tape, black artist's tape, white artist's tape, fishing line, needle and thread, a small spray bottle, paper clips, and a soft eraser.

- **Spray Bottle/Glycerin.** A spray bottle can be used to create dew on close-up subjects. I use a special 2-ounce spray bottle made in China and available for purchase at www.bettysstamppad.com. When searching for small spray bottles, be sure to test the spray and make sure it's to your liking. Not all spray bottles were created equal! Some create very artificial looking droplets that are all the same size. If you want to precisely place water droplets on plants and flowers, then consider using a small syringe. To make water droplets cling better, sometimes I will make a solution of $^3/_4$ water and about $^1/_4$ liquid glycerin (available in most drugstores and pharmacies). See chapter 5 for ideas on ways to use glycerin alone when shooting tabletop macro with props.

- **Stained Glass and Textured Glass.** For a more impressionistic look, and to expand creative possibilities, I have an extensive collection of various pieces of colored stained glass and textured (clear) glass in my home macro studio. (See **image 2-44**.) Look for pieces that are at least 20x24 inches (and preferably 40x40 inches) to allow enough surface area to cover your subject. (You're going to be photographing flowers behind the glass, on top of the glass, and even reflecting in the glass. See chapter 5 for a detailed explanation of these techniques.) Often, you can find smaller samples in scrap bins at stained-glass supply stores. For a list of glass suppliers, see the Appendix and Resource Guide.

- **Glass Stand.** For stabilizing a large sheet of glass, keeping it in an upright, vertical position when shooting flowers and other macro subjects, and for supporting various background materials such as fabric and colored paper, I use a specially designed and built glass stand, which is available exclusively through my website. (See **images 2-45** through **2-47**.) This not only helps prevent breakage but also allows for greater flexibility when changing pieces in and out.
- **Rolling Photo Backpack.** In this post-9/11 world of tightening airline restrictions, I travel with a rolling backpack, LowePro Road Runner AW, and carefully pack all my fragile lenses, detached tripod head, and camera bodies inside. (See **image 2-48**.) Then I check a large duffel bag that contains a smaller, more lightweight LowePro photo backpack,

stuffed with various nonbreakable photo accessories, along with my Gitzo tripod legs.

Once I arrive at my destination before traveling to a given location, I then transfer whatever I will need from the larger camera backpack into the smaller one. This system seems to work well for longer trips when I know I will want all of my gear with me.

According to current TSA regulations (www.tsa.gov/travelers/airtravel/assistant/ editorial_1248.shtm), photographers are allowed to carry on two bags when at least one is photographic equipment, along with a personal item.

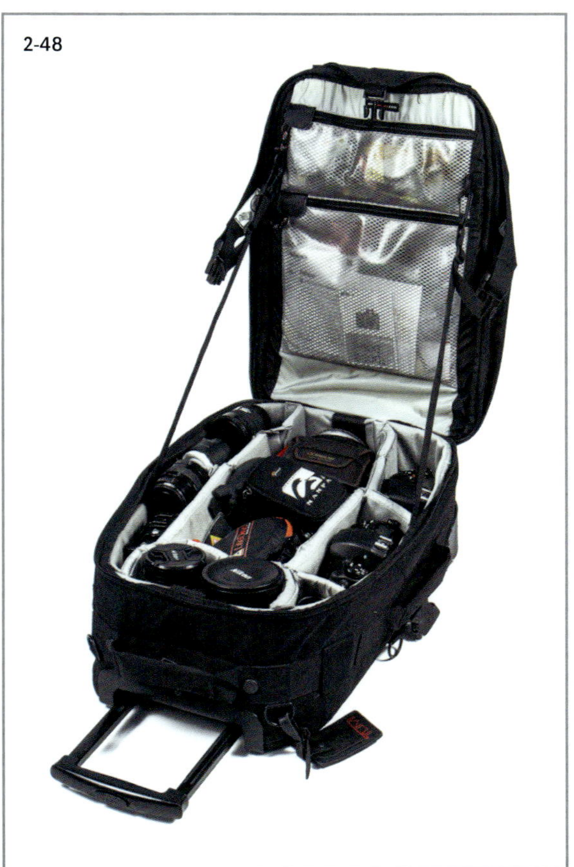

Image 2-48. The LowePro Road Runner AW photo backpack fully loaded with my camera gear.

3. Fundamentals of Macro Photography

Close-up photography is one of the most exciting types of photography because you're given an opportunity to view ordinary subjects with increased magnification, which often reveals far greater detail than the "naked eye" can see. When the camera moves in close, you begin seeing subjects in new, unimaginable ways. What was once familiar is suddenly altered, and you can become awestruck by the incredible beauty in tiny worlds.

You can become awestruck by the incredible beauty in tiny worlds.

Regardless of what type of photography you're most accustomed to shooting—portrait, landscape, architecture, etc.—close-up photography offers several rewards. First and foremost, you'll learn a whole new way of "seeing." By studying details and parts of what we habitually see as whole objects, you'll sharpen your eye as an image-maker. You'll also develop more patience and a greater appreciation for your subject. Instead of merely "taking" snapshots, you'll begin to really "make" images that reveal something about yourself and how you, as a human being and photographer, relate to the world around you.

More than anything else, macro photography expands your creative horizons. Once you learn the fundamentals, you can allow yourself the freedom to break all the rules and venture into the unknown. It's this magical process of discovery that can lead to some of the most stunning and artistic imagery you've ever seen.

This chapter will familiarize you with the fundamentals of macro photography and provide a foundation for thinking outside the box. I encourage you to practice the basics regularly, no matter how mundane it might seem, and get in the habit of observing nature on a frequent basis (with or without your camera). Soon, you'll begin seeing improvement in your work, and studying the results will help you refine your techniques along the way. Whether you're just beginning and are considering purchasing a new macro lens or are a seasoned pro, familiarizing yourself with these basic concepts will help take your close-up photography to the next level.

Close-up vs. Macro

In basic terms, "close-up photography" means focusing on subjects that are very close to the lens. The closer your camera gets to a given subject, the more it fills the 35mm frame.

Often expressed in magnification ratios, close-ups can be life-size or smaller than life-size. If the image of the subject in a final print is exactly the same size as the subject itself in real life, then the ratio is 1:1. This "one-to-one" relationship is commonly referred to as "life-size" and is often expressed as "1X." Therefore, a ratio of 1:2 means that the image is one-half the size of the actual subject and is defined as

"0.5X." Normal close-up photography covers the range from 0.1X to 1X, or $^1/_{10}$ life-size to full life-size.

As a general rule, when the image on the sensor is life-size or greater than life-size, the term "macro" is used. When loosely defined, however (as is often the case among photographers these days), a "macro" image is also a "close-up" image. It's important to remember that the true definition of "macro" refers to a subject rendered 1:1 or greater than 1:1.

A true "macro" lens is a dedicated, fixed-focal-length lens (e.g., 60mm, 100mm, 105mm, 180mm, or 200mm). Many telephoto zoom lenses have built-in "macro features" that allow for close-up work, but technically you are not able to render the subject at life-size or greater with these lenses. With these lenses, the subject covers a smaller area of the frame and appears smaller than life-size.

When it comes to rendering your subject at greater than life-size, there are many accessories available to the macro photographer in addition to a dedicated macro lens. These include:

- **Extension Tubes.** There are hollow metal tubes that fit between the lens and camera body to extend the close-focusing range of the lens.
- **Close-Up Filters (or "Diopters").** These filters screw onto the front of a prime or telephoto lens and increase magnification (I recommend the Canon 500D close-up filter).
- **Teleconverters.** These are auxiliary lenses that multiply the focal length of a lens while retaining its close-focusing distance.
- **Extension Bellows.** This is an adjustable accordian-like device that fits between the lens and camera body for close focusing (similar to extension tubes).

See chapter 2 for a more detailed description of each, as well as an explanation of the advantages and disadvantages of each.

It's also worth mentioning two other inexpensive ways to shoot macro, if you want to experiment without a huge investment: (1) Reversing a lens—either directly on the camera using a reversing ring, or on bellows; and (2) Stacking two lenses by reversing one lens onto another lens using a lens-stacking adapter known as a male-to-male coupling ring. The best combination of lenses in this case is to connect a shorter focal-length prime lens (such as a 50mm lens) to the camera body and then reverse-mount a longer focal-length lens (such as a 100mm lens). In theory, this example would yield a 1:2 magnification ratio—or twice life-size.

I have not experimented much with either of these methods, but they both can yield interesting results without light loss or decreased image quality.

Lens Focal Length

To a certain extent, the focal length of a lens determines magnification. A subject photographed from the same distance with a 200mm macro lens, for example, will produce an image that is roughly twice as large as that produced by a 105mm lens. So logic would tell you that all you need to do in order to shoot close-ups is use a telephoto lens. This is not necessarily the case. Unfortunately, the longer the focal length, the farther away the minimum focusing distance becomes, so any gain in magnification offered by the telephoto lens is erased by the loss of minimum focusing distance.

Having a longer focal-length macro lens definitely has its advantages, however, especially when photographing small creatures such as insects, frogs, and snails. With a greater working distance, you can achieve magnification while not disturbing the animal. There is also the added advantage of more available light falling on your subject, as the camera is farther away.

Depth of Field

One of the keys to creating a successful close-up image is directing the viewer's eye in your frame. Most often, our eyes tend to gravitate toward the brightest and sharpest areas in a picture. So you'll want to pay close attention to the background in your macro image. As a macro photographer, it's easy to get caught up in the subject itself, while ignoring the background. Often, backgrounds are as important—or more important—than your subject. If a background contains too much detail, it can become distracting. Usually a soft, out-of-focus background yields a more pleasing image and helps isolate your subject better, especially when photographing flowers from a close distance. (See **images 3-1** through **3-11**.)

Depth of field refers to the zone of sharp focus in a photograph. As subject magnification increases, the amount of depth of field decreases rapidly. Conversely, stopping down the aperture and/or reducing the magnification increases depth of field.

In macro photography, several factors affect depth of field. Among these are the focal length of the lens and the distance from the camera to the subject. The smaller the focal length of the lens, the greater the depth of field appears. A subject at a greater distance will have greater depth of field than a close-up subject.

The factor that affects depth of field most noticeably when working at high magnifications, however, is the size of the aperture (or f/stop)

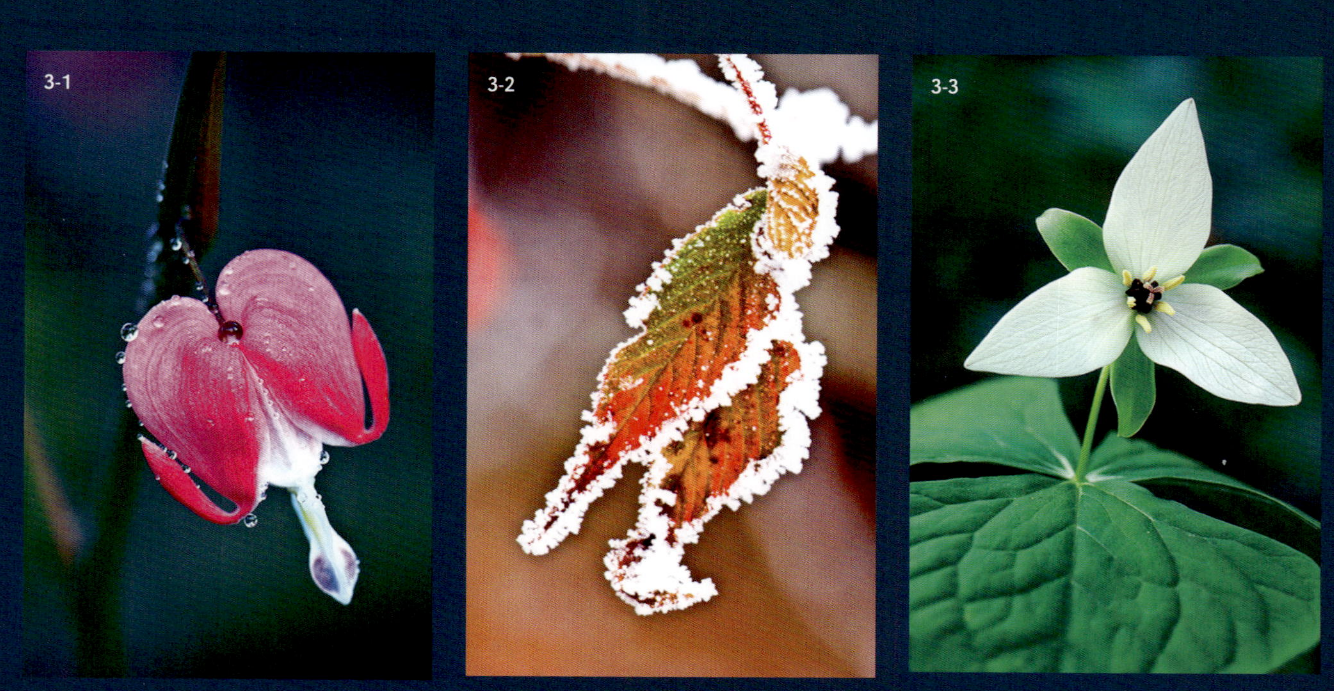

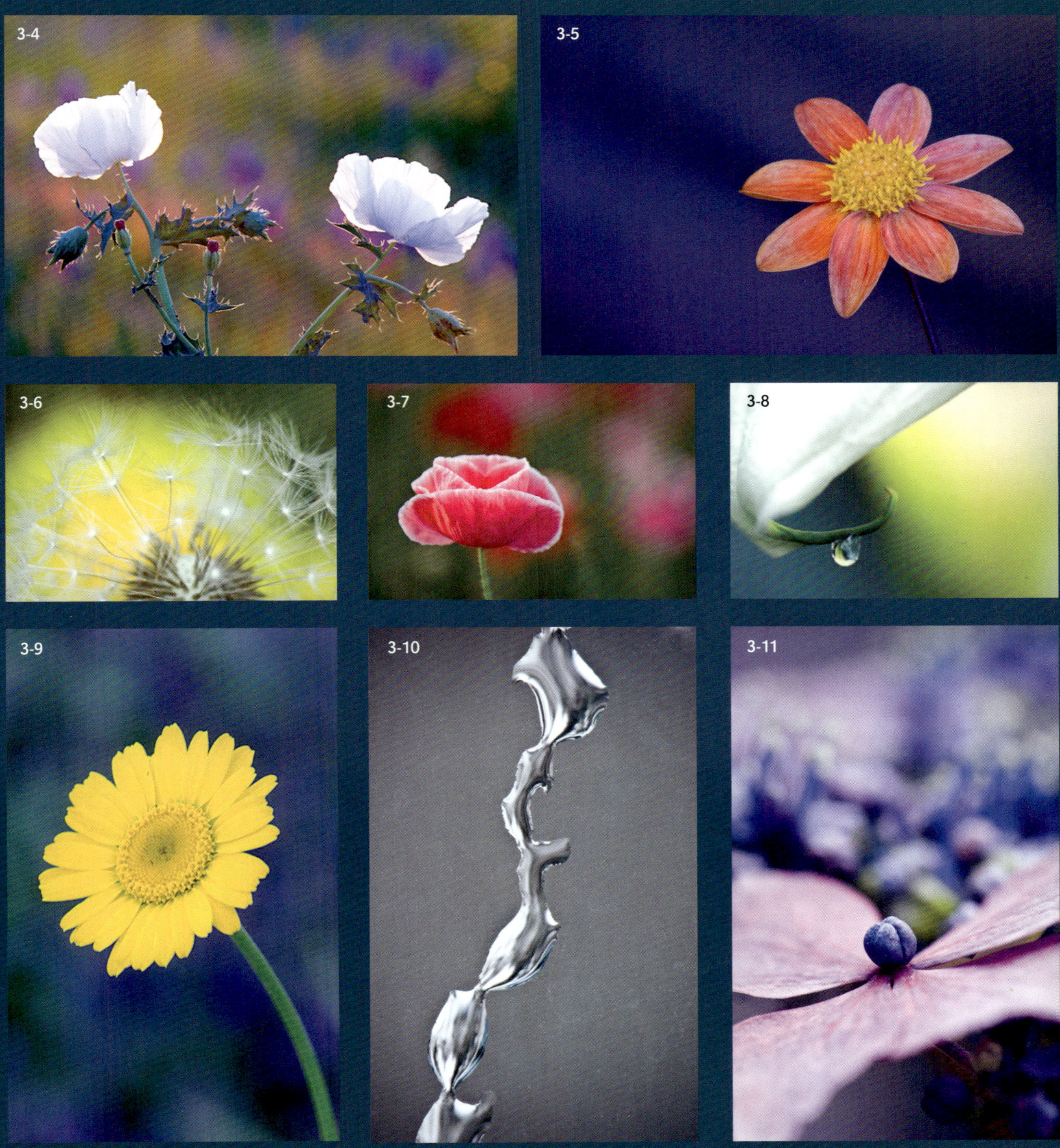

Images 3-1 through 3-11. In each of these close-up images, I chose a wide aperture setting (f/4 or f/5.6) on my 200mm macro lens to isolate the subject and create greater impact with a shallow depth of field. Notice how "clean" and uncluttered each background appears. When composing for macro, it's important to pay very close attention to the colors, shapes, and tones behind your subject. In images 3-2 and 3-7, I was able to stop my lens down one additional stop to f/8 since the background flora was several feet away from the main subject. In image 3-8, I stopped down to f/16 because I wanted to render the water drop sharp but still maintain a soft background of flowers, which were several inches away. The moral of the story here: Be sure to use your depth-of-field preview button often, before you click the shutter, to see just how much detail will be rendered in the background.

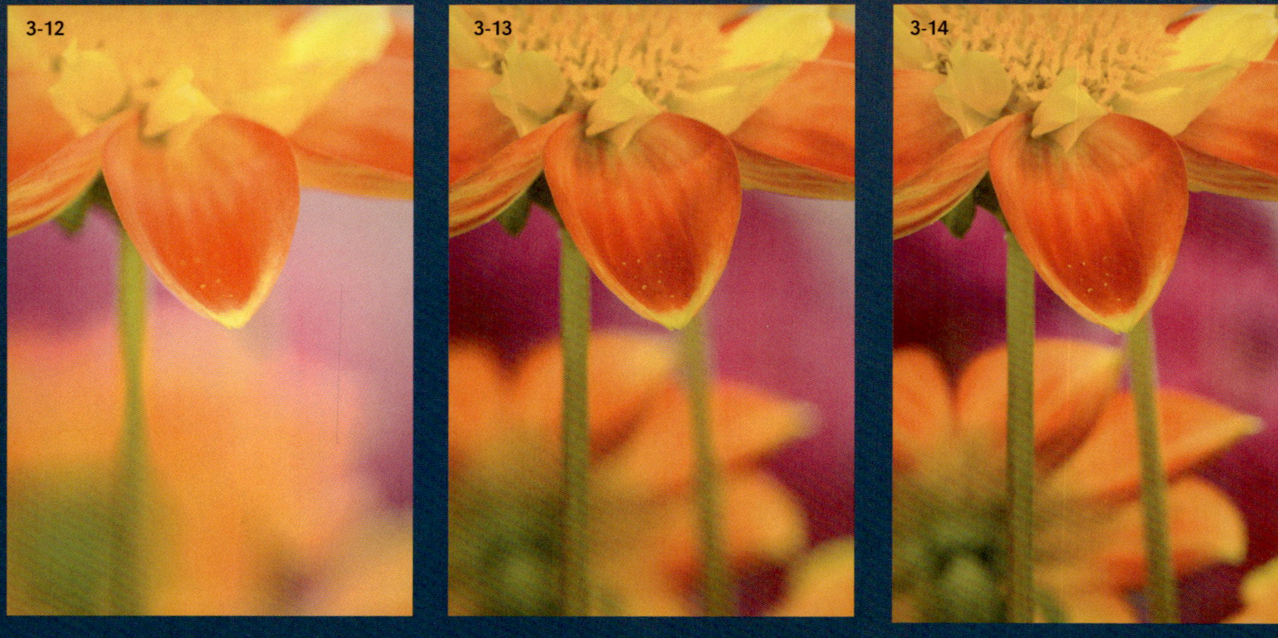

Images 3-12 through 3-14. When working at close range, aperture can dramatically affect how much of the background is in sharp focus. In these three images of a dahlia, I focused on the tip of the foreground petal and made three separate images at three different f/stops: image 3-12 was photographed at f/4.5, image 3-13 was photographed at f/11, and image 3-14 was photographed at f/22. One easy way to remember the basic premise behind depth of field is, "The larger the f-number, the larger the depth of field." The capture details for the three images were: image 3-12. Nikon 200mm macro lens, 1/2 second at f/4.5; image 3-13. Nikon 200mm macro lens, 1.6 seconds at f/11; image 3-14. Nikon 200mm macro lens, 6 seconds at f/22.

on a lens. You can profoundly change the acceptable zone of sharpness by increasing or decreasing the size of the opening on a lens. A wide aperture (smaller f/stop number) will result in less depth of field, while a small aperture (bigger f/stop number) will result in greater depth of field. (See **images 3-12** through **3-14.**) When changing the aperture setting, be sure to adjust the shutter speed also to maintain the correct exposure. I like to shoot in manual mode on my Nikon D3 because I can control the aperture and shutter speed settings myself. Of course, you can also shoot in aperture priority mode (you set the aperture and the camera chooses a corresponding shutter speed based on the amount of available light in the scene). No matter what method you use to make your close-up images, you'll discover that depth of field is very shallow.

Most digital SLRs have a useful feature called a "depth-of-field preview button," which stops the lens down to the aperture selected and allows you to preview the critical zone of sharpness in your image. (See **image 3-15.**) By looking through the viewfinder while pushing the depth-of-field preview button down, you can see what will be sharp and what will be out of focus when you make the picture. You might want to carry a dark cloth in your camera bag to throw over your head, however, because at very small apertures (e.g., f/22 or f/32), what's inside the viewfinder can appear very dark and difficult to see. If you don't have a dark cloth in your camera bag, then consider using any nearby article of clothing such as a jacket. One tip when using the depth-of-field preview button I find especially useful is to try focusing the lens manually while the button is pushed. This way, you can further control how much of the subject is acceptably sharp.

Focusing Techniques

There are other ways to control focus as well. As you'll soon discover, focusing is one of the biggest challenges you'll encounter in macro photography. To create sharp images, your focusing has to be accurate because you're dealing with such a shallow depth of field— especially at wider apertures such as f/2.8 or f/4. Sometimes, the focusing ring on your lens is not enough to render sharpness, so you need to move the entire camera closer or farther away from your subject. In these cases, a focusing rail can be a helpful tool. (A focusing rail is a rack-and-pinion-driven system that attaches to a tripod and moves the entire camera backward and forward in small, precise increments.)

Image 3-15. Depth-of-field preview button (top) on my Nikon D3.

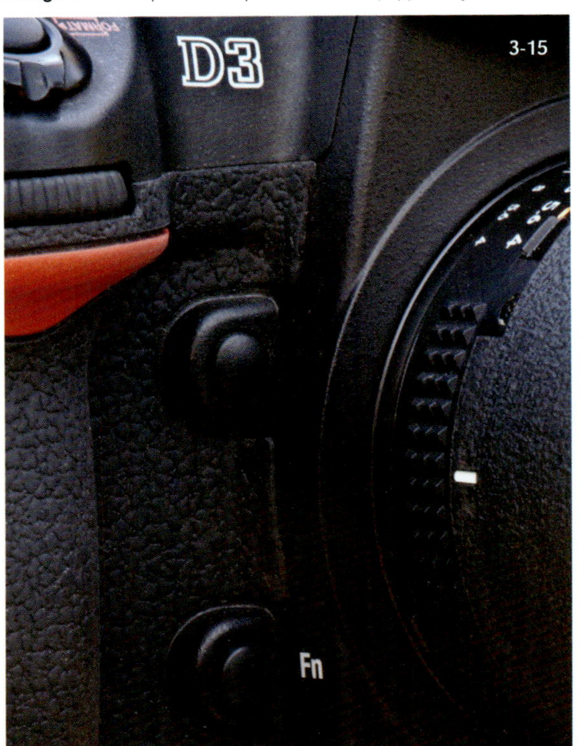

Before I make an image, I will often remove the camera and lens from the tripod, set my lens to its minimum focusing distance, then hand-hold the camera while looking through the viewfinder and move my body closer to and farther from the subject until it comes into sharp focus. Once I have determined roughly how far the tripod needs to be from the subject (and at what height), I'll position the tripod at that spot, re-attach the camera to my tripod, and then fine-tune my focus by loosening the quick-release plate and moving the camera back and forth in small increments while viewing my subject through the viewfinder.

As a general rule, I always set my camera to manual focus for macro shots. By shooting in manual-focus mode, you can determine where to place your focus, rather than relying on the camera to pick some arbitrary point of focus.

So where should you focus when working at magnified views? As is the case much of the time with photography, the answer is, "It all depends."

Suppose you're going for maximum sharpness in your close-up image. Some flower subjects, such as orchids, are difficult to render completely sharp because they have great "depth." Even if I were to stop my macro lens down to f/99 (if there were such an aperture), I could not render the entire flower sharp since the flower's depth spans several inches. On the other hand, if I wanted to make a sunflower or daisy sharp throughout, this would be possible since these flowers are relatively "flat" and do not have as much depth as some other flowers. Their "depth" is only about an inch, so by stopping my lens down completely (to, say, f/22 or f/32), I can achieve sharpness in each flower petal as well as the center of the flower.

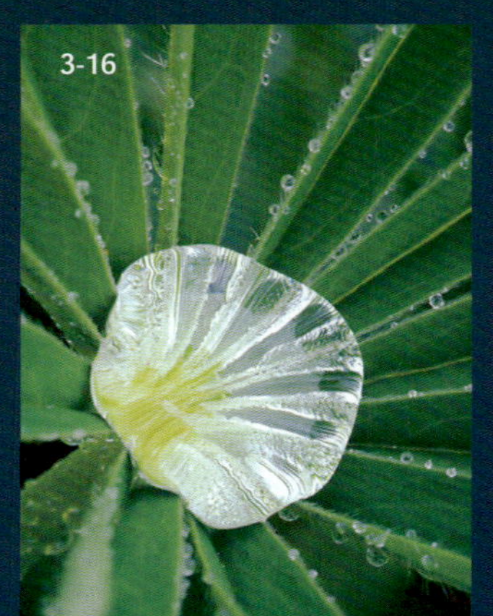

3-16

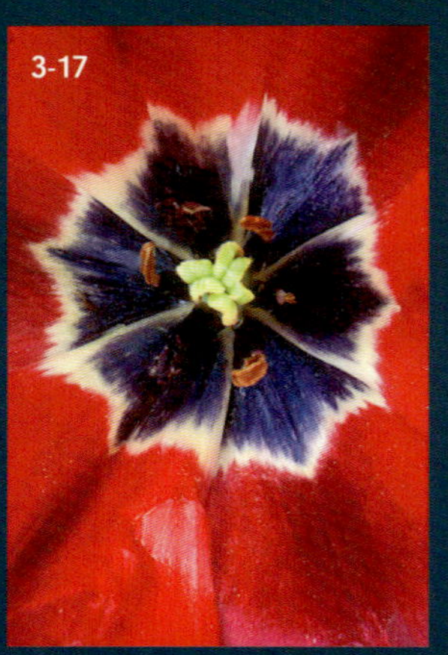

3-17

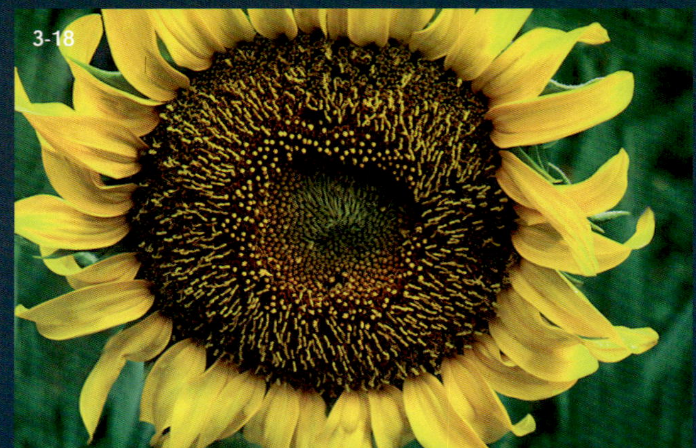

3-18

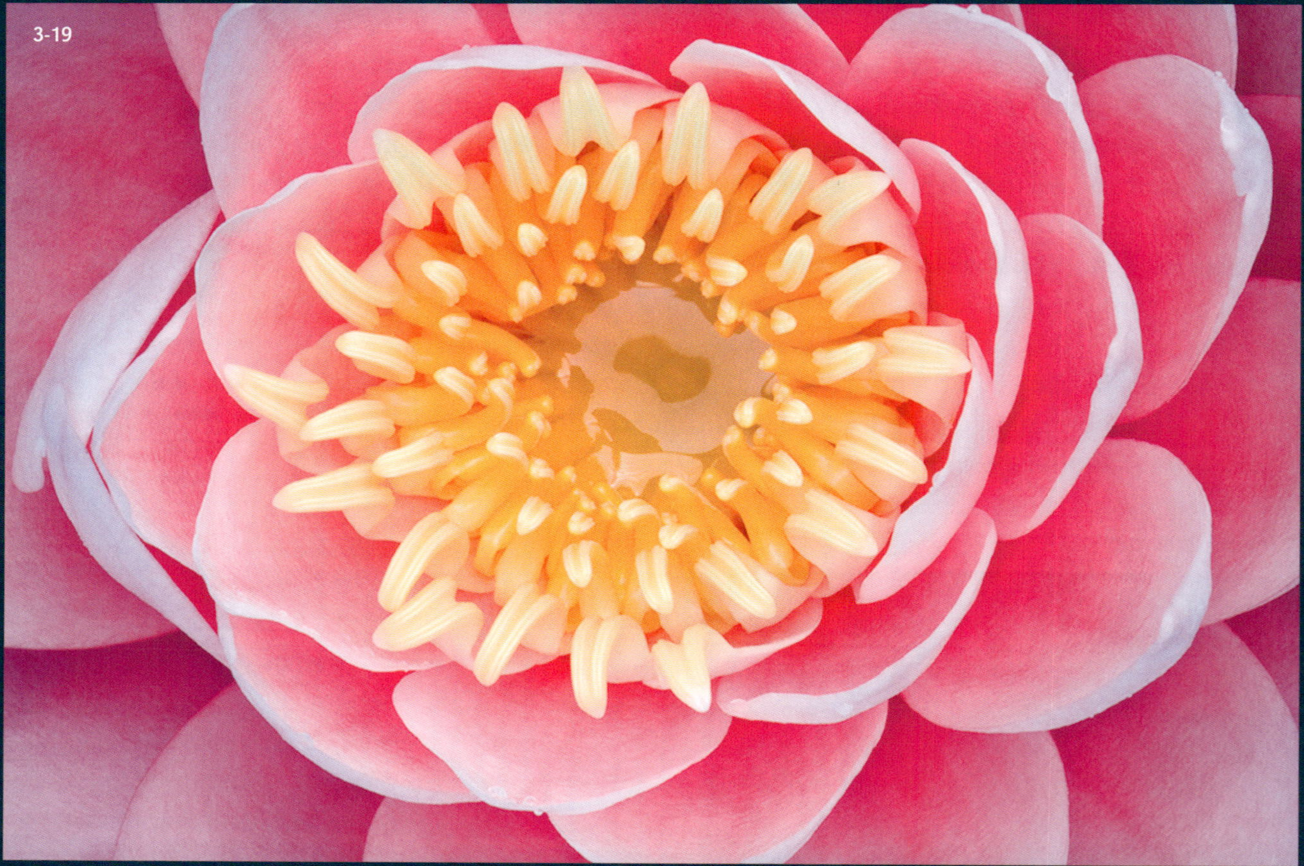

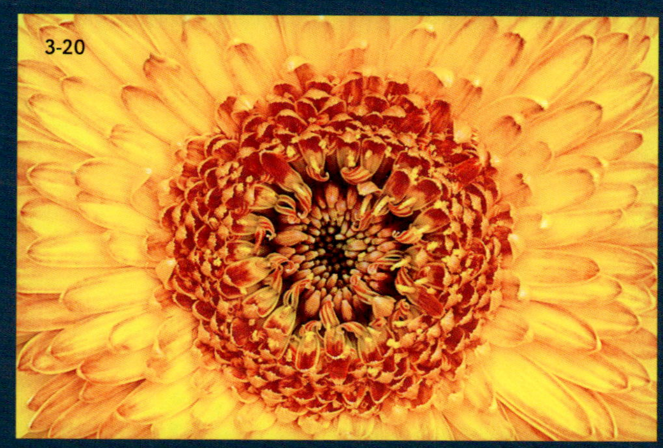

3-20

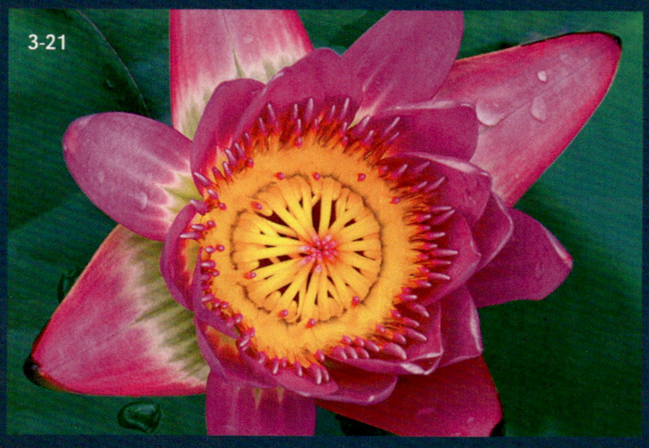

3-21

Note: You could achieve total sharpness of the orchid in the example above by using "focus stacking," which involves shooting the orchid at various planes of focus, then combining them in postproduction using a third-party software program such as Helicon Focus.

Since macro photography is similar to shooting a mini landscape, I always advise that if you're going for maximum sharpness, you want to focus the same way you would in a traditional grand landscape shot, using what's known as "hyper-focal focusing." This involves looking through the viewfinder once you've composed your shot, moving your eye one-third of the way up the side of the frame on either side, and then placing your focus at whatever falls at that one-third point. By stopping down to the smallest aperture on your lens, you're then able to increase sharpness throughout as much as possible.

Images 3-16 through **3-21** were all photographed at either f/22, f/32, or at f/45. Each subject presented its own set of unique challenges due its inherent varied "depth." A tulip, for example, has a depth of several inches, while the surface of a sunflower has only an inch or so. In each case, my intention was to show as much detail as possible, so I made the conscious choice to stop my lens down completely.

Many telephoto zoom lenses have built-in "macro features" . . .

Another way to ensure your images are sharply focused is to place your camera back in the same plane as your subject. When the image sensor plane is parallel to the plane of your subject, you increase the odds of getting a sharp image. (See **images 3-22** through **3-29**.) If your subject has little-to-no depth, such as a pane of glass or the flat surface of a shell, then use a mid-range aperture such as f/11 to create maximum sharpness. Once you're all set and ready to press the shutter, get in the habit of first walking around to get a side view of your

Image 3-16. In order to render detail in this drop of dew that settled in the crevice of this miniature palm plant, I needed to stop-down my lens to f/22 and focus sharply on the pattern "inside" the drop. Nikon 200mm macro lens. Exposure: 1/2 second at f/22. **Image 3-17.** In this image, I was going for maximum detail and sharpness when shooting the inside of this tulip bloom. I focused my 200mm macro lens as parallel as possible to the bottom plane of the flower (pointing my lens straight down inside the flower) and stopped down to f/22. Because there was a slight breeze, I used a Plamp to stabilize the flower so that I could render sharp detail. I also used the mirror-lockup feature on my camera to minimize shutter vibration inside the camera, making the final image even sharper. Nikon 200mm macro lens. Exposure: 1 second at f/22. **Image 3-18.** Again, in order to capture as much detail in this sunflower as possible, I positioned the camera so that the sensor plane would be as parallel as possible to this sunflower. Because the green plants in the background were several feet away, even at f/16, they were not rendered sharp because of the extremely shallow depth of field. Nikon 200mm macro lens, 1/4 second at f/16. **Image 3-19.** In order to make each lotus petal sharp in this image, it was necessary to stop my macro lens down as much as possible. The beautiful soft, diffused light was created by positioning a LiteDisc (a portable diffuser) as close to the flower as possible without seeing it in the viewfinder. Nikon 200mm macro lens. Exposure: 2 seconds at f/22. **Image 3-20.** Here, I also stopped my macro lens down all the way and focused on the center of this gerbera daisy to capture as much detail as possible. Nikon 200mm macro lens. Exposure: 3 seconds at f/45. **Image 3-21.** I photographed this lotus floating in a pond at a small botanical garden near Hana, Hawaii. The most challenging aspect of this shot was trying to position my tripod legs and camera directly above the flower so the sensor plane of the camera would be parallel to the flower. I had to work quickly because the light was fading fast near the end of the day, and the bloom was beginning to close. The other challenge was maintaining a relatively clean and uncluttered background. I used a stick to move some of the surrounding lily pads under the lotus and waited until there was no water movement in the pond. Again, to achieve maximum depth of field, it was necessary to stop my lens down completely. Nikon 200mm macro lens. Exposure: 4 seconds at f/45.

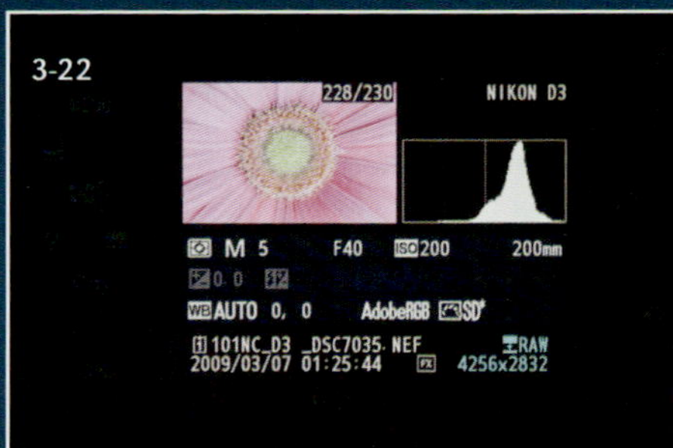

Images 3-22 and 3-23. When the sensor plane of your camera is parallel to the flower, as shown in this example, you can achieve maximum sharpness and depth of field. Nikon 200mm macro lens. Exposure: 4 seconds at f/22.

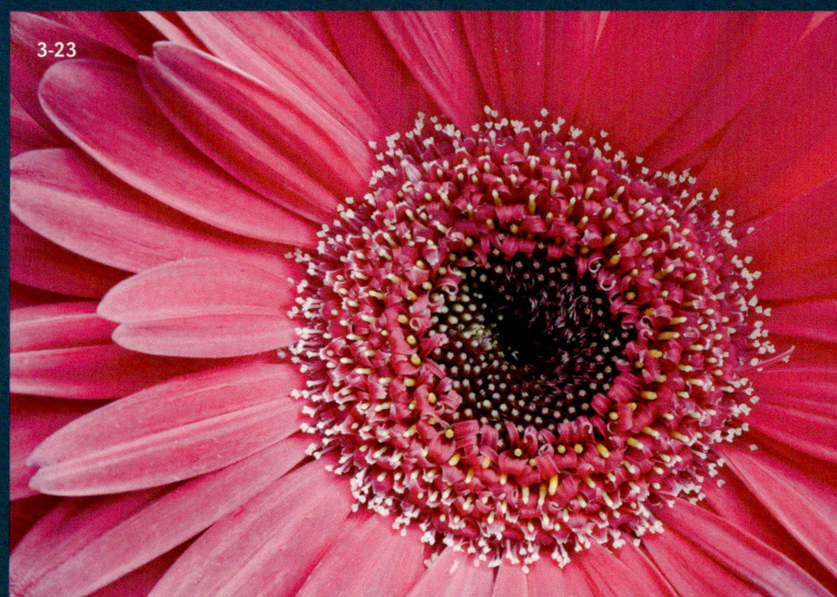

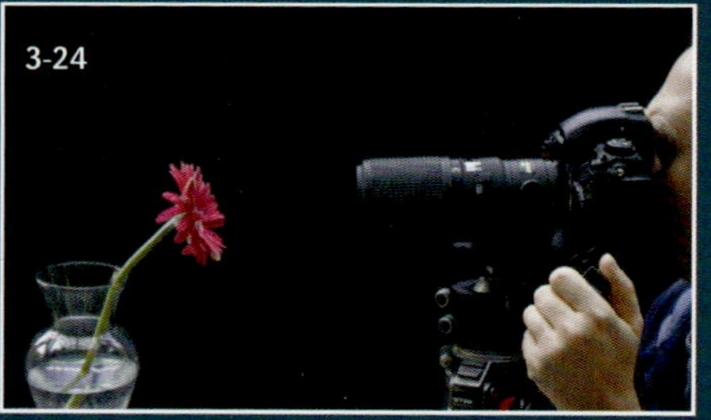

Images 3-24 and 3-25. In this example, the camera is not parallel to the flower. The resulting image is not sharp throughout. Only the lower portion is sharp, even at f/22, because that side of the flower is closer to the lens. Nikon 200mm macro lens. Exposure: 3 seconds at f/22.

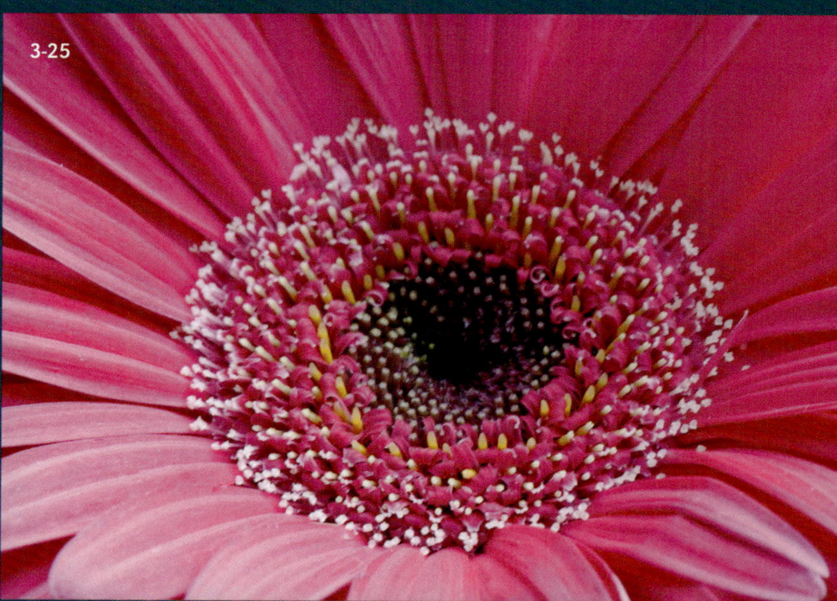

setup and then examining whether or not the camera back is, in fact, parallel to the subject plane.

Oftentimes, you might want to deliberately tilt the camera so that it is *not* parallel with the subject. This is known as selective-focus macro and can be a very effective way to direct the viewer's eye to what you want them to see (see chapter 4). Keep in mind, however, that you don't want lack of sharpness to appear to be a mistake or near-miss. If you don't want things sharp, be bold and throw them completely out of focus. Otherwise, the viewer might be confused, and you will have failed to

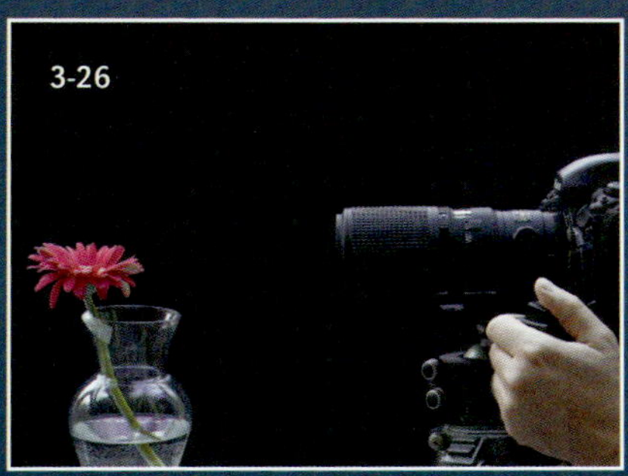

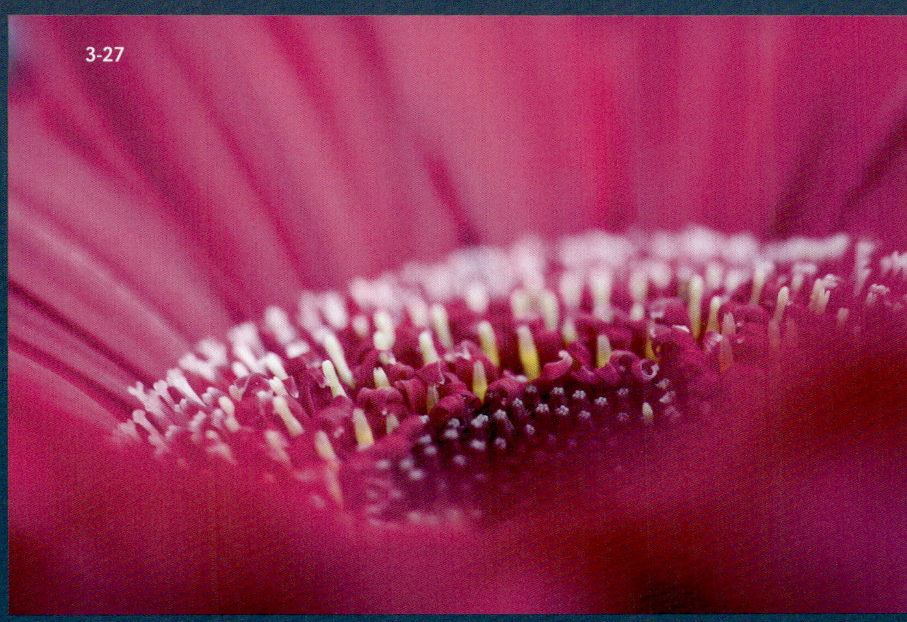

Images 3-26 and 3-27. Here, I chose a wider aperture and decided to shoot straight across the surface of the daisy, placing my focus near the center of the flower. The front edges of the petal help to "frame" and anchor the image, drawing the viewer's eye toward the center. In this case, I made a deliberate decision to break the rules and show only a portion of the flower in sharp focus. Nikon 200mm macro lens. Exposure: 1/8 second at f/5.

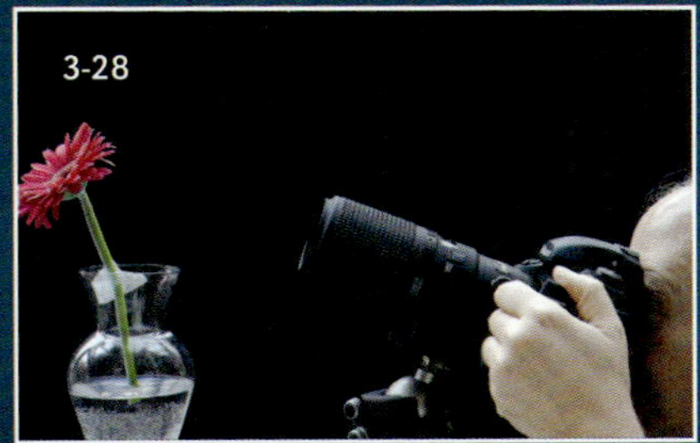

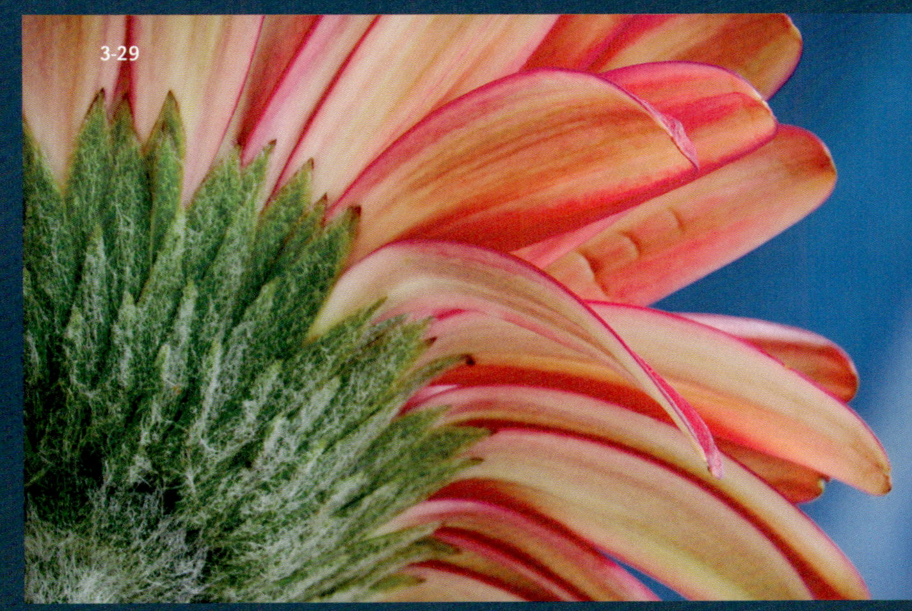

Images 3-28 and 3-29. Often, one of the most neglected camera angles when shooting flowers is the underside. Here, I positioned my camera under the daisy and stopped my lens down completely to capture as much detail as possible and render the flower completely sharp. Nikon 200mm macro lens. Exposure: 8 seconds at f/38.

communicate your visual message clearly and effectively.

Exposure

No discussion about macro photography basics would be complete without a word about exposure and histograms.

A histogram is probably one of the most useful tools available in digital photography. It's a graphic representation of the range of tones in a given image. The left side of the graph represents shadows (darker tones), and the right side represents highlights (lighter tones). The horizontal axis indicates the brightness level

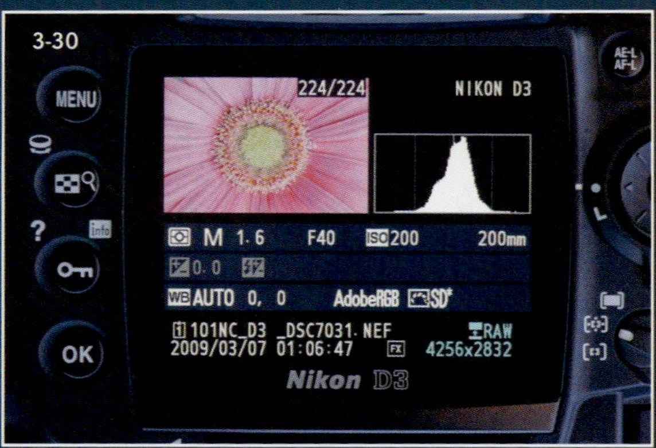

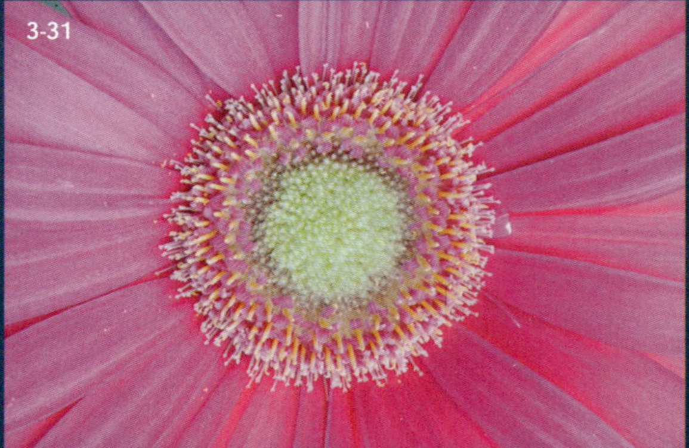

Images 3-30 and 3-31. A properly exposed image with shadow and highlight detail. Shadows fall on the left side of the histogram curve, while highlights fall on the right side. Nikon 200mm macro lens. Exposure: 1.6 seconds at f/40.

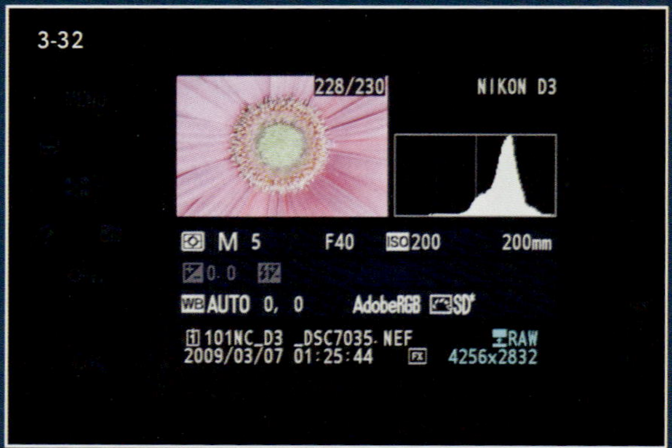

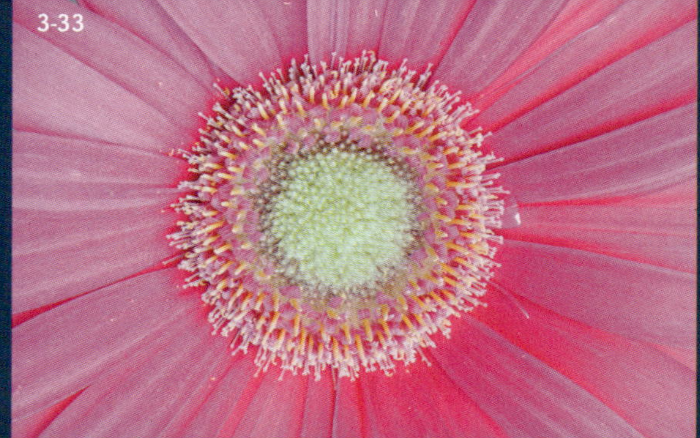

Images 3-32 and 3-33. Increasing the exposure by 1 stop causes the histogram curve to shift to the right. Notice that I am still not "clipping" highlights on the right side of the curve. Nikon 200mm macro lens. Exposure: 0.6 second at f/22.

(darker on the left and brighter on the right), while the vertical axis indicates how many pixels exist for each brightness level.

Therefore, the darker the image, the more spikes you'll have on the left, and the brighter the image, the more spikes you'll have on the right. If the spike is too far to the left, you'll lose shadow detail, and if the spike is too far to the right, you'll lose detail in the highlights. This is called "clipping," and when you lose detail, you lose pixels which usually cannot be recovered. This is why it's so important to check your histogram regularly. As a general rule,

you want to expose for highlights in a digital photograph so that there are pixel values on the histogram as far to the right as possible without clipping. If you see clipping on either side of the graph, then you'll need to adjust your exposure accordingly by overexposing or underexposing. (**Images 3-30** through **3-37** illustrate four different exposures of a gerbera daisy with corresponding histograms.)

Because brightness varies from LCD to LCD, it's not enough to rely solely on the thumbnail that you see once an image has been exposed. You need to see the "composite histogram"

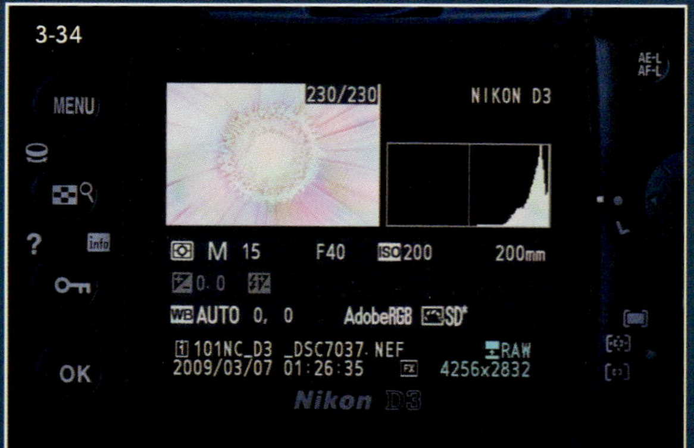

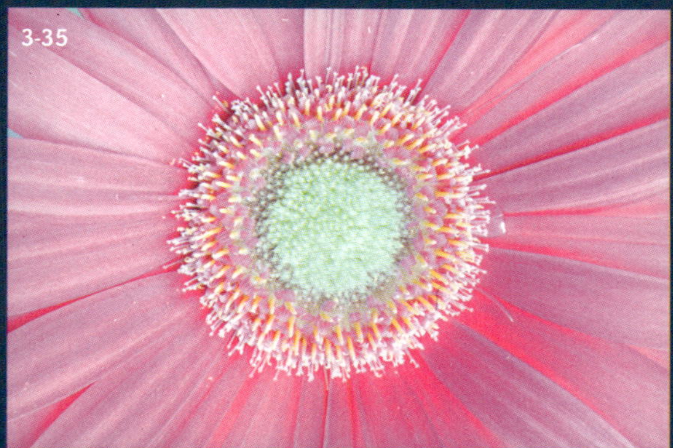

Images 3-34 and 3-35. Increasing the exposure by 2 stops does cause "clipping," which means the image is overexposed and the histogram curve has shifted to the far right. Notice there is no detail in most of the highlights, with few mid-tones and no shadows present. Nikon 200mm macro lens. Exposure: 1/10 second at f/11.

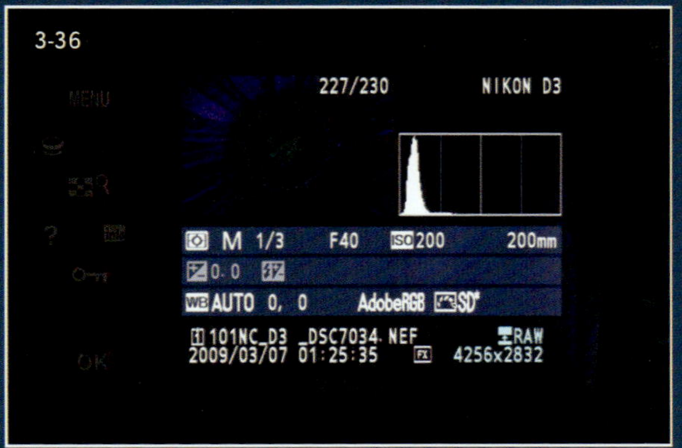

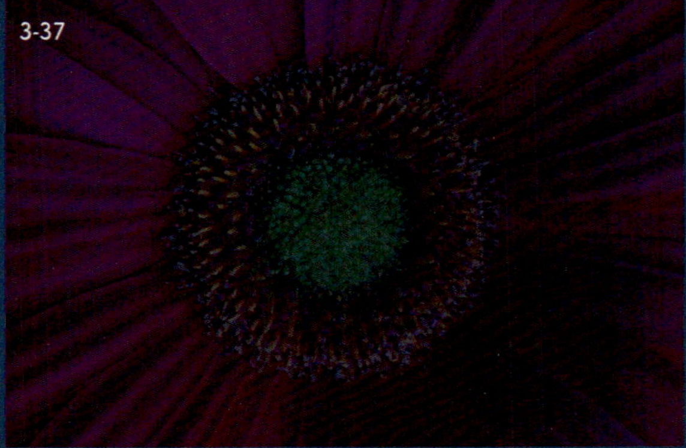

Images 3-36 and 3-37. Conversely, by decreasing the exposure 2 stops, the histogram curve shifts to the left, and the image becomes underexposed with mostly shadow detail but no mid-tone or highlight detail. Nikon 200mm macro lens. Exposure: 1/3 second at f/40.

(which combines the Red, Green, and Blue color channels and is usually rendered white). So I recommend highly that you set your LCD to a viewing mode that will allow you to see a composite histogram after each click of the shutter.

One final thought about exposing for macro photography: Because of the close working distance and the optics of a macro lens, I've found that often you'll need to "fool your camera meter" by overexposing by 1 to 2 stops, which is why it's particularly important to pay close attention to your histogram when shooting macro. Another reason for this is that you're often extending the lens farther than normal from the sensor plane when focusing close, which also reduces the amount of light reaching the sensor.

Lighting

As is the case with all types of photography, lighting is a crucial component for success. For the majority of my macro images, I prefer natural daylight over artificial light whenever possible. Direct sunlight can be difficult to work with because it's tricky to control, bathes the

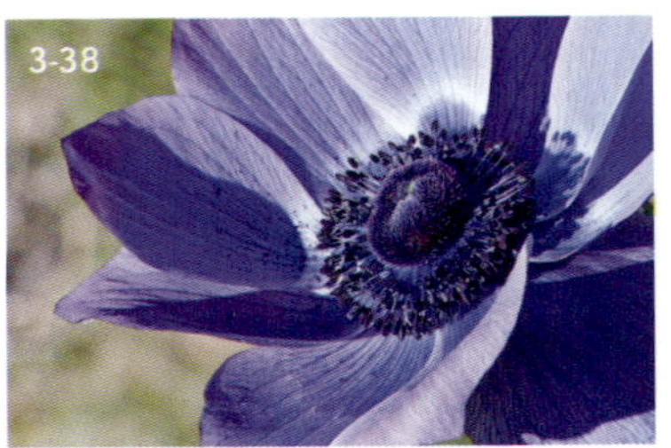 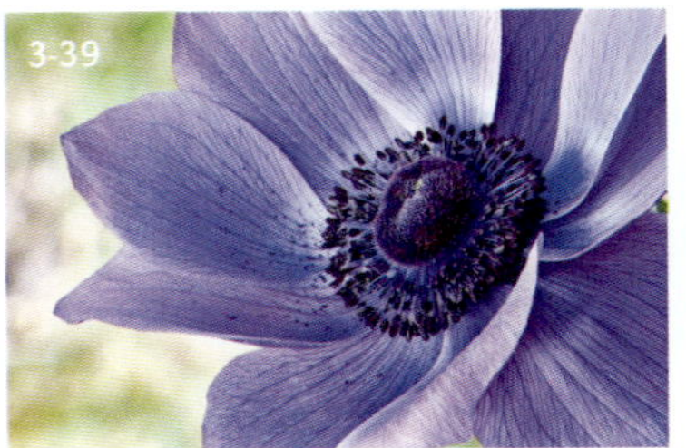 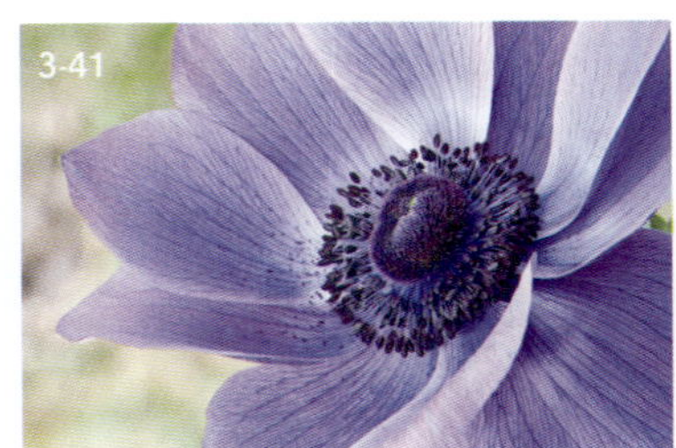

Image 3-38. Poppy in harsh sunlight.

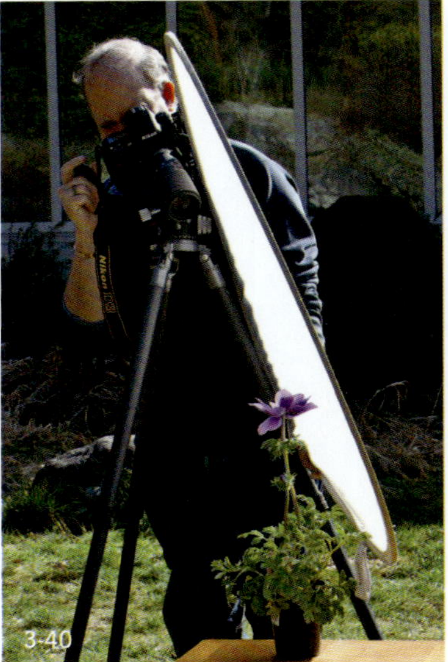

Images **3-39 and 3-40.** Holding the 42-inch diffuser far from the subject does not soften the light but really only casts a shadow.

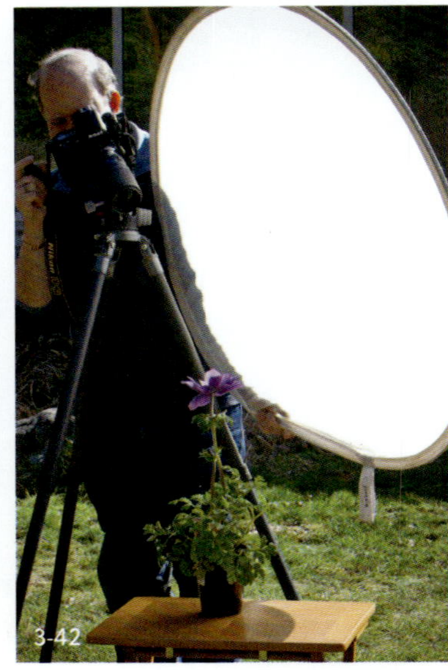

Images **3-41 and 3-42.** Positioning the diffuser much closer to the flower made the light falling on the subject much brighter and softer.

subject in strong, contrasty light, and casts dark shadows. (See **image 3-38**.)

By far, the best light for macro photography is a bright, overcast day. The clouds serve as a giant diffuser, softening the light evenly with no harsh shadows. And if you're lucky enough to photograph close-up in bright overcast light just after a rainfall, you'll receive the added bonus of beautiful water droplets that cling to your subjects and sparkle like jewels or prisms!

Because I shoot RAW format images, I set my camera to auto white balance when making macro photographs. RAW allows me to change the white balance in Adobe Photoshop's Raw converter post-capture if there are irregularities in the light. White balance refers to the camera's interpretation of what is "white"—or rather, what you would perceive as neutral white in a particular scene. Colors are captured, therefore, as close as possible to what the human eye sees.

If you are not shooting in a RAW format (say, JPEG, for example), then I suggest you use "manual" or "daylight" white balance settings for your macro photography, because then you'll avoid the camera being confused by the prevalence of a particular color in the frame. If you're unsure which white-balance setting would work best in a given situation, some

DSLR cameras allow you to take photos that use "white-balance bracketing." (Consult your owner's manual to see if your camera has this capability.)

If you're shooting setups indoors, pay attention to various light sources. You might have a mix of fluorescent and incandescent lights, or natural window light. Whenever possible, even indoors, I try to shoot next to a window or under a skylight so there's as much natural light falling on the subject as possible. When in doubt, bracket white-balance settings if you're shooting in any format other than RAW.

In my camera bag, I carry a few tools to help control the light on close-up subjects. One is a 42-inch diffuser disc, which is like having a "portable cloud" at my disposal. The white semi-transparent material of a diffuser can transform harsh light on a bright, sunny day into soft, omni-directional light instantaneously. I prefer the larger 42-inch size to smaller diffusers because I can cover a wider area—especially helpful if I am shooting in a field of wildflowers and want to also shoot an intimate landscape. One tip when using a diffuser for close-up work is to make sure you hold the diffuser as close as possible to your subject without it being in the shot. The closer you hold it, the better the softening effect. You're going for a bright overcast quality of light, so holding the diffuser farther away defeats the purpose and creates more of a shadow on your subject than a nice soft bright white light. (See **images 3-39** through **3-42**.)

Another useful lighting tool for the macro photographer is a 12-inch gold reflector disc. A reflector allows you to bounce warm, glowing light onto subjects, which helps add a three-dimensional feel and assists in bringing out its best qualities. Outdoors, reflectors work best when you're shooting in open shade with sunlight nearby to be reflected back in.

Even on a cloudy day, however, you can add subtle warm fill light to your subject and increase shadow detail with a gold reflector disc. I like the 12-inch reflector because it's small enough to position close to flowers and other tiny macro subjects. (Feel free to experiment with using the reverse silver side as well. The silver is designed to increase specular highlights

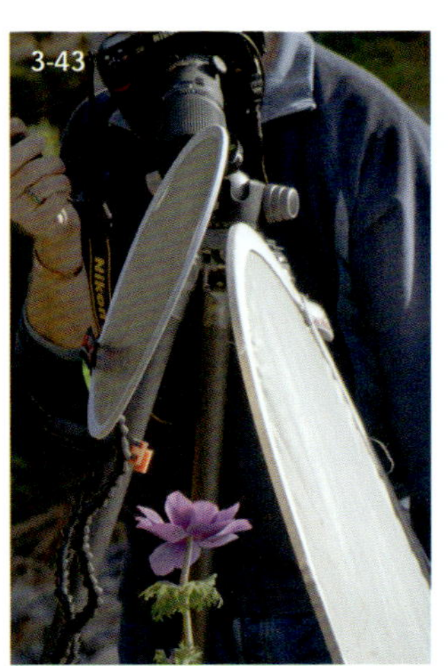
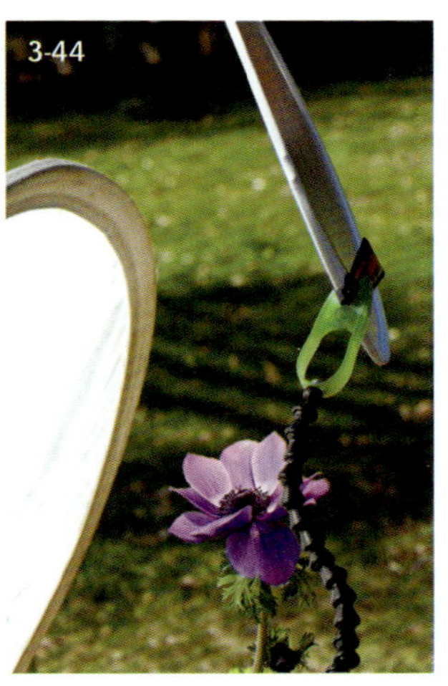
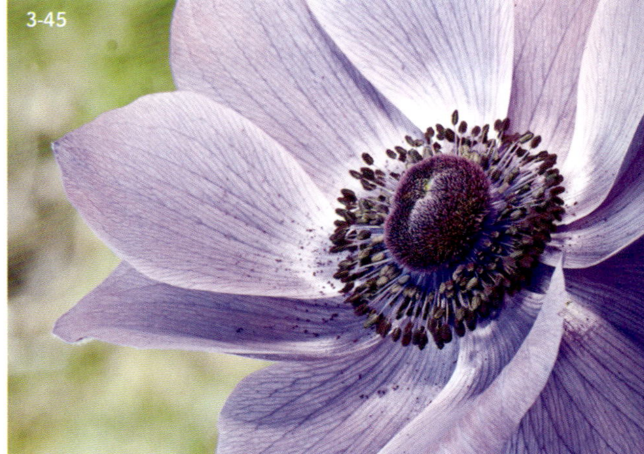

Images 3-43 through 3-45. Here, I used a gold reflector and diffuser simultaneously. This gave the flower a much warmer tone.

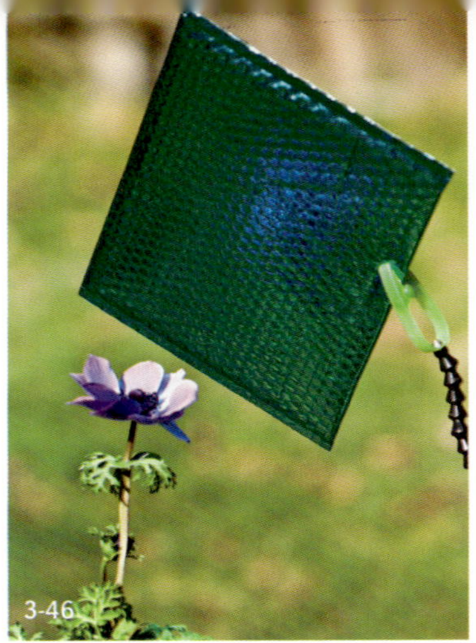 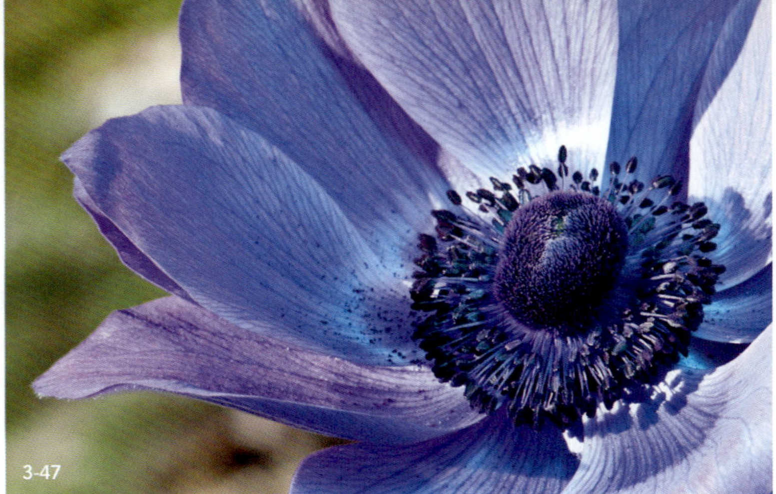

Images **3-46** and **3-47.** Using a metallic foil green bubble envelope mailer created a cool color cast on the poppy.

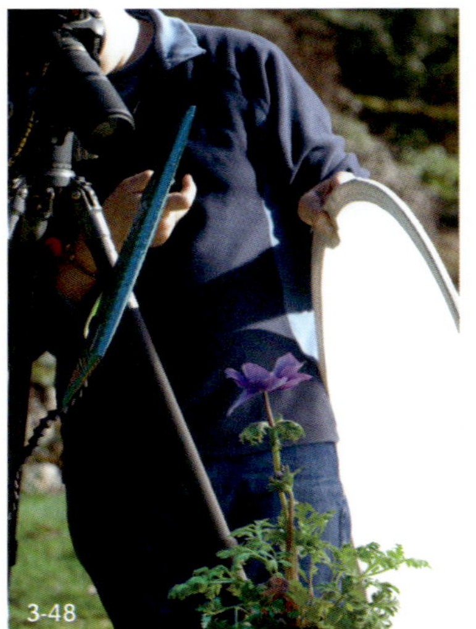 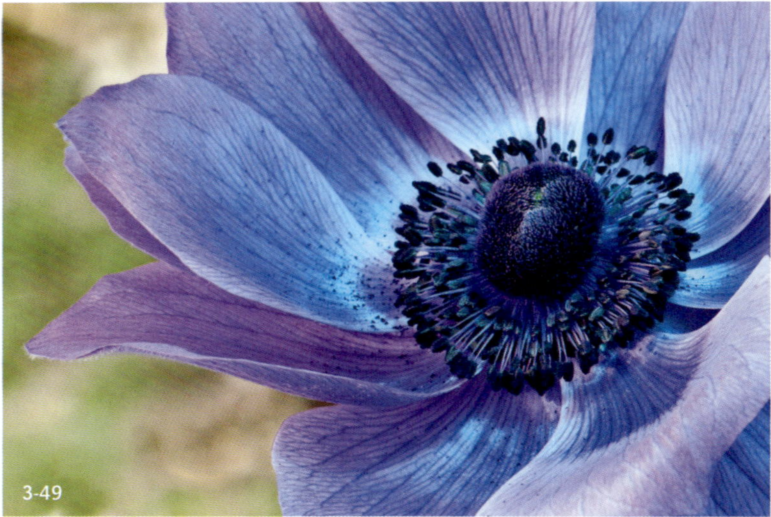

Images **3-48** and **3-49.** Using the same green bubble envelope mailer plus a diffuser softened the overall image for a more pleasing result. **Image 3-50.** Using a pink foil metallic bubble envelope mailer to bounce warm pink light upon a white orchid.

and add more contrast to your image, but overall I've found the results less pleasing.)

Often, I will use a diffuser and gold reflector at the same time to soften shadows and create a warm glow. **Images 3-43** through **3-45** show how both of these lighting tools can be used in combination with each other.

You might also wish to experiment with using other colored surfaces to reflect light back onto your subject. In **images 3-46** through **3-49,** I used a green foil metallic bubble envelope mailer to bounce cool light into a purple poppy. Similarly, **image 3-50** illustrates what happens when using a pink foil metallic bubble mailer to reflect light onto a white orchid.

Every serious macro photographer also will want to equip himself or herself with some sort of small LED flashlight. My personal favorite is a multi-colored LED flashlight made by Coleman, which allows you to add red or blue light to any small subject. (See **images 3-51** through **3-64.**) The advantage in using

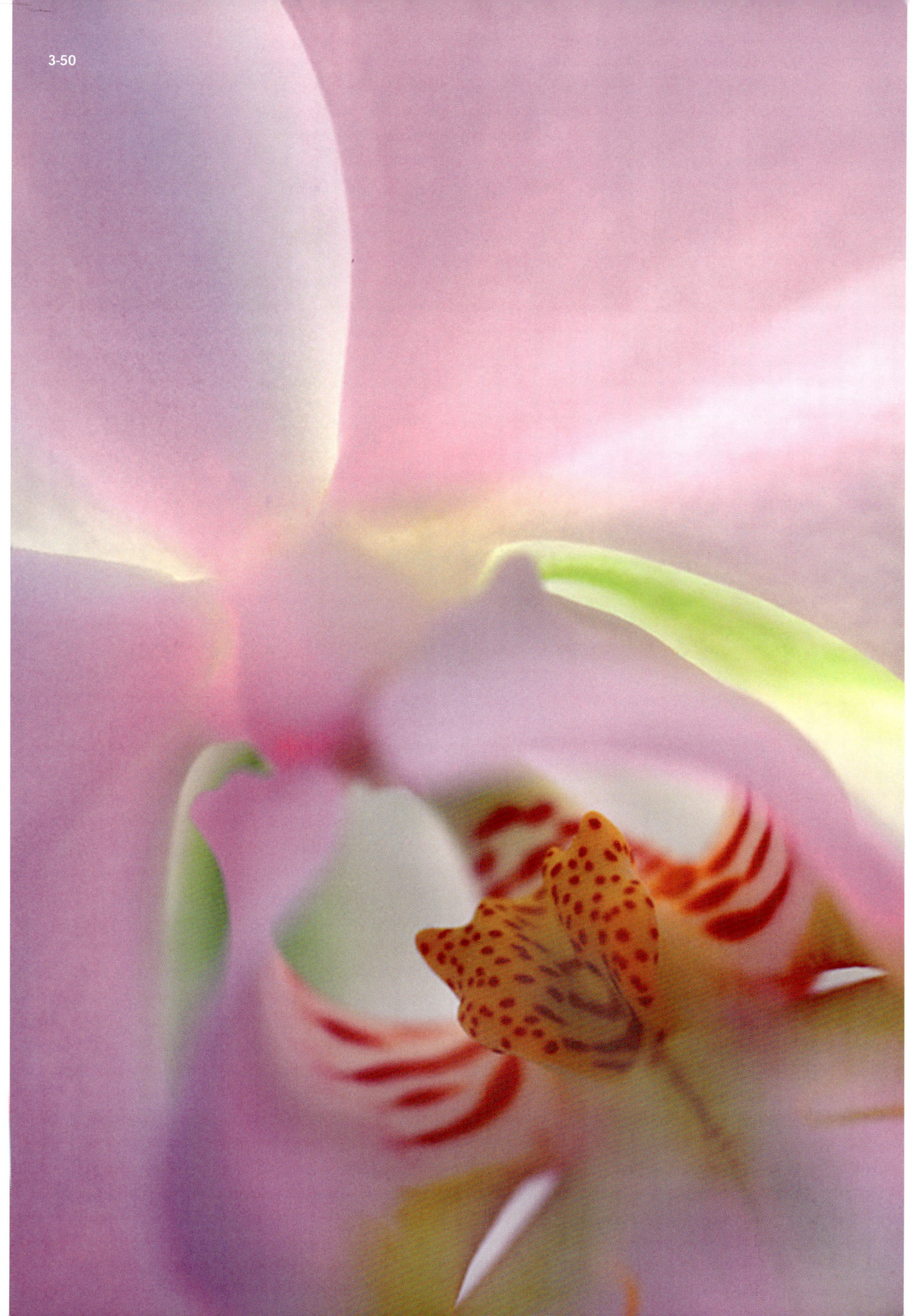

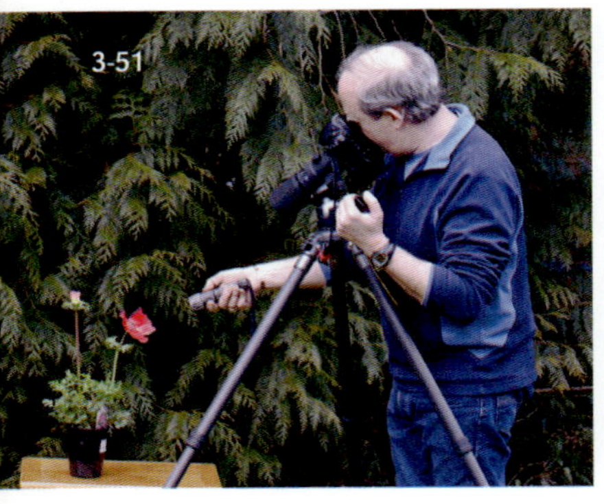 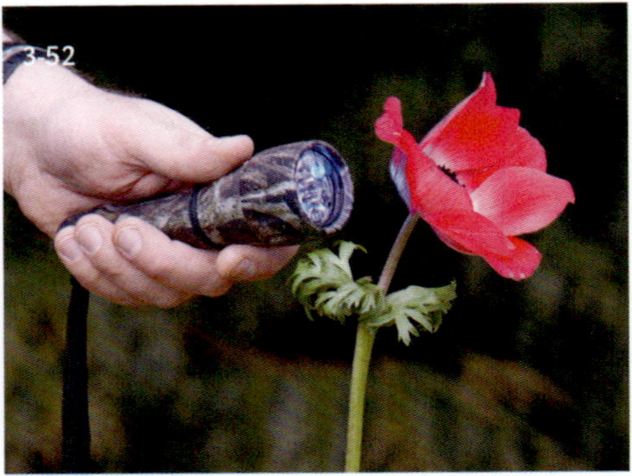 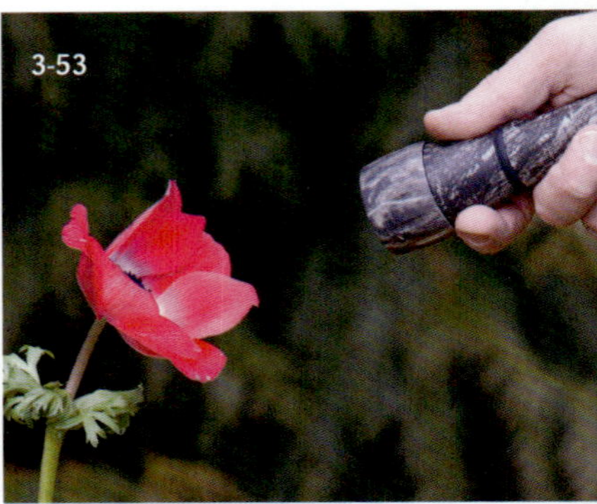

Images 3-51 through 3-53. A multi-colored LED flashlight allows you to add a subtle hint of red or blue light to any small subject. By varying the distance from your subject, you can change the intensity of the light. Don't forget to move the light around during exposures of 1/2 second or longer for a more subtle effect.

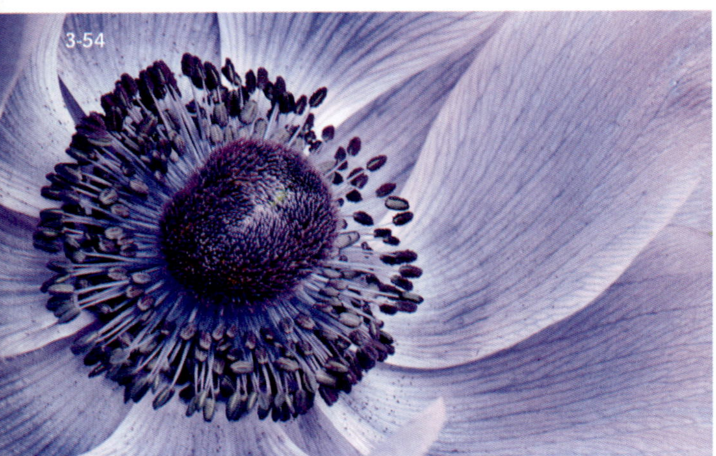 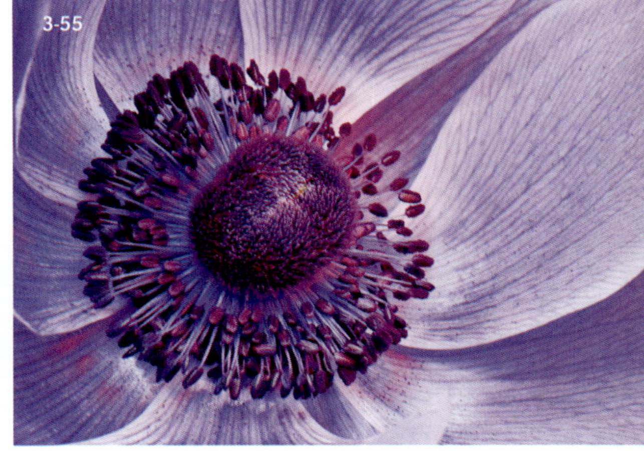

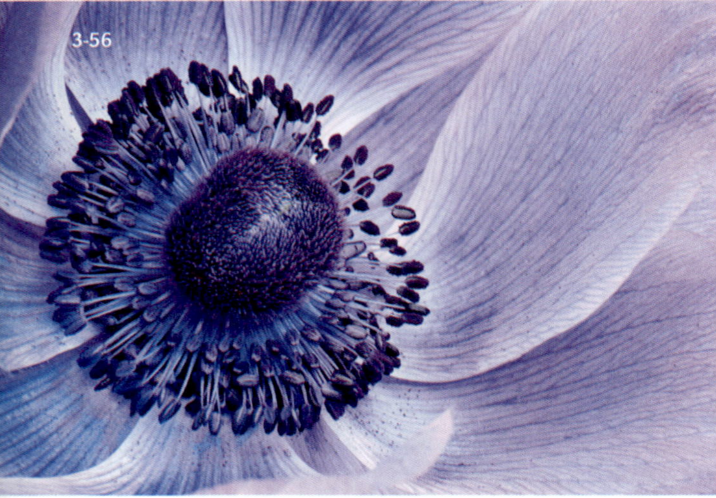

Image 3-54. No flashlight. **Image 3-55.** Red flashlight. **Image 3-56.** Blue flashlight. All three of these images were taken using the same exposure settings: 1 second at f/36.

Image 3-57. Blue flashlight on dahlia. This dahlia already had some red and yellow coloration, so I decided to add a subtle hint of cool color for contrast. Photographed indoors to allow for longer exposure time and to avoid having to battle the wind. Nikon 200mm macro lens. Exposure: 4 seconds at f/36. **Image 3-58.** Blue flashlight on dahlia. Here, I intentionally used a shallower depth of field to lead your eye into the center of the flower. Only the center portion is illuminated. Nikon 200mm macro lens. Exposure: 1/20 second at f/5.3. **Image 3-59.** Blue flashlight on dahlia. Nikon 200mm macro lens. Exposure: 2 seconds at f/16.

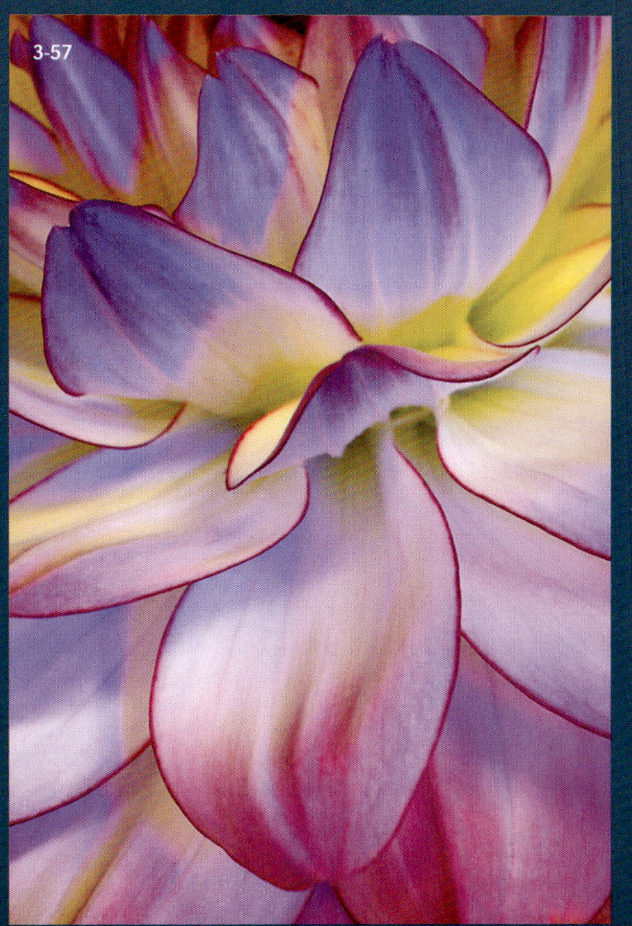

3-57

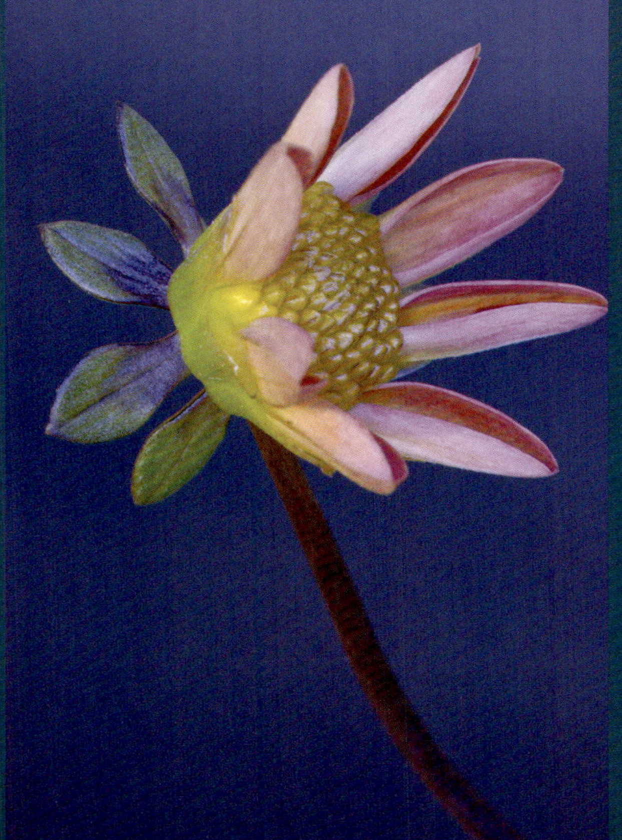

3-59

3-58

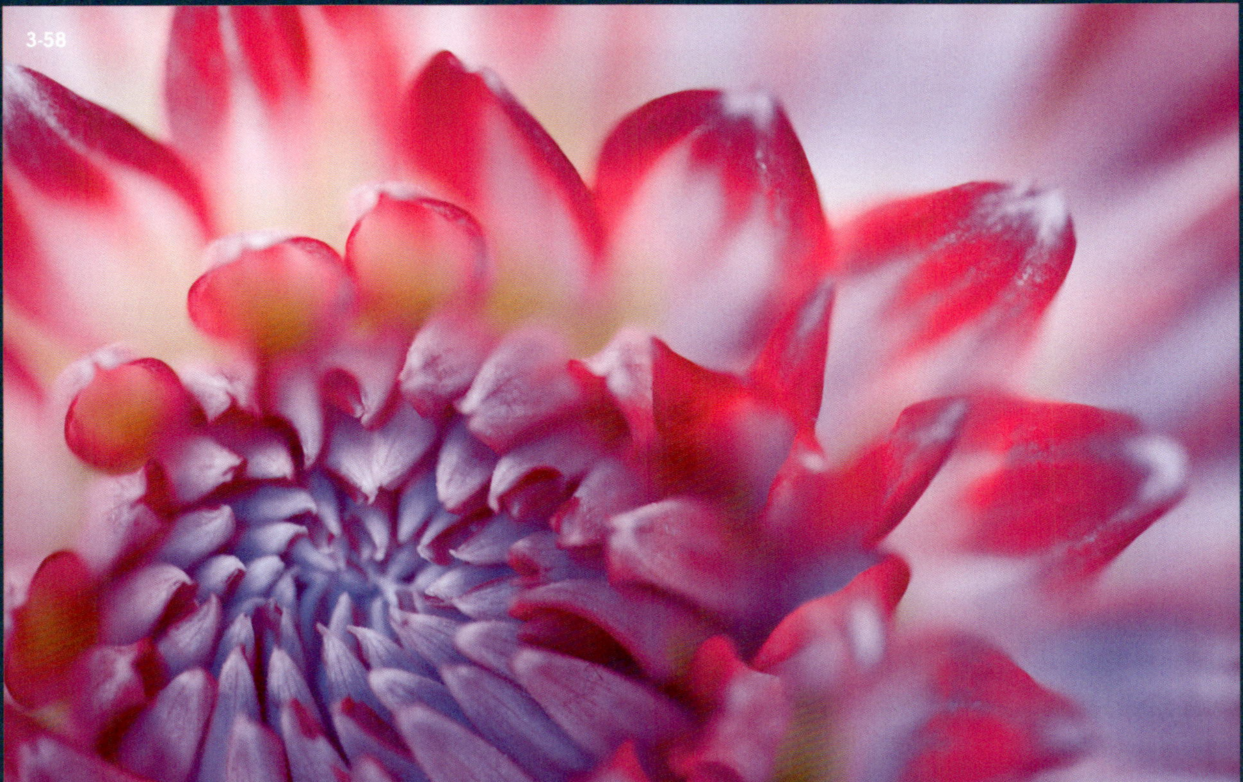

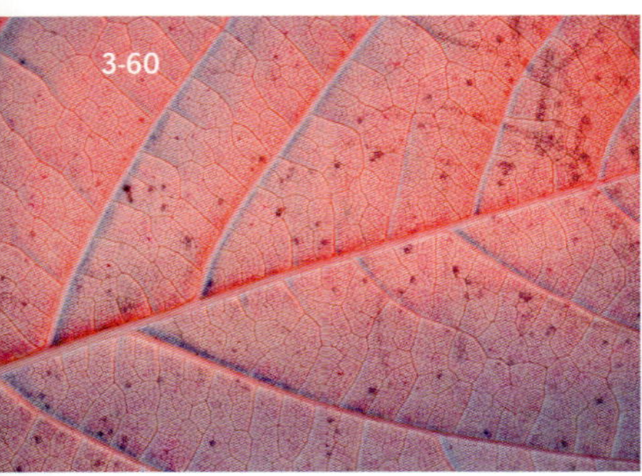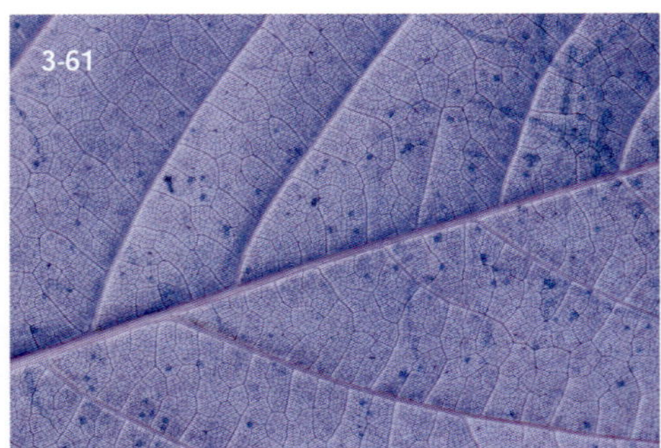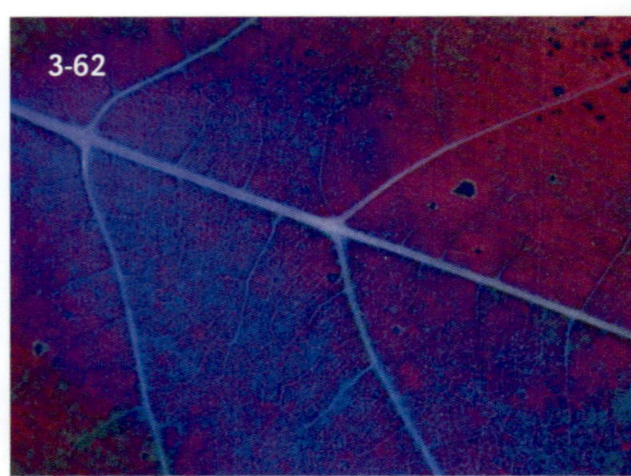

Image 3-60. Red flashlight on leaf in Great Smoky Mountains National Park. The light was positioned low and to the side to create dramatic side lighting. Nikon 200mm macro lens. Exposure: 1/8 second at f/11. **Image 3-61.** Same leaf with blue flashlight. Nikon 200mm macro lens. Exposure: 1/6 second at f/11. **Image 3-62.** Same leaf, underside up, with blue flashlight held stationary during the exposure. Nikon 200mm macro lens. Exposure: 1/2 second at f/13.

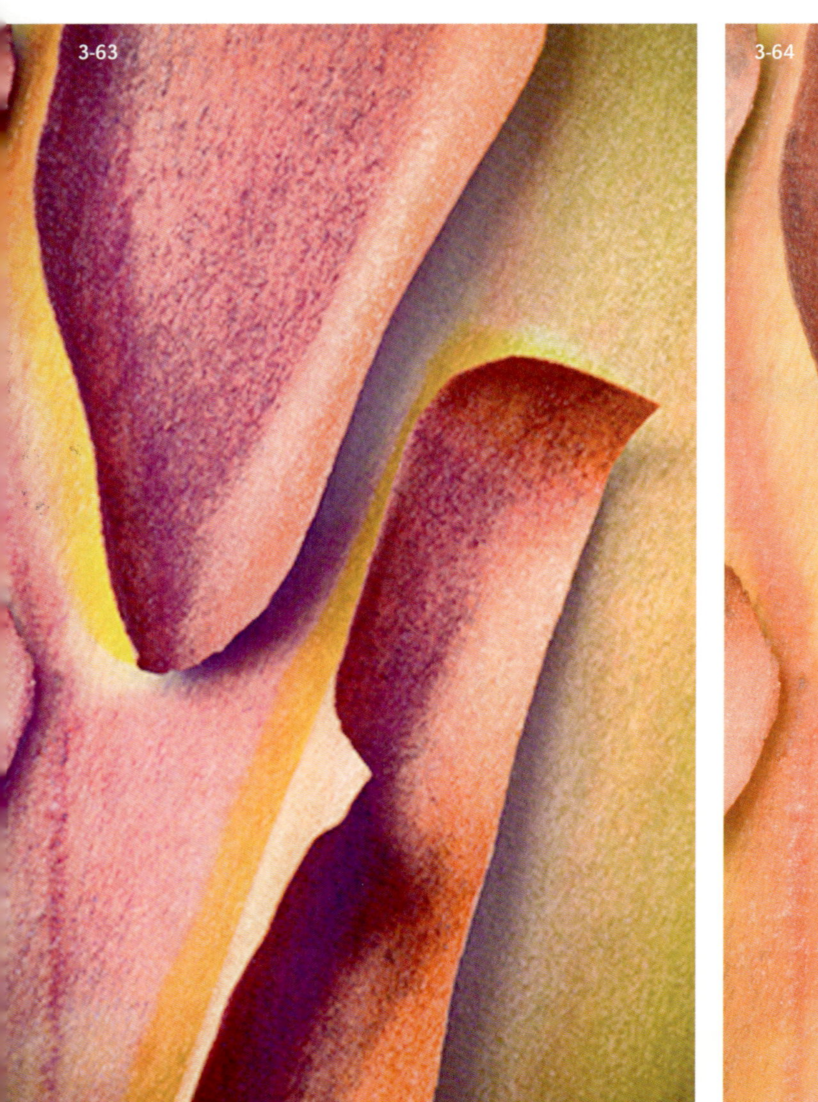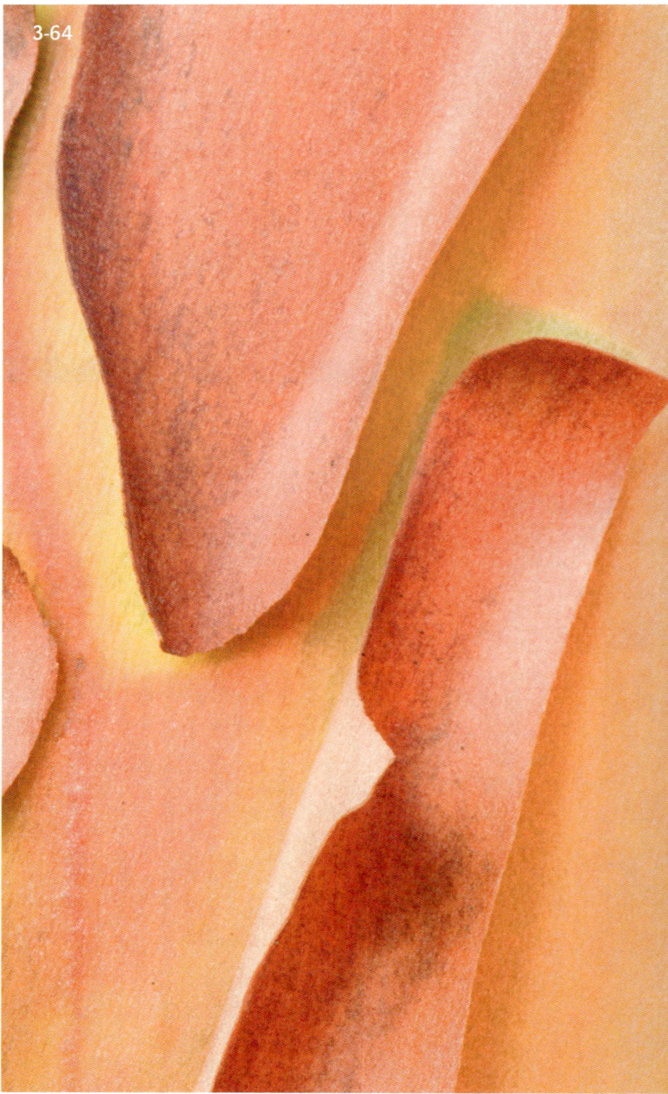

Images 3-63 and 3-64. The multi-colored LED flashlight works well on subjects such as the bark on a madrone tree, photographed one summer afternoon on Whidbey Island, WA. The blue flashlight setting was used for image 3-63, while the red setting was used for image 3-64. Exposure settings were the same for both images. Nikon 200mm macro lens. Exposure: 5 seconds at f/36.

such a simple tool is that you can selectively illuminate any small portion of your image or background. By varying how close/far you hold the flashlight, you can also control the intensity of the light. This flashlight also has a white (halogen) beam to which you could also add a colored gel and/or illuminate the throat of a flower or backlight your subject. I "paint" with light by moving the flashlight around during an exposure of $\frac{1}{2}$ second or longer. *Caution:* When using a multi-colored flashlight, be careful not to exaggerate the effect because your image will look too artificial. You'll need to experiment some before you get the subtle desired effect.

For more on lighting and macro lighting tools, see chapter 2.

Flash and Close-up Photography

I use flash only about 10 percent of the time in my macro photography because I prefer natural light over artificial light. Photographing flowers with an electronic flash tends to look clinical and unrealistic, unless you're able to control the flash and use it as a secondary light source rather than a primary one.

There are several types of flash units available with increasing sophistication as technology improves. Some cameras come equipped with a built-in flash, but I recommend as a general rule that you turn this off when shooting close-ups because you'll get boring frontal lighting, which looks too artificial. Instead, I suggest you purchase a basic single flash unit that can be manually operated and has TTL (or "through the lens" meter reading) capability. I use the Nikon SB-800 as my supplemental light source in such cases.

Over the years, some students have asked me about ring flash units, which mount on the end of a macro or telephoto lens and wrap 360 degrees around the lens. These were traditionally used in the medical and dental industries and provided nice evenly-lit photo illustrations. Today's newer more modern ring lights are much better because you can vary the light output on either side of the lens. Some models, such as Nikon's R1, a wireless close-up speedlight, feature two removable lights to allow for more creative lighting effects.

Regardless of which type of flash you choose, avoid attaching your flash directly to the camera's hot shoe because this produces boring frontal lighting and the light tends to overshoot the subject, illuminating past the subject and striking the background rather than the subject. The solution is to remove the flash unit from the hot shoe and attach it to a sync cord (a cable that allows the flash and camera to communicate). Some of the newer flash units are wireless, so a sync cord may not be necessary.

To make flash usage even easier, I use a special macro flash bracket that allows me to easily move the flash in any direction and place the light exactly where I want it to fall. This bracket, along with an extra extension arm, mounts directly to the lens plate on my Nikkor 200mm macro lens and works better than any other flash bracket system I've tried for macro. Unlike some of the other brackets on the market, which are primarily designed for

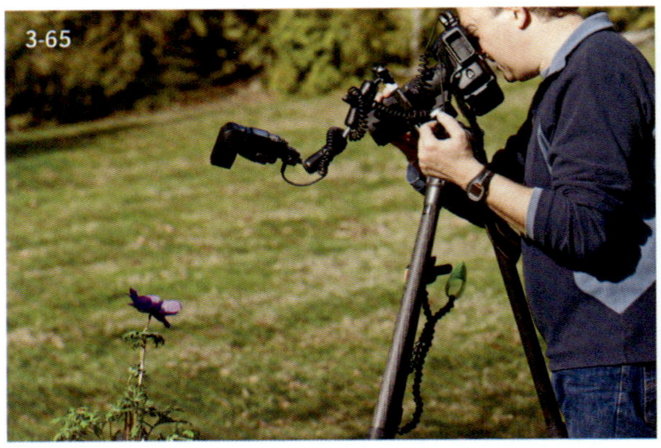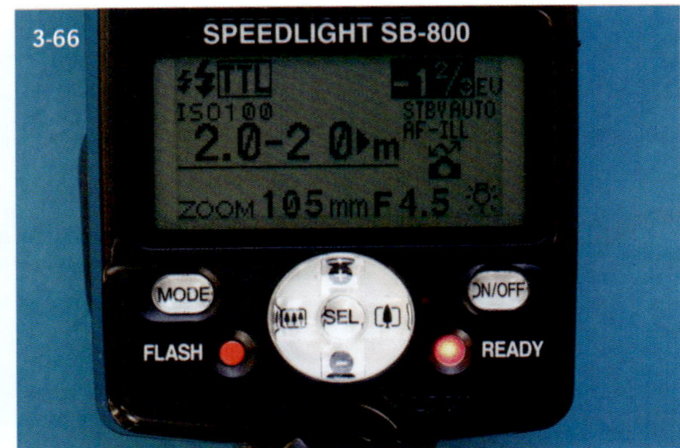

Image 3-65. Because I shot this purple poppy in sunlight, I needed to "fill in" the shadow areas using fill-flash to make the light more even and less contrasty. **Image 3-66.** Nikon SB-800, set in TTL exposure mode at -1²/₃ stops flash exposure compensation. The camera automatically balances available light in the scene with artificial light from the flash unit.

portrait and wedding photographers, this one offers a practical solution with optimal results because of the infinite number of ways you can position the flash. (Note that in order to use this particular flash bracket, your lens plate must be Arca-Swiss compatible, which means the plate must have small angled grooves on either side.)

When using a digital SLR, there are several ways to make flash look more natural. If you are indoors, bouncing the flash off the ceiling by aiming the flash-head upward gives a much softer and more pleasant light. You can also use a mini diffuser, which slides onto the head of the flash unit. (My Nikon SB-800 flash unit comes with such a device.)

When working on close-up subjects outdoors, the best way to make flash appear more natural and subtle is to decrease the output on the flash itself. This produces "fill light," which complements the natural light and reduces some of the heavy shadows. Because working distances are short when shooting macro subjects, you'll need to decrease the flash output to anywhere from a -1.7 to -2

flash compensation setting. (Consult your flash manual to learn more about flash compensation and how to achieve these settings.)

Images 3-67 through **3-74** illustrate how various flash exposure compensation settings on my Nikon SB-800 impact shadow and highlight detail on a blue poppy photographed outdoors in direct sunlight.

The general steps for creating fill light are below, but you'll need to adjust accordingly, depending on what flash unit you're working with:

1. With the flash unit turned off but attached to the camera and aimed at your subject, take an ambient light meter reading (as if you were going to take a picture using no flash). You can use any exposure setting, but I prefer working in manual mode for this application.
2. Turn the flash unit on and make sure it's set to TTL meter reading.
3. Dial minus flash compensation into your flash unit (not the camera). I suggest starting with -1 flash compensation.
4. Take a picture and then evaluate the image and histogram. If there's too much flash

output and the image looks "artificial" with certain highlights overexposed, continue dialing in more minus flash compensation in $\frac{1}{3}$ stop increments and taking pictures along the way until you reach the desired flash output level.

5. If necessary, adjust the spread of light (how wide the light is dispersed) on your flash unit. This can make a difference if you're trying to illuminate a wider area versus a very narrow, smaller area.

That's really all there is to it! No calculating fancy foot-candles. In TTL exposure mode, the camera automatically balances available light with the artificial light. Since digital SLRs provide instantaneous visual feedback via the LCD on the back of the camera, you don't have to guess in the same way you might have had to do using a film camera. The key is to produce a subtle, yet pleasing balance of natural light and fill light.

One other note: If you do decide to hand-hold the flash unit rather than using a flash bracket, be careful not to cover the front sensor on the flash with your hand (a common mistake!).

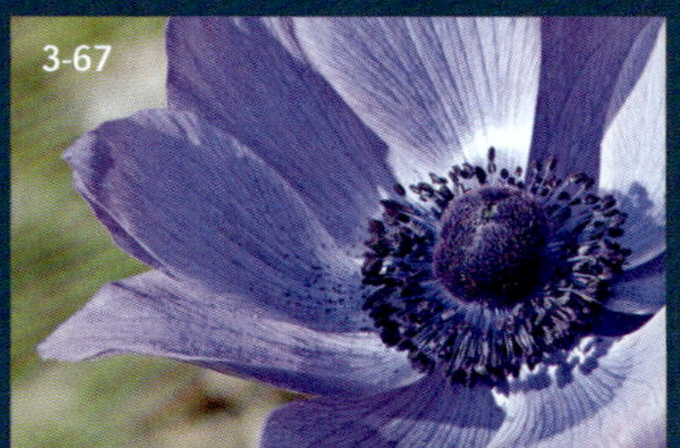

Image 3-67. No flash, Nikon 200mm macro lens, 1/10 second at f/40.

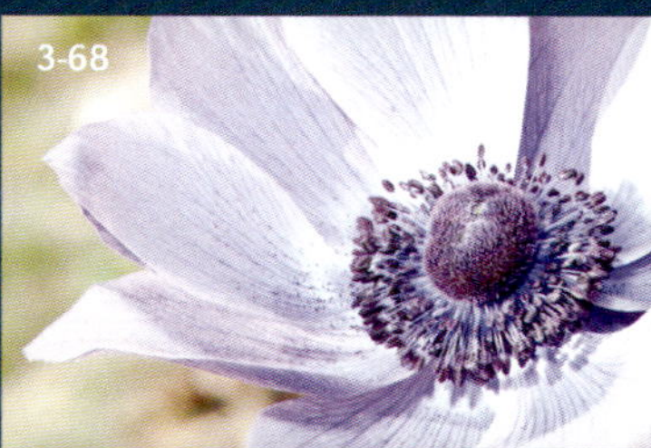

Image 3-68. +2 stops flash exposure compensation—no highlight detail.

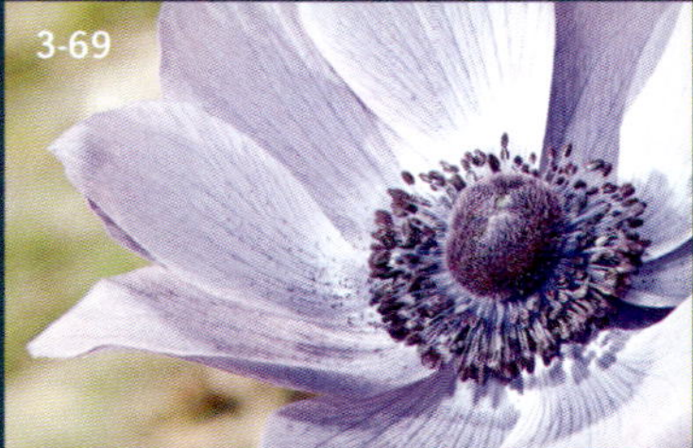

Image 3-69. +1 stop flash exposure compensation—still too bright.

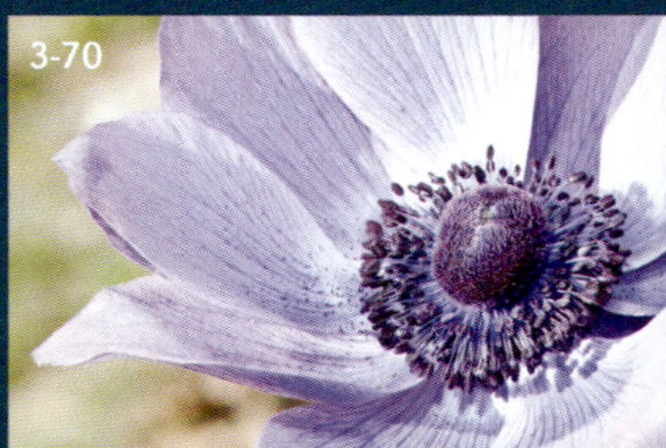

Image 3-70. Full flash (no flash exposure compensation)—highlights still blown out.

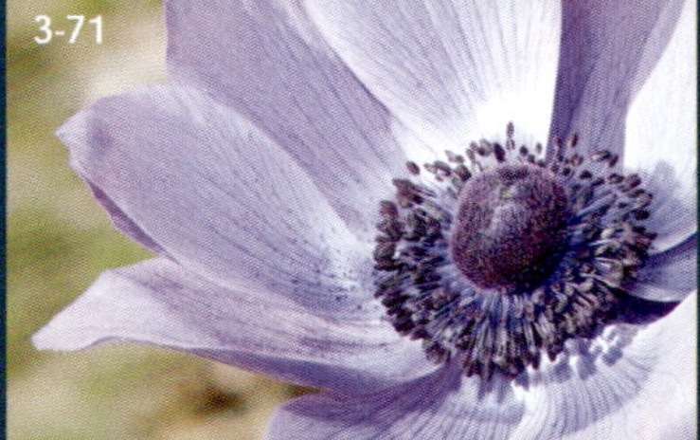

Image 3-71. -1/3 stop flash exposure compensation—better, but still rather bright.

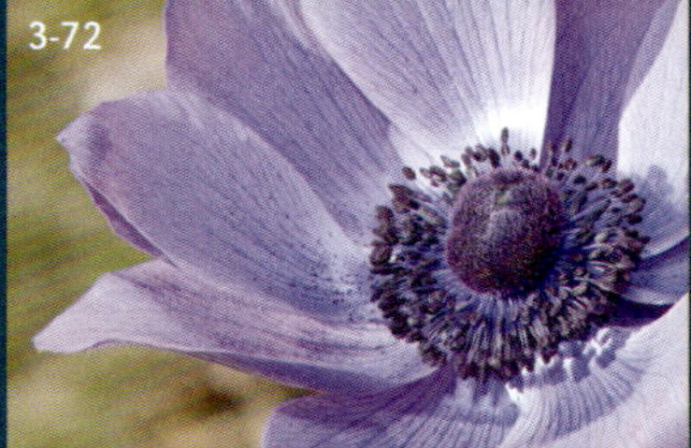

Image 3-72. –2/3 stop flash exposure compensation—acceptable.

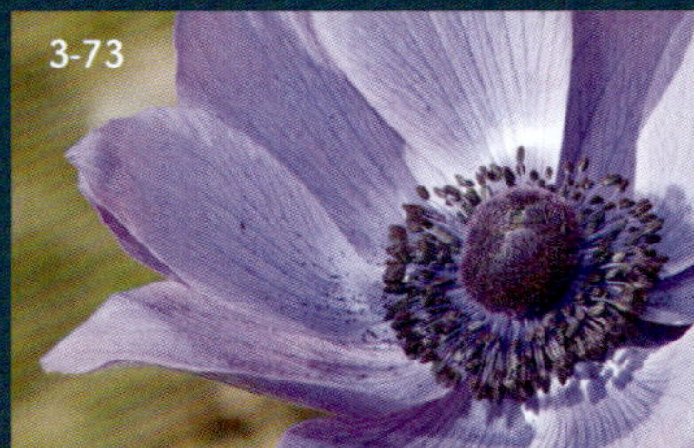

Image 3-73. -1 stop flash exposure compensation—looking more "natural" with highlight detail.

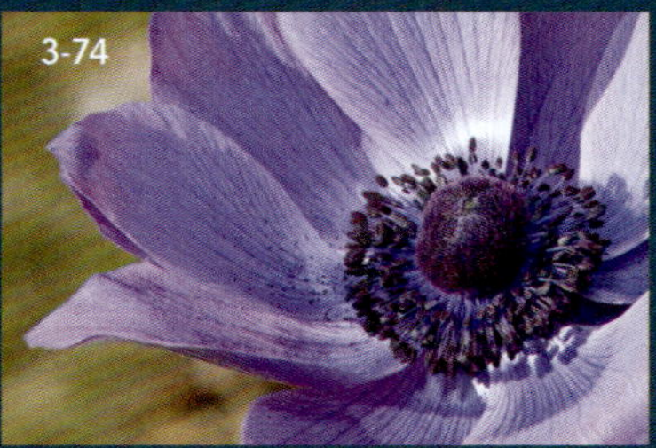

Image 3-74. -1-1/3 stop flash exposure compensation—not quite enough shadow detail.

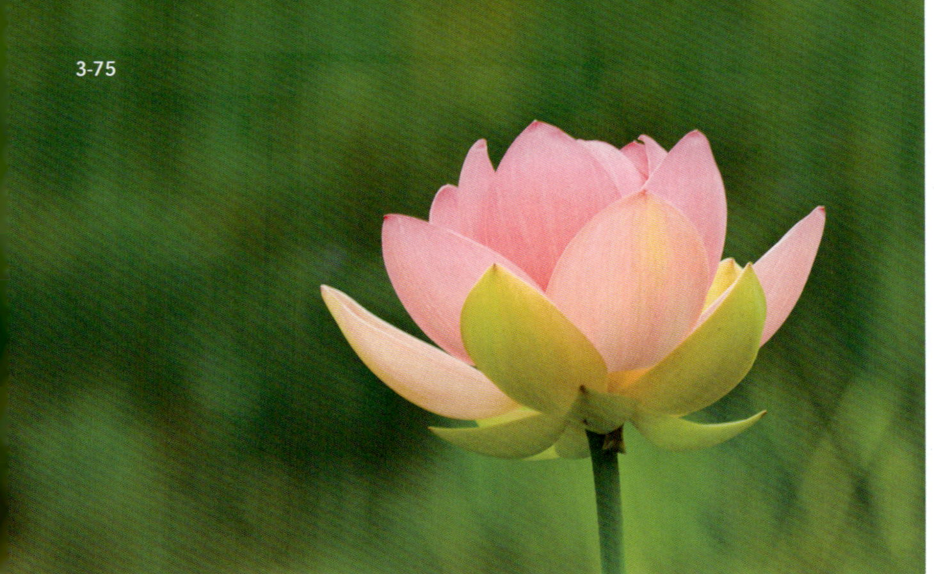

Image 3-75. Using the Rule of Thirds, I placed the lotus in this image on a "power point" (place where two lines intersect) in the lower part of the frame to add more visual interest and create greater impact. Note the amount of negative space surrounding the flower. The distance from the edge of the far right petal to the right edge of the frame is the same as the distance from the bottom of the bloom itself (excluding the stem below) to the bottom edge of the frame. Careful placement of your subject, such as this, can make all the difference between good composition and superb composition.

Composition

Composition is defined as the union of several visual elements to collectively make a photograph better. You don't need fancy equipment to design and compose a beautiful image. All that's required is an understanding of several design elements, a lot of practice and refinement, and most importantly, an innate cultivated sense of what works and what doesn't work.

In macro photography, particularly, composition plays a critical role in successful image making because you are directing the viewer to witness beauty in a miniature world with reverence. To convey such reverence, you'll need to pay close attention to every small detail within your viewfinder. Unlike some other forms of art, such as painting, photography requires you to eliminate all that's distracting within the frame and "distill" the true essence of your subject.

So what is the "essence" and how do you go about communicating that essence visually? One of the biggest mistakes I see among macro photographers is that all too often, they aren't paying close enough attention to what's in the viewfinder. They will quickly compose an image, set the correct f/stop, create just the right type of lighting, wait for the breeze to die down (if shooting a close-up subject outdoors), and then click the shutter. You need to get in the habit of really studying your compositions after you've made the first series of images and before you move on to the next subject.

Composing an image successfully is a process that requires a lot of fine-tuning. You can't expect to get "the shot" the first time. Often, I'll make twenty to thirty images of one subject without moving the camera much, only to make very subtle minor adjustments using my ballhead. All the while, I am asking myself if what I am looking at through the viewfinder really conveys the essence of what I was seeing. In the end, it's those subtle adjustments that can make all the difference between a good shot and an excellent one. The key is to simplify, simplify, simplify. Ask yourself, "Is every single element I am looking at through the viewfinder an integral part of what I am trying to convey to the viewer?" If not, then you'll need to somehow eliminate all of the small pieces that don't contribute to the visual whole.

Since macro images are mini landscapes, the same rules of composition in landscape photography generally apply. Of course, as in all types of photography, once you understand the rules, it's okay to think outside the box occasionally and break the rules deliberately.

Here are ten important rules of composition to consider when making a close-up image:

1. **Every photograph needs to have a central point of interest.** Before you ever set up your camera, study your subject. Walk around it several times. Examine it from every possible angle. Ask yourself, "What is drawing me to this subject and why?" For example, if it's the lighting, then what is it about the lighting that's so intriguing? Is it the quality of light or the direction of light? Is the subject backlit, side-lit, softly lit? Is the tone of the light warm or cool, or a combination of both? Then ask yourself how you can best emphasize this quality using the camera as an extension of your "vision" that you find so appealing.

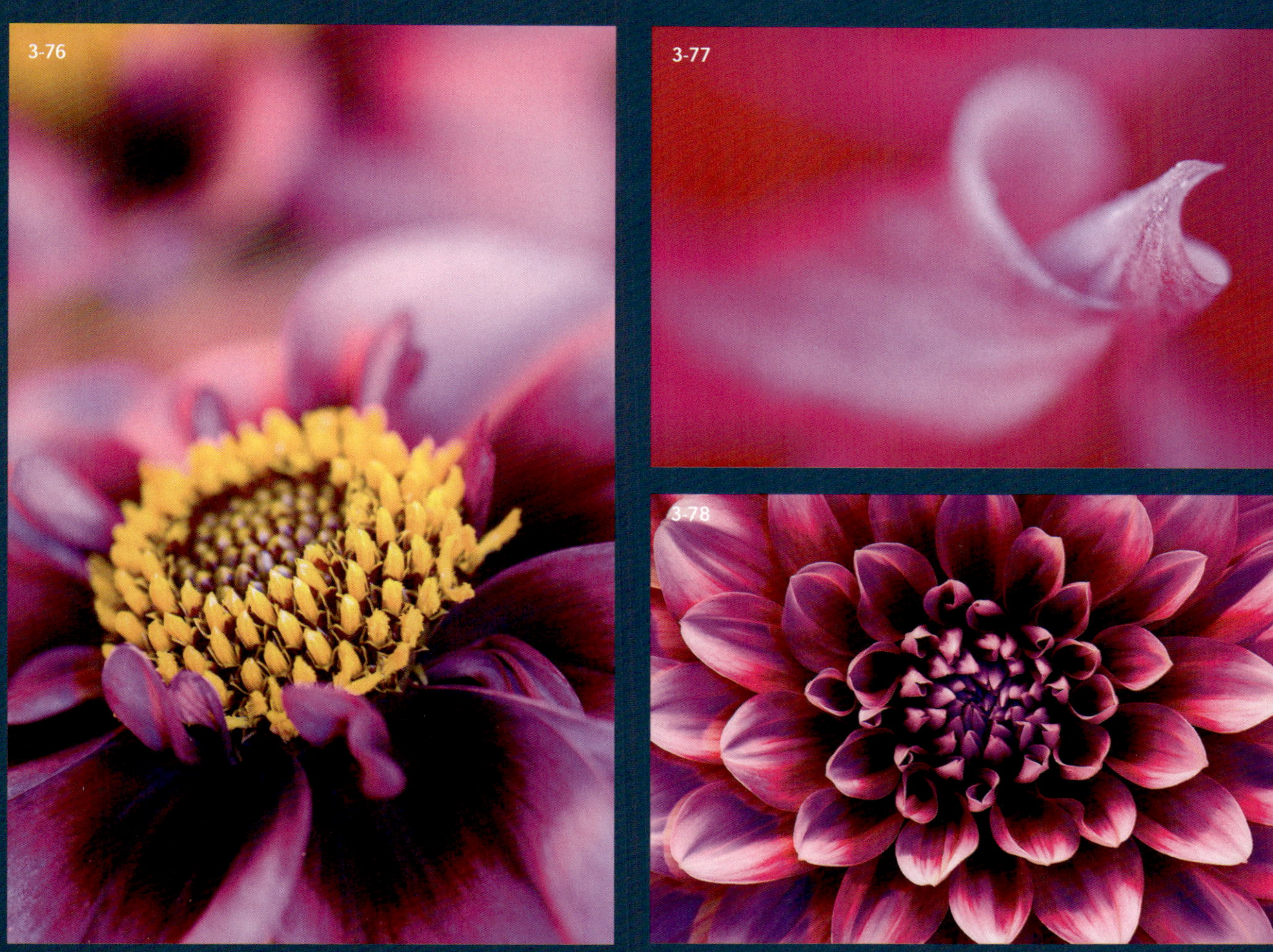

Image 3-76. In this image (photographed with a Lensbaby and two macro filters stacked), I purposely placed the bloom in the lower portion of the frame to give it more visual weight. By using shallow depth of field and turning the camera in a slightly oblique position, I was able to draw the viewer into the photograph even more. **Image 3-77.** Again, using the Rule of Thirds, I placed the sharpest part of this rose petal on a power point. Positioning the petal in front of a darker-toned background helped isolate the subject even more. **Image 3-78.** All rules of composition are meant to be broken. In general, you would not want to place a subject dead-center, because it can be rather dull and static. In this case, however, I deliberately chose to place the subject in the middle to emphasize the radiating pattern of the dahlia. I added a touch of blue flashlight to this image to help hold the viewer's attention.

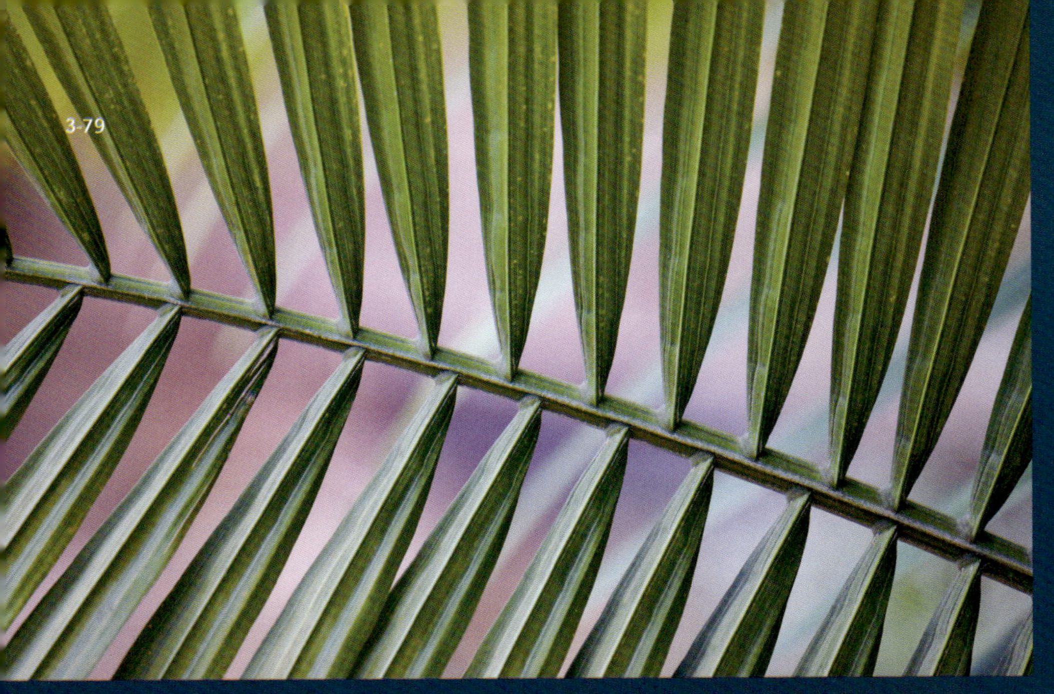

Image 3-79. The dominant oblique line in this close-up photograph of a palm frond helps add impact and hold the viewer's attention. Notice that neither end of the line lands in the corner of the image. This placement in the frame adds impact, making the top half larger and more dominant than the lower half. Dividing the frame in two equal halves would not have been as visually appealing because there would have been too much symmetry, too much predictability.

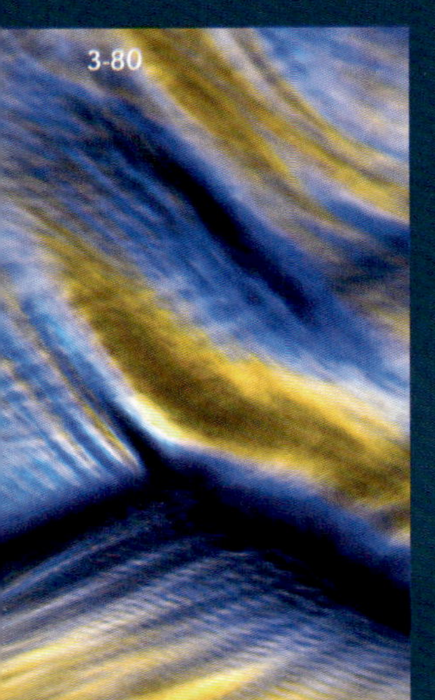

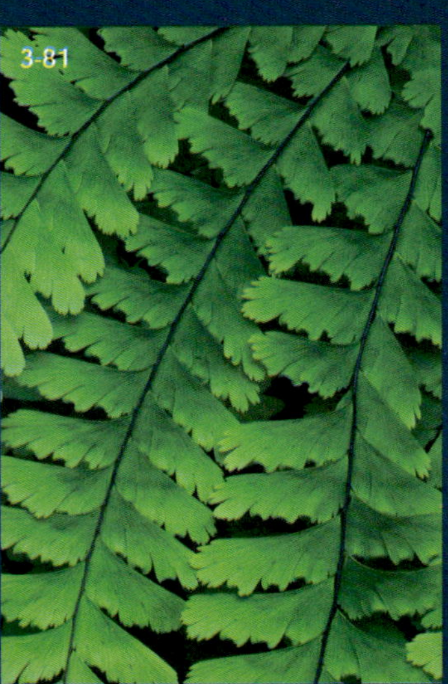

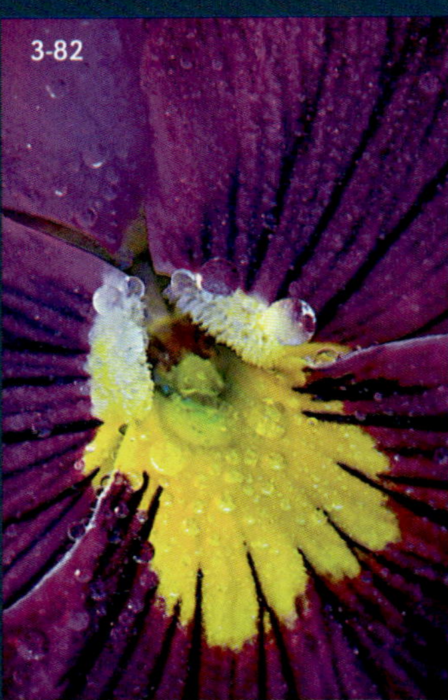

Image 3-80. This abstract image of fall foliage reflecting in running water (Great Smoky Mountains National Park) also illustrates the use of oblique lines to help convey energy and movement. Again, no dominant oblique lines intersect with the corners of the frame. **Image 3-81.** In this image, the repetition of three dominant oblique lines makes this a more dynamic composition. Filling the frame also creates greater impact. Again, no dominant oblique lines intersect with the corners of the frame. **Image 3-82.** In this pansy image, turning the camera at a slight angle created an implied oblique line that adds energy to the overall composition. **Image 3-83.** Another strong, implied oblique. Complementary colors, yellow and purple, also help to draw the viewer's eye into the image.

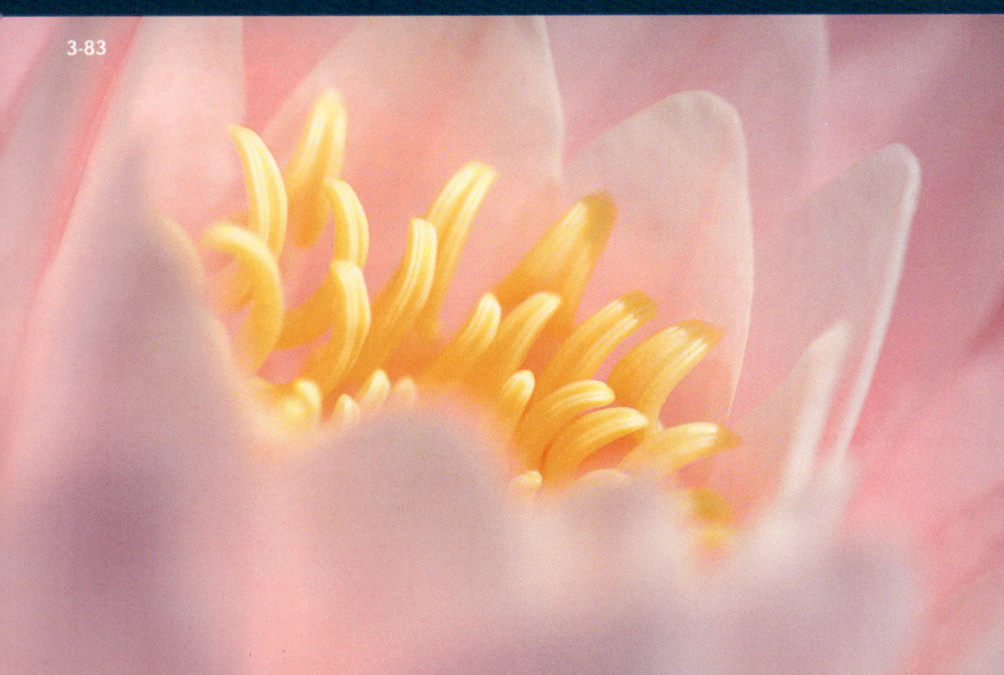

If, for example, it's the oblique lines or textures that are drawing you to photograph a particular subject, then make your image all about the lines or textures. By continually asking yourself these kinds of questions, you'll find that your compositions become more refined and that you are able to communicate exactly what you were feeling or thinking to your viewer much more effectively.

One other tip is to handhold your camera and study what's in the viewfinder without feeling constrained by a tripod before you ever click the shutter. Once you've found a pleasing composition, then set up your tripod from that particular vantage point.

2. **Pay close attention to backgrounds.** Once you understand how aperture controls depth of field, you can use this to your advantage when composing an image. When shooting at wider apertures, you can certainly isolate subjects. However, keep in mind that even the softest of backgrounds can contain distracting elements. There might be something bright, such as another flower or a tree limb, that can detract from the main subject. As a general rule, you want a very "clean" and uncluttered background in macro photography. To address these concerns, I find that often a simple minor adjustment in camera angle can make all the difference. Don't get so caught up in your subject that you forget to study the background. Especially when working close-up, what's behind the main subject can be as important—or more important—than the subject itself.

3. **Get in the habit of rigorous "border patrol" before you press the shutter button.** I'm a real stickler for this one! Sometimes, unwanted distractions are located around the perimeter of your viewfinder. Unless you're in the habit of scanning all four edges before you make the picture, you're likely to overlook them. This rule applies to objects that might appear around the edges, such as single stems, tree branches, or flower petals, as well as situations where brighter tones appear near the edges (pulling your eye out of the frame) or when the tip of a flower petal appears right on the edge of the frame (creating tension for the viewer). A couple of rules to remember here: Your eyes are drawn to the brightest areas within the frame first. Also, keep anything that comes to a sharp point away from the edges of the frame.

4. **Pay attention to placement of your subject within the frame.** One of the most common tenets in photographic composition is the Rule of Thirds. This rule states that an image should be imagined as divided into nine equal parts by two equally-spaced horizontal lines and two equally spaced vertical lines and that important compositional elements should be placed along these lines or at their intersecting points. This technique creates more tension, energy, and adds interest to the composition than simply centering the subject would.

Another consideration when deciding where to place subjects in the frame is visual weight. In general, large subjects and darker tones should be placed in the lower portion of the frame to avoid causing an image to appear too top-heavy and less stable. (See **images 3-75** through **3-78**, pages 60 and 61.)

5. **Learn the "squinting technique."** When I am just beginning to think about composing

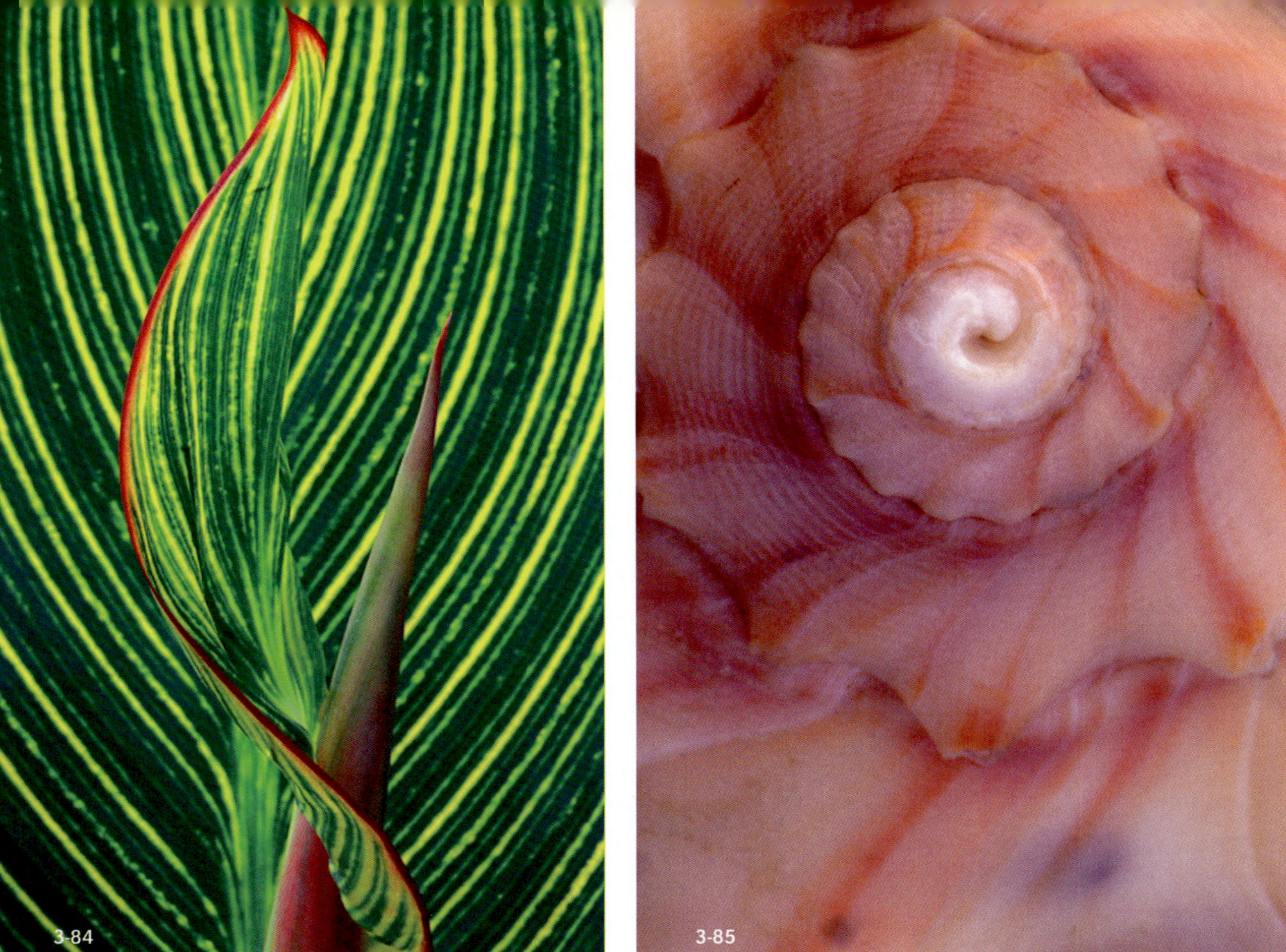

Image **3-84.** S-curves are always compelling. The stripes of this canna lily provide symmetry in the background, but the graceful curve of the leaf in the foreground dominates the composition. **Image 3-85.** Spiral shapes consist of repeating S-curves emanating from a central point. The geometric pattern within this conch shell draws the eye inward.

an image, squinting helps me see lighter and darker tones within an image, as well as the overall shapes within that image. This is one way of "abstracting" your subject, breaking it down into forms and shapes so you don't see it quite as literally as you might first see it. To quote Impressionist painter Claude Monet, squinting helps you "forget the name of the thing you are seeing," which is precisely what you want when designing an image for maximum impact. Once you've seen areas of light/dark tonality and what shapes dominate within the frame, you can adjust your composition accordingly.

6. **Work those obliques!** One of the most effective ways to create impact in a close-up image is to use actual or implied oblique lines. (See **images 3-79** through **3-83**, page 62.) Macro lenses with rotating collars, such as Nikon's 200mm or Canon's 180mm, come in handy when trying to compose a shot with strong diagonals, as you can rotate the lens slightly to put a subject at more of an angle in the viewfinder. As a general rule, perpendicular lines in a photograph are more predictable, stable, and "static" to the viewer. Angular lines create more interest, are dynamic, and carry a certain energy or

direction in a photograph. Remember, there are a million more camera orientations other than just "horizontal" or "vertical."

7. **Use contrast as a compositional element.** When you think of contrast in an image, usually it refers to tonal contrast. An image with great contrast has lots of tonal variation, from the deepest shadows to the brightest highlights.

    There are other forms of contrast, however, that are often overlooked among photographers. You can use these to your advantage when composing an image, or even as you search for subject matter in the field. Some of these more esoteric forms of contrast are: smooth against rough, bright color over dull colors, vertical and horizontal, large and small, soft and hard, sharp and blurry.

8. **Use color as a compositional element.** Although it's often overlooked as a design element, color plays an integral role in the overall effectiveness of a macro image. Color can dictate where you look first and the order in which you look at things. Warmer colors (such as red, yellow, and orange) tend to advance toward the viewer, while cooler colors (such as blue, green, and lavender) tend to recede or appear farther away.

    Warm colors are bold and energetic, while cool colors are soothing and give an impression of calm. By combining warm and cool colors in your photograph, you can evoke certain emotions and create more interest because of color contrast.

    Changing the white balance setting in-camera or post-capture using image-editing software also can impact the degree of warmth or coolness in a color when one color stands in relationship to another color.

Conversely, lack of color in a photograph or images that are predominantly one color (or monochromatic) can be equally as compelling.

9. **Use S-curves to help lead the viewer's eye through an image.** The human eye loves circles and roundedness, especially when these lines repeat themselves. Many macro images have implied or actual winding S curves in them, which create added interest and give the eye someplace to travel. (See **images 3-84** and **3-85**.)

Learn the difference between positive and negative space, and use it wisely.

10. **Learn the difference between positive and negative space, and use it wisely.** If something has more "visual weight," that is to say, it is more of a dominant element in the frame, then pay attention to the space surrounding that dominant element and balance it with the amount of space the subject occupies. Sometimes it's okay to have lots of negative ("empty") space in an image because it contributes to the overall cohesiveness in the image.

    One of the most common mistakes I see when evaluating student workshop images is that there is not enough "breathing space" for subjects. Be sure to leave some negative space around the main subject and do not overfill the frame. Otherwise, you will create a crowded feeling, which can leave the viewer feeling uneasy.

Practice Good Habits

Now that you've learned some of the fundamentals of macro photography, there are still a few tips I'd like to share from my 10+ years of shooting close-ups:

1. **When shooting flowers, choose the freshest and best-possible specimens.** Avoid ones that have blemishes, are wilting, or have missing parts.
2. **Choose flowers that are at least 3–4 inches in diameter.** Anything smaller than that will only frustrate you—especially when first starting out—because you'll probably need extension tubes or other more advanced macro accessories to allow the flower to fill the frame.

3. **When working with glass, keep it clean (especially when shooting reflections and/ or shooting through textured glass).** Always use a good glass cleaner prior to shooting.
4. **Use the lowest possible ISO, such as 100 or 200.** This will help minimize digital "noise."
5. **Use mirror lock-up when shooting close-ups.** Every movement is exaggerated when working at close range, and sharpness is critical. Mirror lock-up will ensure you get minimal vibration within the camera, resulting in the sharpest-possible image.
6. **Use the depth-of-field preview button often and bracket depth of field during your every shoot.** By practicing this habit early on, you'll be able to study images on the computer later on and become much more comfortable with which apertures produce which visual effects.
7. **Don't overdo artificial water droplets.** Always shoot the subject without water droplets first. Then add water droplets carefully. Try to make your droplets appear as natural as possible. By shooting two versions (with and without), you'll have a means of comparison and might decide post-capture that you prefer the image without droplets over the one with water added.
8. **Rely on your histogram more than your eye for "correct" exposure.**
9. **Use a sturdy tripod for 99 percent of your shots if you want the sharpest, most carefully composed images possible.** Handhold your camera only when initially composing your image or when sharpness is not important.
10. **If a subject doesn't excite you in some way at first, give it time and effort anyway.** Sometimes it takes a while to "warm up," and magic can happen when you least expect it, as long as you remain open and alert.
11. **Don't get caught up in technology.** Remember the joy and magic of the creative process. Take time to savor present moments in the field and discover your own unique artistic vision.
12. **Have fun and don't be afraid to break all the rules.** Venture into the unknown with passion, boldness, and open-mindedness.

4. Selective-Focus Macro

In close-up photography, one of the most effective ways to isolate your subject is to use selective focus. With selective focus, you can literally become "lost" in another world—a completely altered dimension of reality. By peering through the lens with no preconceived ideas and being open to all possibilities, you'll discover new meaning if you just "let go" and allow your eyes, mind, and heart to become synchronized.

As a general rule, selective-focus macro is best achieved at wider apertures such as f/5.6, f/4, or f/2.8 to allow for very shallow depth of field and to blend and blur the background. The overall effect can be quite stunning, especially if the foreground or background contain vivid colors. By doing this, you're distilling the essence of your subject, breaking it down into its simplest form, thereby evoking an emotional response from your viewer.

In my experience, too many camera club judges immediately discard images because they are not tack-sharp. Even the slightest "fuzziness" in one small portion of a photograph is deemed unacceptable. This is unfortunate, in my opinion, because it inhibits creativity and causes you, the photographer, to view the world in only one way.

In life, there is a great deal of uncertainty we all experience on a daily basis. Making images with soft-focus can teach you to embrace this uncertainty and, in fact, enjoy it! Throw in a lot of patience, and watch the magic happen. Adding soft-focus to an image immediately transports your viewer one step away from reality, giving him/her an ethereal, impressionistic feeling. Rather than seeing the scene literally, it forces you to think outside the

Image 4.1. By using very shallow depth of field, I was able to isolate this bleeding heart, which caught my eye as I was leaving the parking lot of the Atlanta Botanical Garden one spring evening. Placing the flower at an oblique angle added interest as well. Be careful to make sure your background is relatively clutter-free. This ensures greater overall impact. Micro-Nikkor 200mm at f/4.

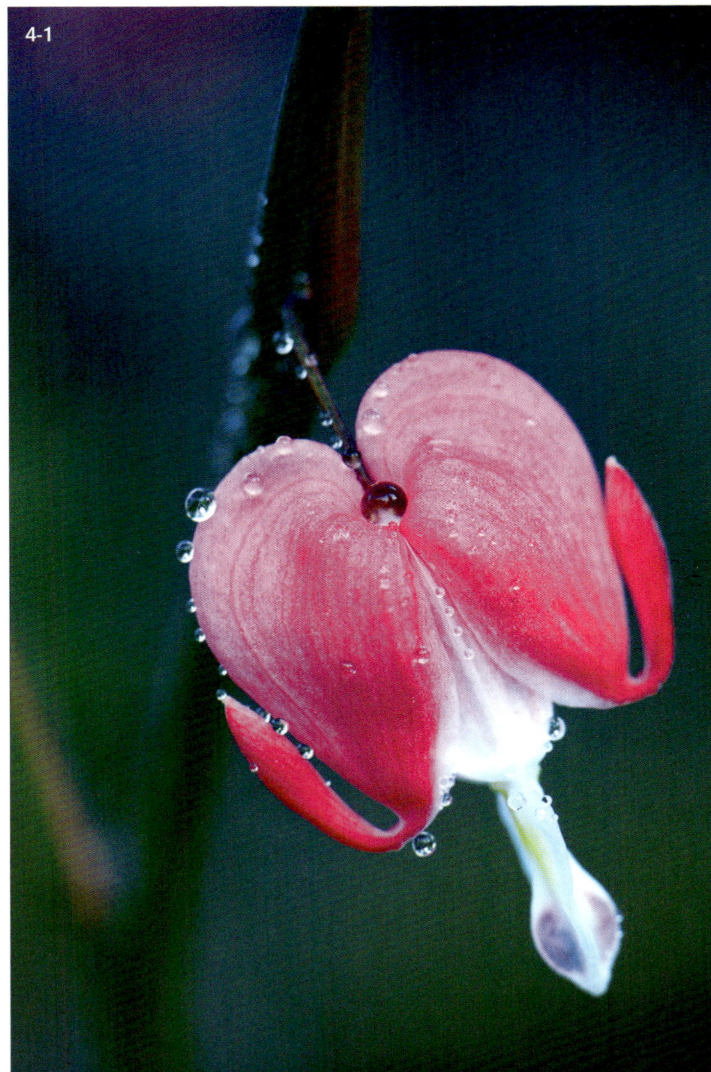

box and attempt to translate feelings into pixels.

Soft focus should not be used in every photograph; however, some flowers or scenes will lend themselves to this technique more readily than others. Look for foreground/background relationships in terms of tonal contrast. Lighter-toned flowers such as pink and yellow stand out better against dark-toned backgrounds such as green and gray. In a studio setup, you can control this much more than in the field because you can use colorful potted flowers and plants, as well as colored papers, as foreground or background elements that become an integral part of the composition.

From a technical standpoint, selective-focus macro is controlled by aperture. You can work in either manual or aperture priority mode to adjust the aperture, starting with the lens wide open at its largest-possible aperture. Often, I'll experiment by taking the same image at several different apertures, or at several different focusing points, to compare results.

Images **4-1** and **4-2** illustrate using a telephoto lens at a wide aperture to selectively focus and isolate the subject. In both examples, I used my 200mm macro lens, focusing much farther away from the subject in the first example than in the second one. Both isolate the subject by blurring the background effectively. This is the more "traditional" and conventional way of achieving selective focus.

However, through experimentation in the field and in my own backyard garden studio, I've discovered five methods for creating unusual and striking selective-focus macro images in-camera. Each of these renders radically different effects, and I encourage you to give it a whirl and take these even one step further by combining more than one technique in a single image.

Telephoto Lens

If you have grown tired of using the same old macro lens for your close-up photography, try using a telephoto lens to break the monotony. Telephoto lenses of 100mm or longer work best for this technique. By carefully positioning your camera right in front of colorful flowers or other foliage in the foreground and focusing the lens on your subject in the background, you can create a beautiful wash of color in your image. I use this technique of "shooting through" quite often with varying results, depending on just how close the foreground element is to the lens. As a general rule, place foreground objects 2–12 inches from the end of your lens. Be careful not to cover too much area within the frame. You want to be able to see and focus on your main subject in the background. (See **images 4-3** and **4-4**, as well as images **4-5** through **4-7**.)

Using the depth-of-field preview button on your camera allows you to see the effect at various apertures. If you don't have a

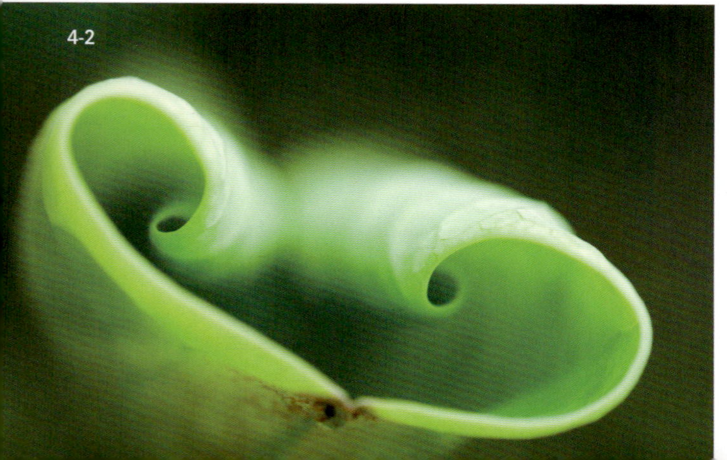

Image 4-2. You can still achieve shallow depth of field when focusing close with a macro lens. In this example, I chose an aperture of f/5.6 when shooting the edges of the petals of this tropical water lily because I wanted to emphasize the beautiful heart-shaped formation. Since I was at the minimum focusing distance, the background remained in soft focus. Micro-Nikkor 200mm at f/5.6.

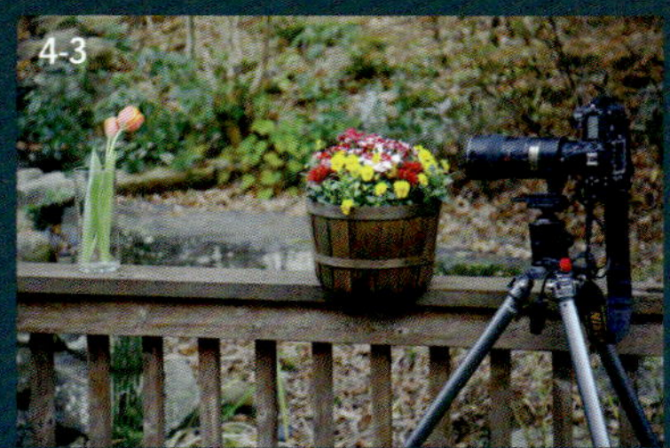

Images 4-3 and 4-4. This setup illustrates the technique of "shooting through" flowers. By positioning my camera in front of the flower-pot and maintaining a low camera angle, I was able to use the pink flowers in the foreground to create a soft color vignette around the orange tulips. Micro-Nikkor 200mm at f/2.8.

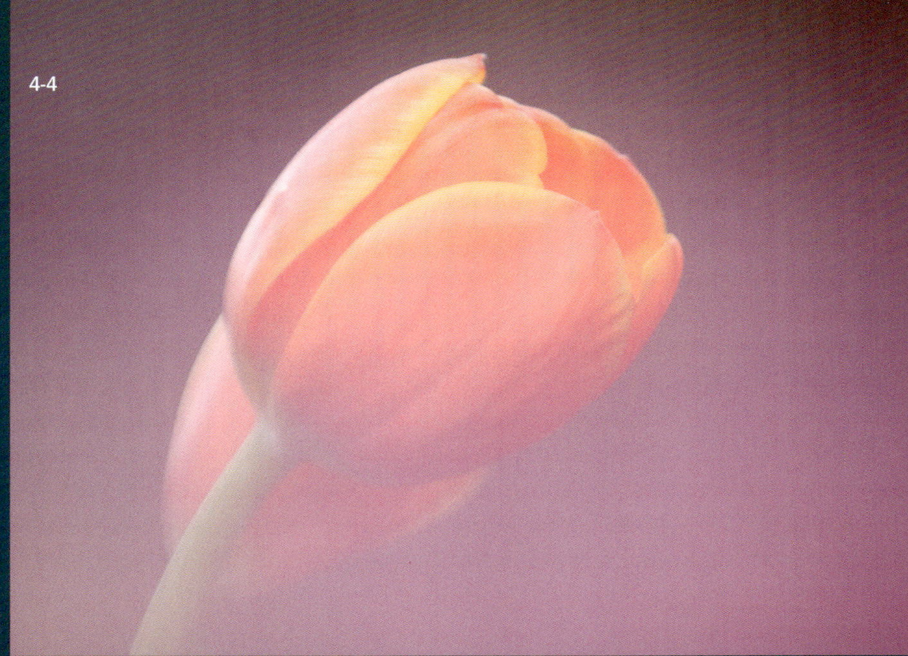

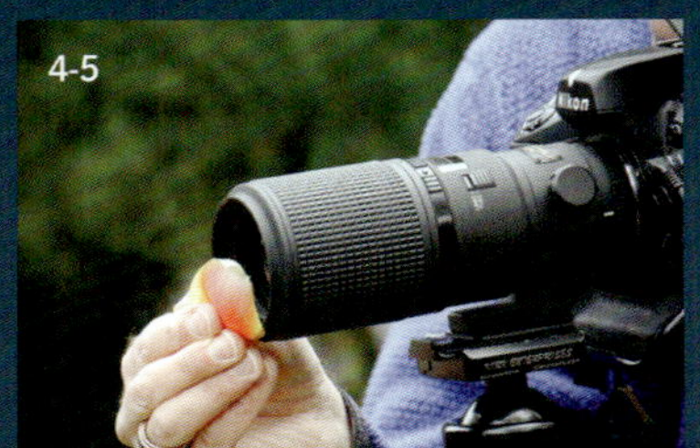

Image 4-5.

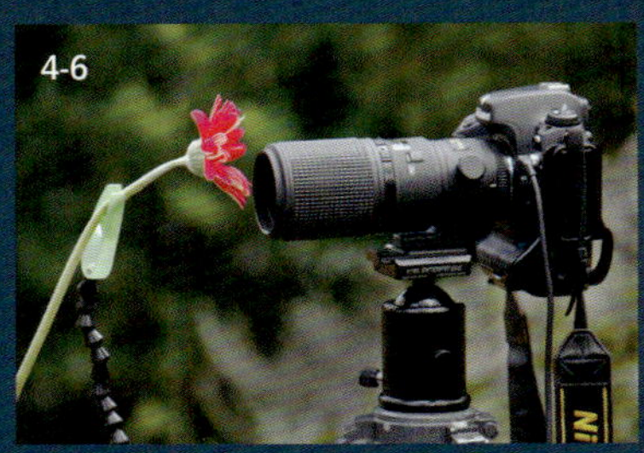

Images 4-6 and 4-7. This time, using a Plamp attached to my tripod leg, I positioned a pink flower a couple of inches from the lens and "shot through" with the lens wide open and focused on the orange flower in the distance. I was careful to position the flower low enough so that the vignetting effect appeared only across the lower portion of the frame. This technique is especially effective when you want to soften or minimize the visual impact of certain elements in the picture, such as the flower stem in this case. Instead of using a Plamp, you could hand-hold a flower petal, as illustrated in image 4-5.

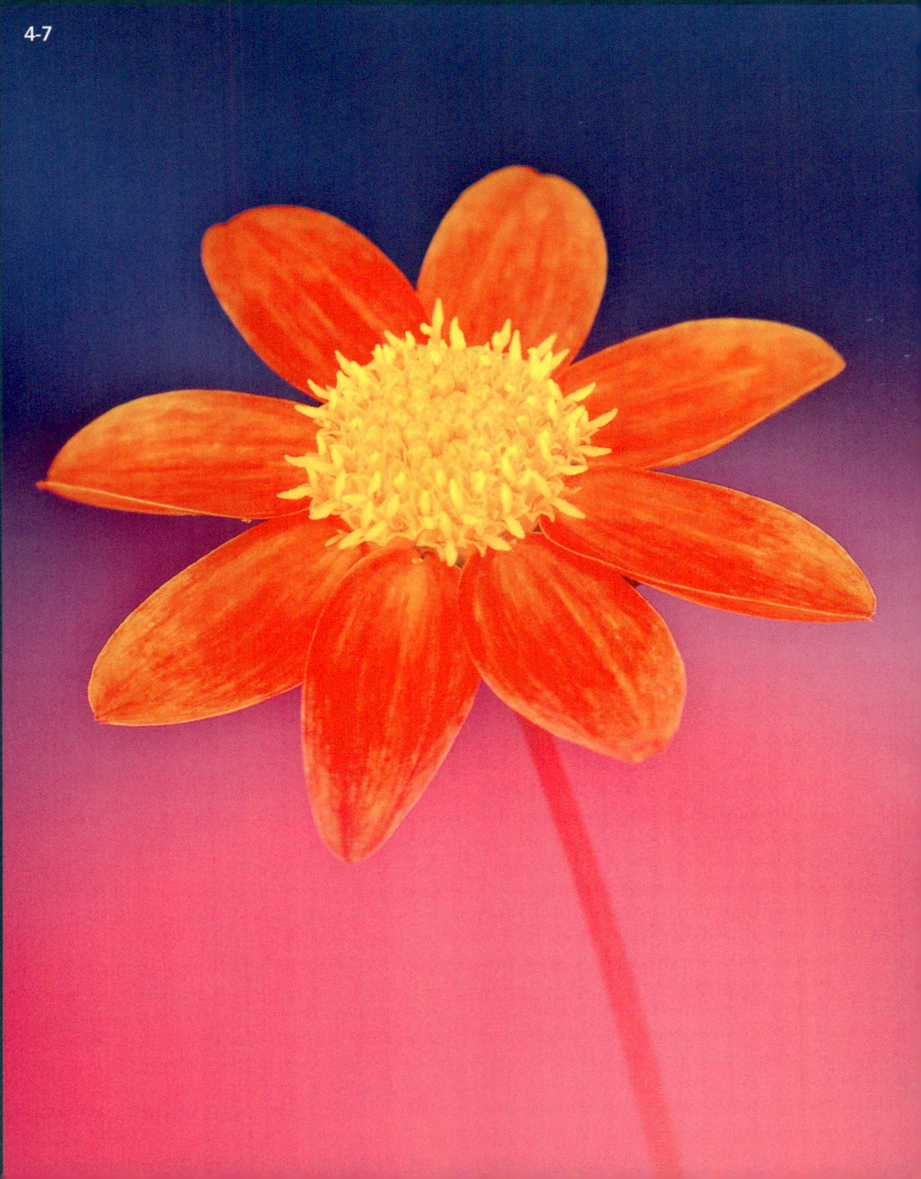

preview button, use the LCD on the back of your camera to determine just how much "unsharpness" you want. Typically, I'll start out by shooting at the widest aperture first, and then shoot several frames, each stopped down in 1-stop increments. (Be sure to decrease the shutter speed accordingly as you stop down the lens.) You'll want your camera on a tripod for sure!

Remember to be creative with what you use in the foreground to "shoot through." Besides flowers and other foliage, I've experimented with everything from sheer fabrics and other articles of clothing (see **image 4-9**) to a colorful placemat with holes in it (see **image 4-8**). In essence, you're creating your own soft-focus filter. Have fun and use various objects from around the house!

Here are some additional examples where the technique of "shooting through" other flowers in the foreground was used.

Macro Lens with Extension Tube

Traditionally, extension tubes are used to allow a lens to focus closer, thus giving you greater

Images 4-8 and 4-9. In addition to flowers, I have experimented with holding various colorful objects in front of the lens to achieve a vignetting effect. In image 4-8, I held my arm close to the top portion of my macro lens to create a bluish soft-focus effect from my blue sweatshirt. In image 4-9, a green placemat with holes in it also did the trick! Feel free to let your imagination go wild. Remember to use the widest-possible aperture on your lens and look through the camera to check for exact positioning to achieve the desired effect.

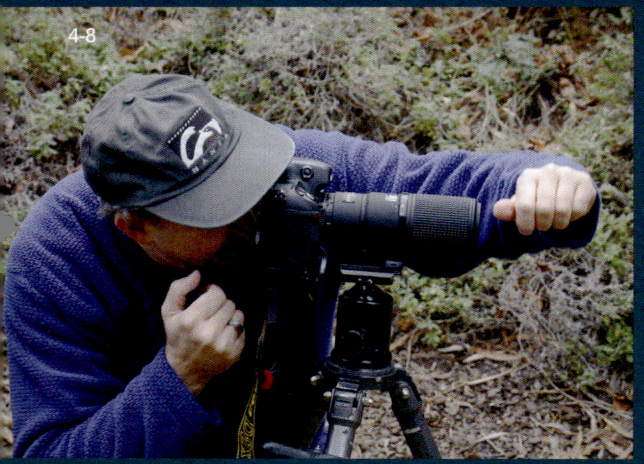

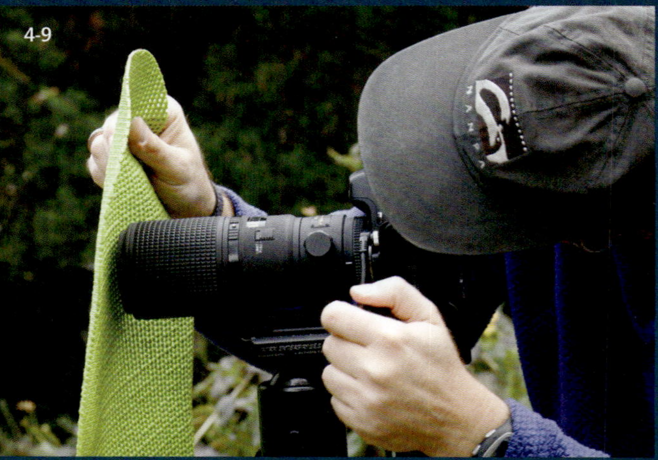

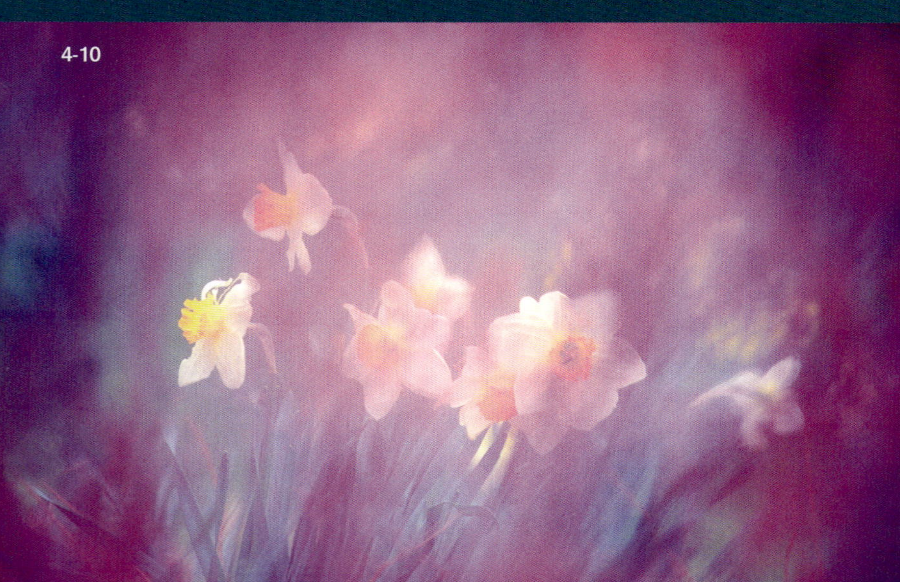

Images 4-10 and 4-11. Here are two more examples of how you can "shoot through" other flowers to achieve soft-focus. In both of these cases, however, I used my 70–200mm lens, rather than my macro lens, which still resulted in pleasing effects. With the daffodil image, I crouched down low and literally stuck my lens into some fairly dense foliage (a shrub with purple flowers), changed the focus on my lens to about 20 feet, and focused on the daffodils in the distance at the widest aperture, f/2.8.

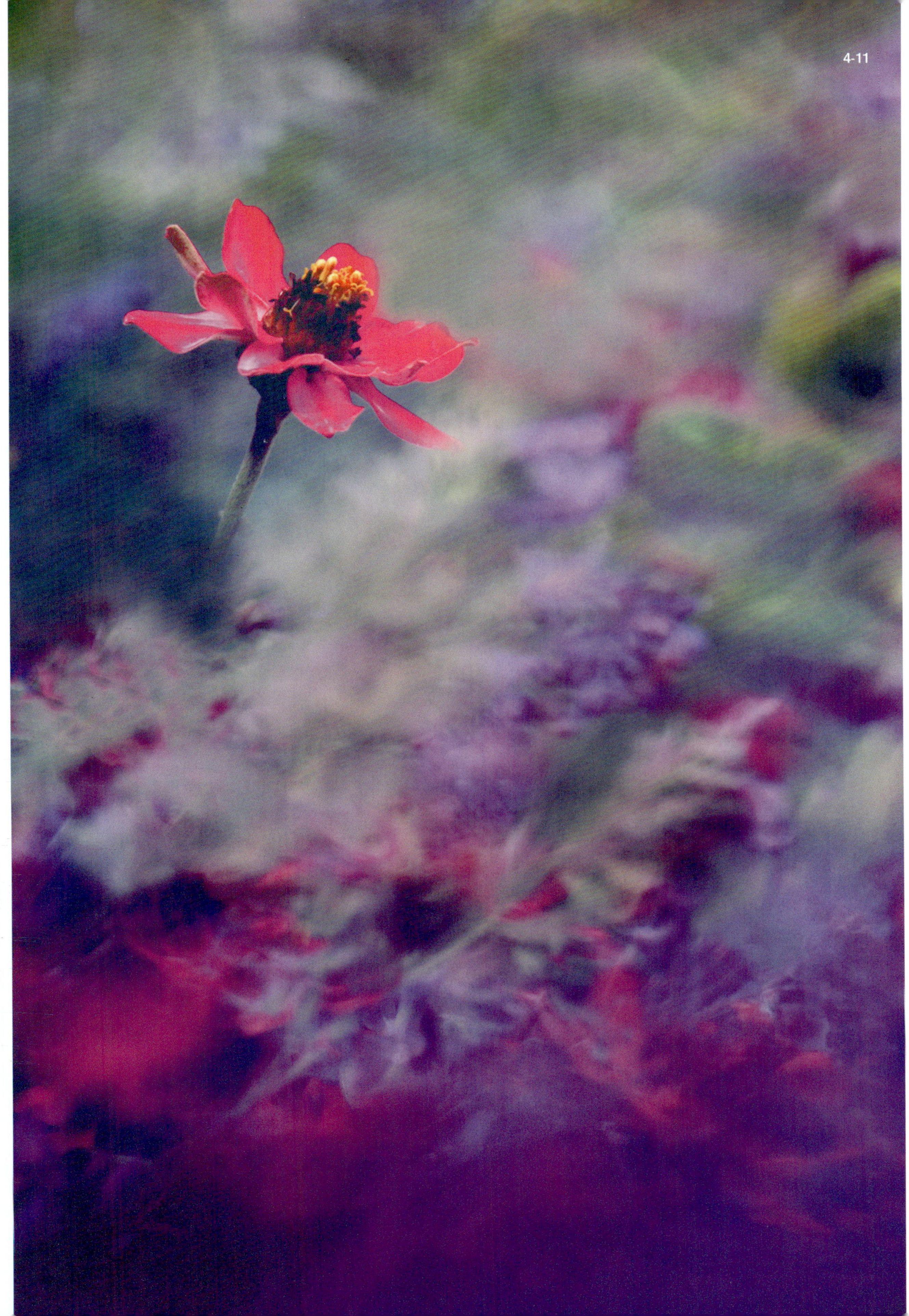

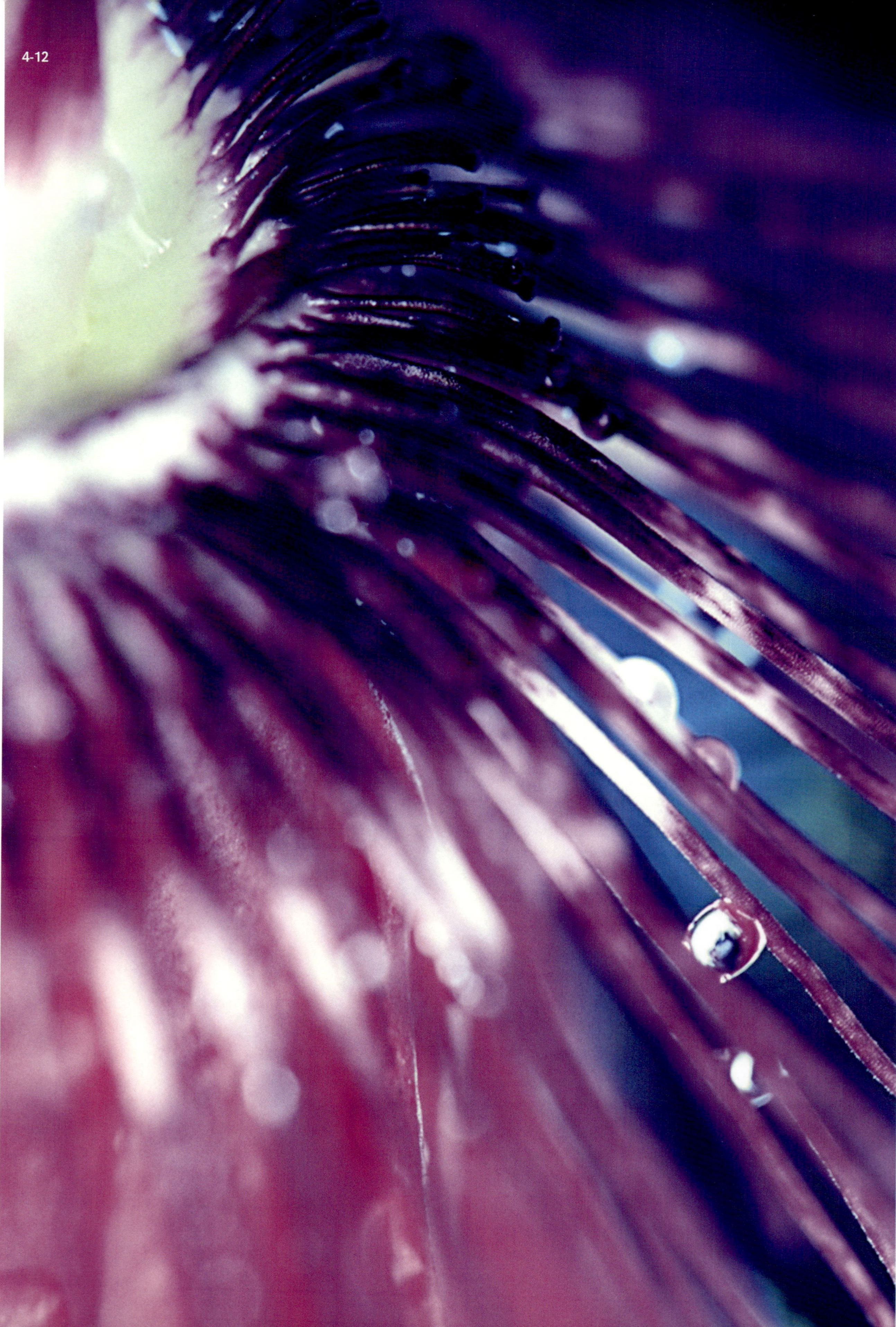

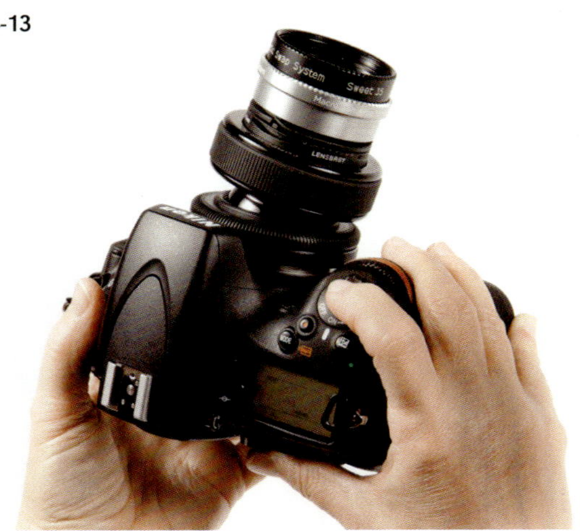

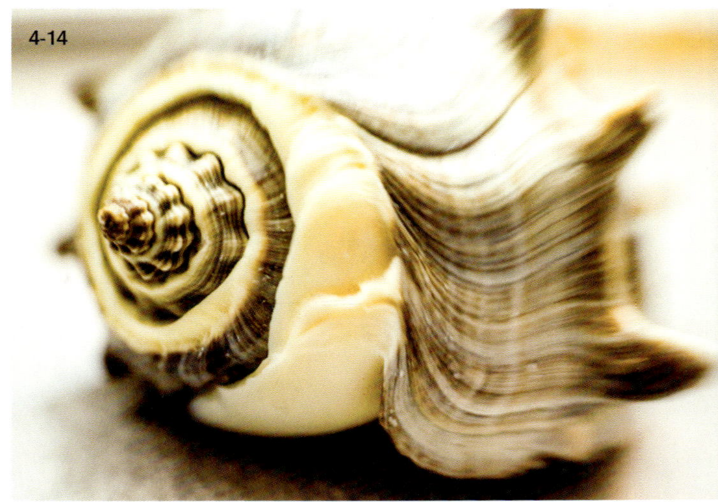

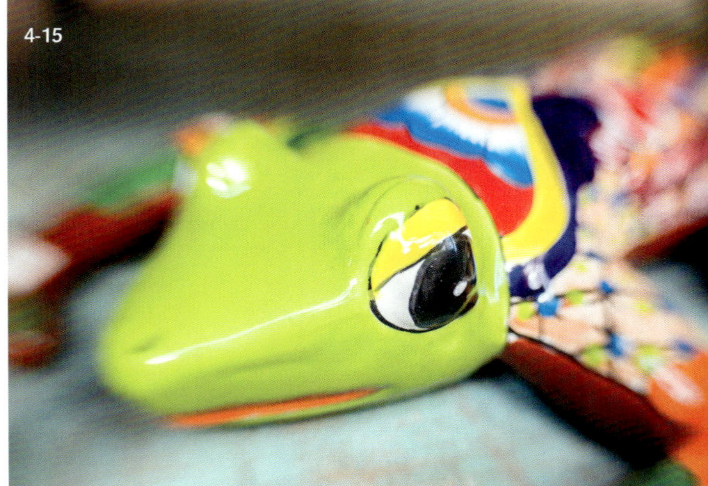

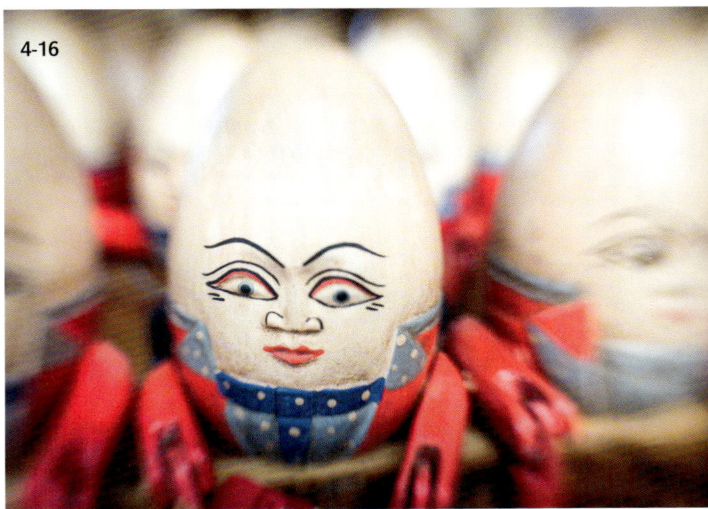

Image 4-12. For this image, I used a 500D close-up lens and 200mm Nikon macro lens. **Image 4-13.** Lensbaby Composer Pro with Sweet 35 Optic and Macro Converters (8mm and 16mm).

magnification. I've experimented with using one or more extension tubes between the camera body and macro lens, moving in very close to the subject (closer than the minimum focusing distance of your lens plus the extension tube). This configuration creates some beautiful, abstract, artistic soft-focus close-ups and is particularly effective when photographing flowers. (See **image 4-12**.) Be sure to adjust your exposure accordingly to compensate for light loss. Typically, I open up anywhere between $\frac{1}{2}$ to 2 stops, depending on how much extension I'm using. I also bracket the depth of field using various aperture settings, beginning with the lens wide open.

Lensbaby

The Lensbaby is a specialized selective-focus SLR lens that brings one area of your photo into sharp focus, with that "sweet spot" surrounded by gradually increasing blur. You

Images 4-14 through 4-16. Lensbaby Composer Pro/Sweet 35 Optic with 8mm and 16mm Macro Converters installed.

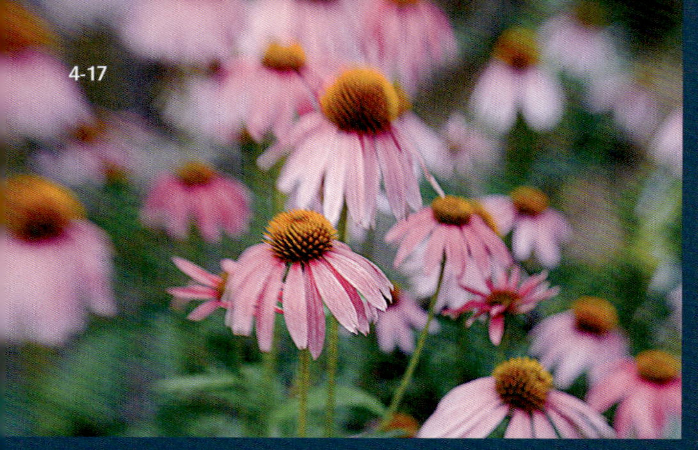

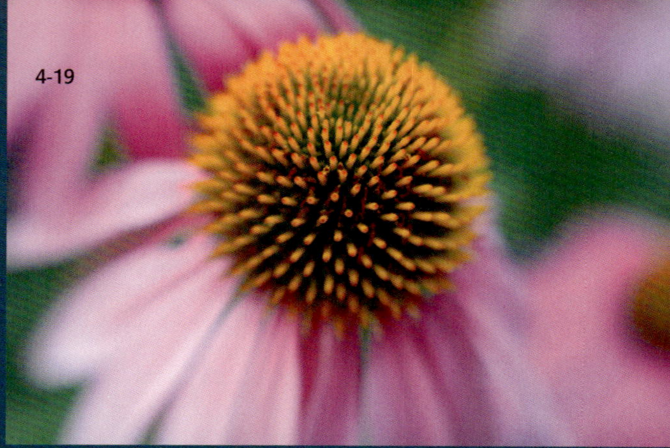

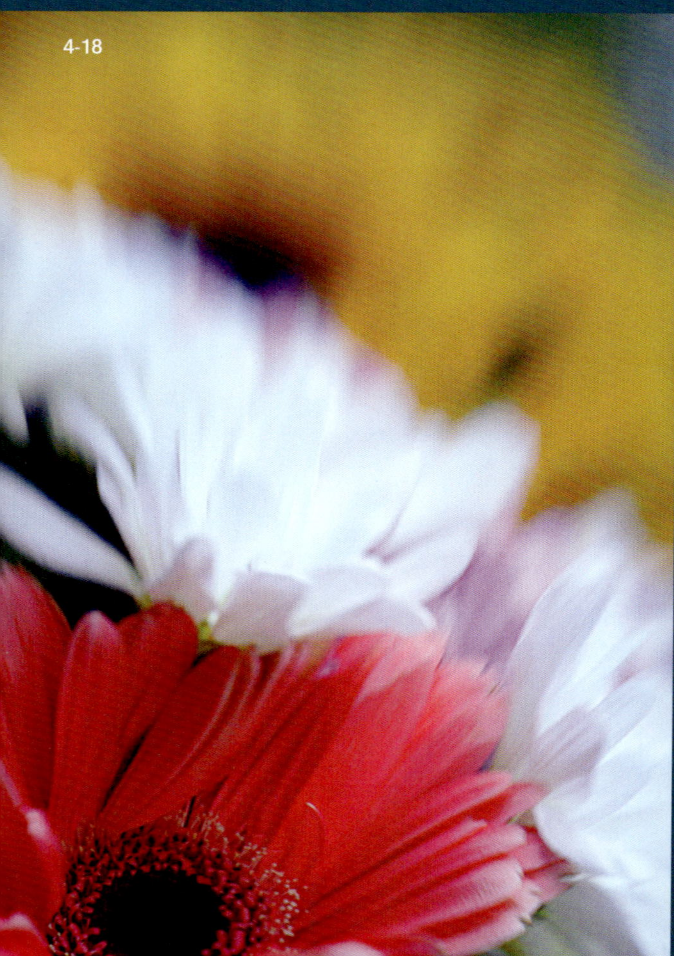

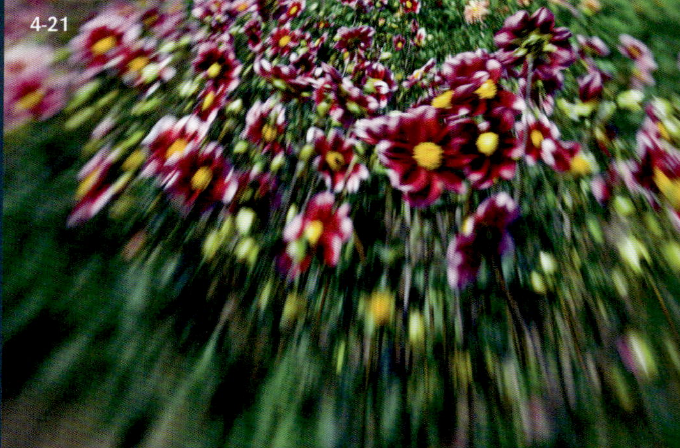

Image 4-17. Lensbaby Composer Pro/Double Glass Optic with f/5.6 aperture disk installed, partly extending the Lensbaby forward but being careful not to bend the lens left, right, up, or down. **Image 4-18.** Lensbaby Composer Pro/Double Glass Optic with f/4.0 aperture disk installed and +10 macro lens.

Image 4-19. Lensbaby Composer Pro/Double Glass Optic with f/4.0 aperture disk installed and +10 and +4 macro lenses stacked together. **Image 4-20.** Lensbaby Composer Pro/Double Glass Optic with f/4.0 aperture disk installed, tilting the lens down radically using my middle two fingers. **Image 4-21.** Lensbaby Composer Pro/Double Glass Optic with f/4.0 aperture disk installed, tilting the lens upward radically using my middle two fingers. **Image 4-22.** Lensbaby Composer Pro/Double Glass Optic with f/5.6 aperture disk installed, partly compressing the Lensbaby and tilting it downward.

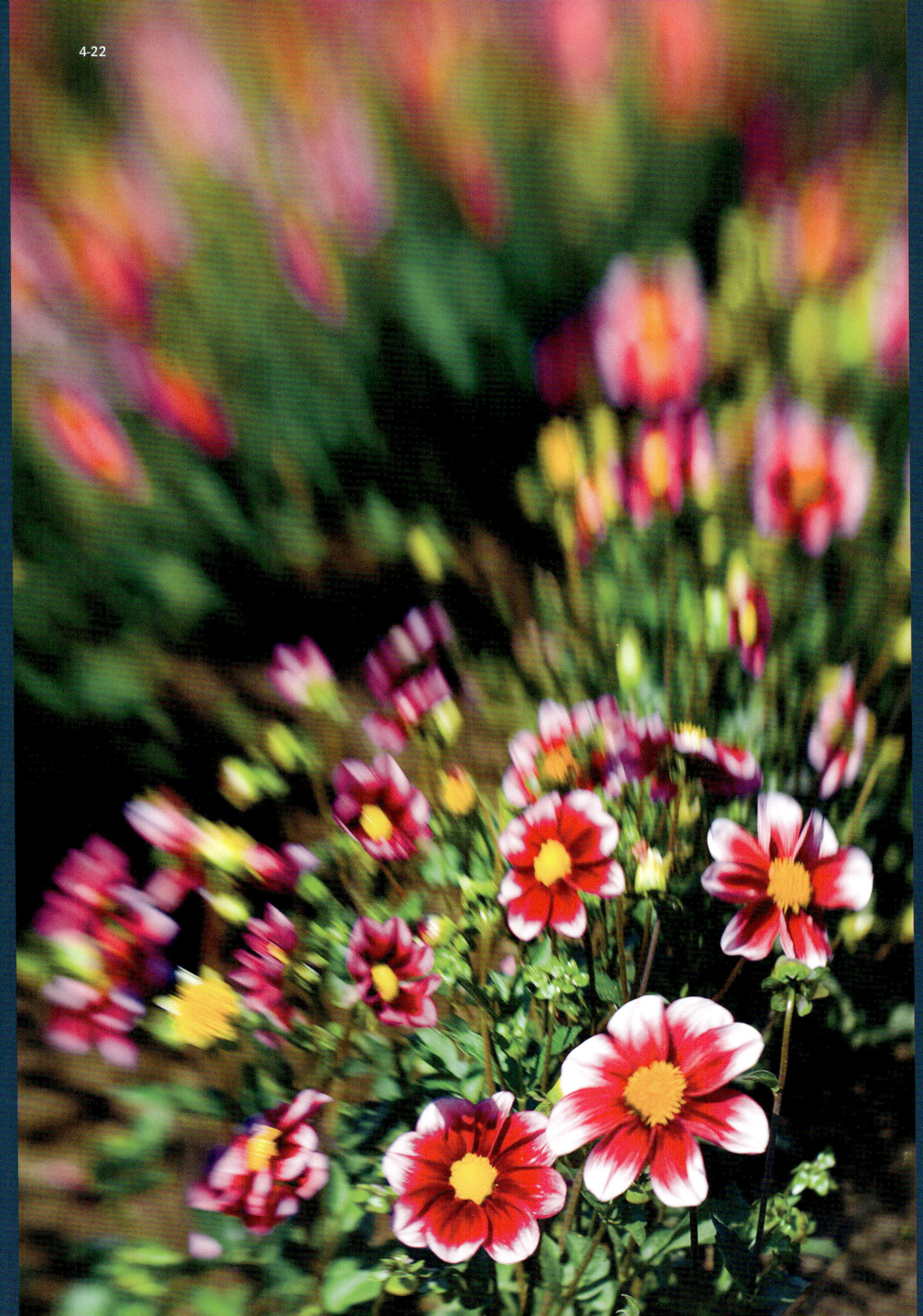

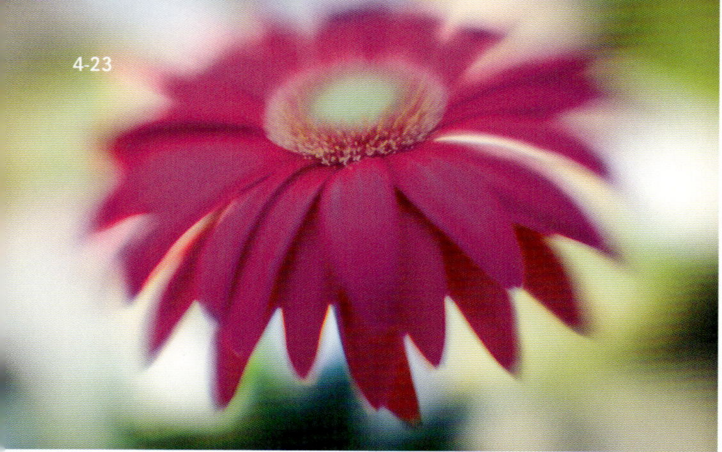

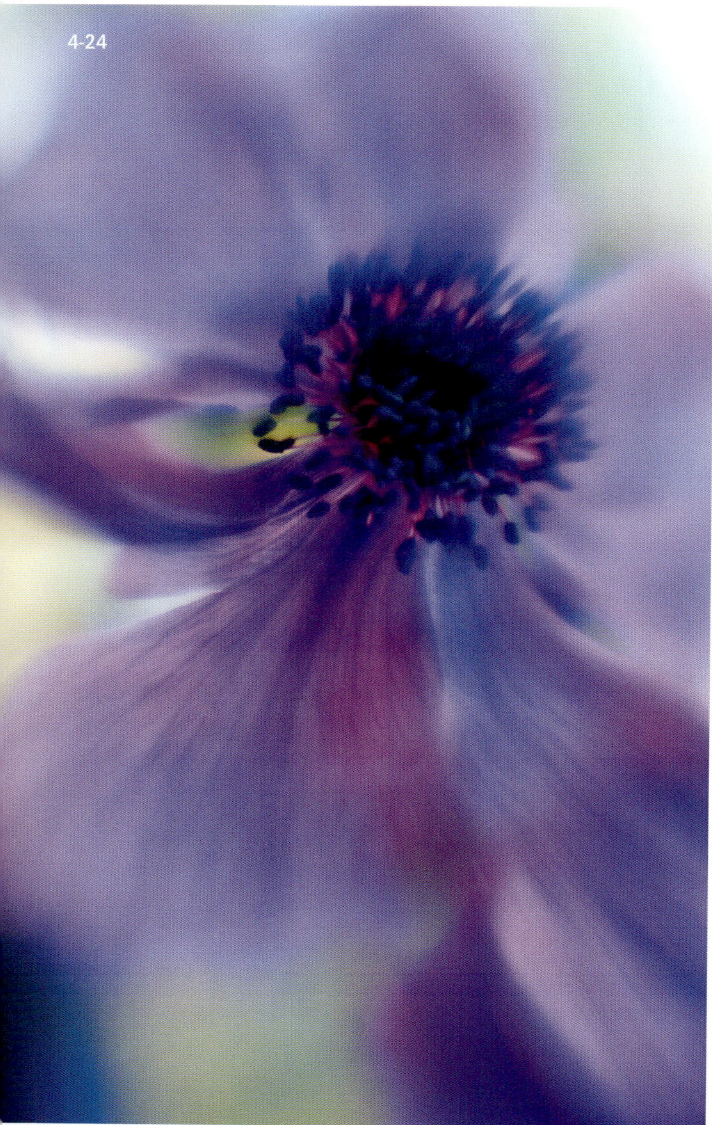

can move the sweet spot to any part of your photo by literally bending the lens. The beauty of this nifty little accessory is that you can shoot hand-held or on a tripod in any lighting situation—even bright sun at high noon!

Keep in mind, you'll need to operate your camera in aperture priority mode (with most Canon cameras) or manual mode (most Nikon cameras) when using a Lensbaby and change apertures on your Lensbaby Optic by turning an aperture ring (using a Sweet 35 Optic or Edge 80 Optic) or dropping in various aperture rings manually (using a Double Glass Optic). Since you'll be hand-holding in most situations, you'll need to adjust the ISO and shutter speed settings to achieve at least $\frac{1}{60}$ second shutter speed for a sharp sweet-spot of focus. Be sure to evaluate the LCD screen and histogram on the back of your camera to ensure proper exposure.

Lensbabies come in three basic styles: swivel, squeeze, and straight.

Lensbabies come in three basic styles: swivel, squeeze, and straight. The swivel variety features a metal swivel ball-and-socket design; it is my current personal favorite because it allows you to tilt the lens and quickly make aperture changes with ultrasmooth, precise focus. I recommend the Composer Pro with Sweet 35 Optic configuration to achieve creative selective-focus effects. For close-ups, I place two Macro Converters (8mm and 16mm) between the Composer Pro shell and the Sweet 35 Optic. (See **images 4-13** through **4-16**.) You can literally focus within 1–2 inches with this setup and take your macro photography to a whole new level.

Images 4–23 and 4-24. Lensbaby Composer Pro/Double Glass Optic with f/5.6 aperture disk installed with 0.42x Super Wide Angle Conversion lens, holding a Canon 500D close-up filter in front.

Close-up Lenses

If you don't currently own a macro lens or are looking to extend the creative possibilities of your existing macro lens, then you may want to consider purchasing a high-quality, dual-element glass close-up lens, such as the Canon 500D or Nikon 6T close-up diopter. The advantage of dual-element glass is that it minimizes chromatic aberrations and does not degrade image quality.

The 500D lens has become my personal favorite (after using the 6T for years and trying to replace it, only to discover that Nikon stopped manufacturing the 6T diopter!). The 500D comes in 72mm or 77mm filter diameters and can easily fit on the end of my Nikon 200mm macro lens with a step-down ring. (*Note:* The Canon 500D close-up lens is recommended for use with lenses in the 70–300mm range. If you want to use it with lenses in the 50–135mm range, I suggest you go with the Canon 250D. Keep in mind, however, that you won't have as much working distance with this type of setup.)

What you'll immediately notice when using this lens is that you get greater magnification at an extremely shallow depth of field. This can be a good thing when you wish to artistically blur a single or entire portion of an image.

Here's the general procedure to follow when using a close-up lens:

1. Set your lens and camera to manual focus.
2. Move the lens to its closest focusing distance.
3. Attach the close-up filter to the front of your lens using a step-up or step-down ring, if necessary. (See **image 4-25**.)
4. While hand-holding the camera, move your body forward and backward while looking

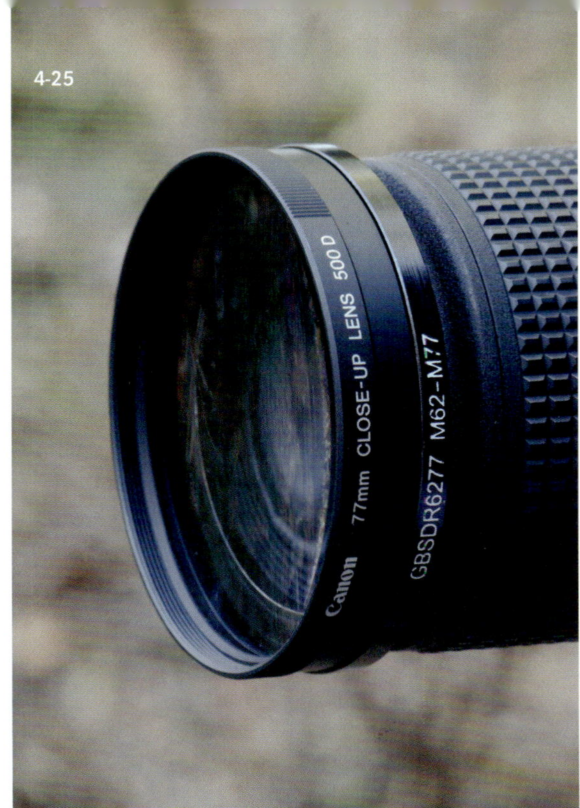

Image 4-25. Canon 500D close-up lens mounted on the end of my Nikon 200mm macro lens with a 77-62mm step-down adapter ring.

through the lens. (Or, if your camera is on a tripod, use a focusing rail.) Be sure to get very close to your subject (within 1 to 2 feet). At first, everything will appear as a big blur, but if you move back and forth slowly, you'll begin to see that small portions of your image will magically emerge into sharp focus. You may have to adjust the focus of your lens to see the effect more clearly.

5. Once you've found the sweet spot of focus, set your camera on the tripod at that exact position and click the shutter.

Through experimentation, I've discovered that often you'll need to stop down the lens by 1 or 2 stops from the widest aperture to bring an area into sharp focus and translate your artistic

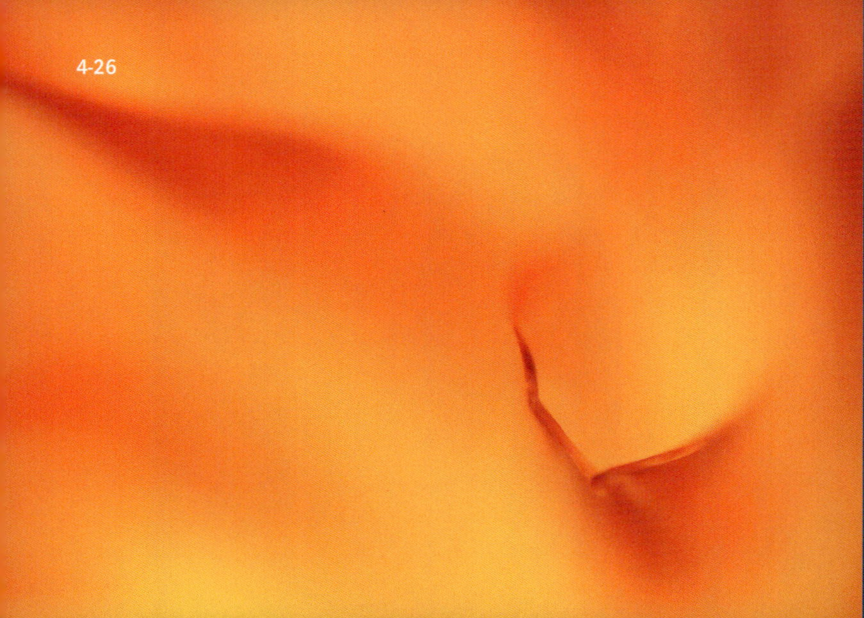

4-26

4-27

Images 4-26 through 4-30. Each of these images was created using a Canon 500D close-up lens attached to my 200mm macro lens at various aperture and focus settings. With very limited depth of field, I created some unusual abstract close-ups of flowers. In the first image (4-26), I was able to artistically isolate the curl of a tulip petal while leaving a faint hint of more petals in the background. The remaining four images were all created using the same technique from flowers on my kitchen table one cold winter day! You don't need to have much in focus with this soft-focus technique, but with limited depth of field, it's a good idea to bracket the point of focus when shooting at a minimum depth of field and bracket apertures, going from widest to smallest.

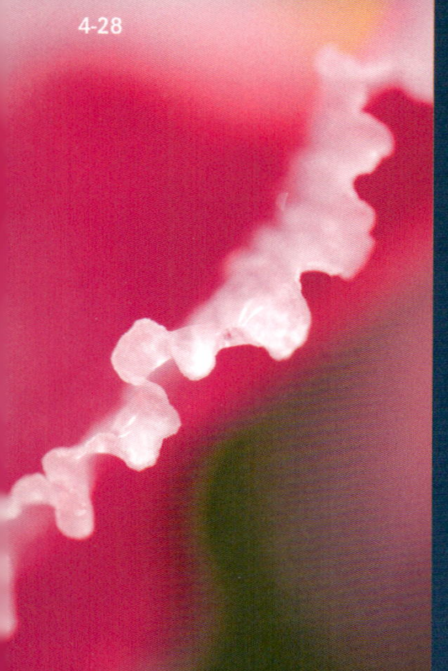

4-28

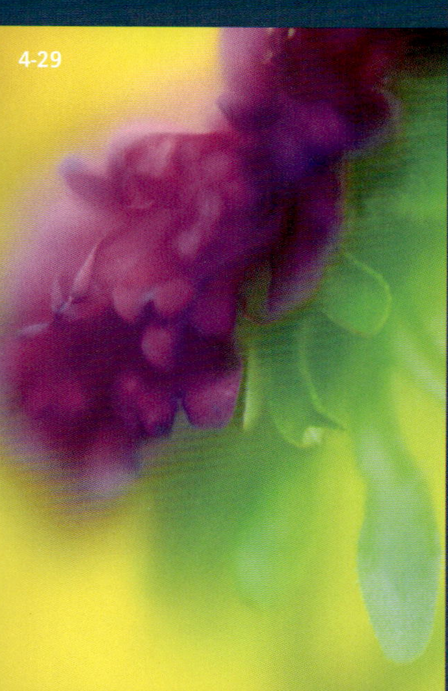

4-29

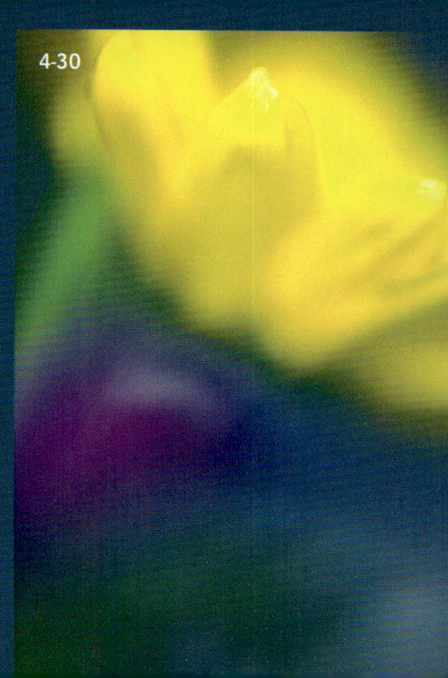

4-30

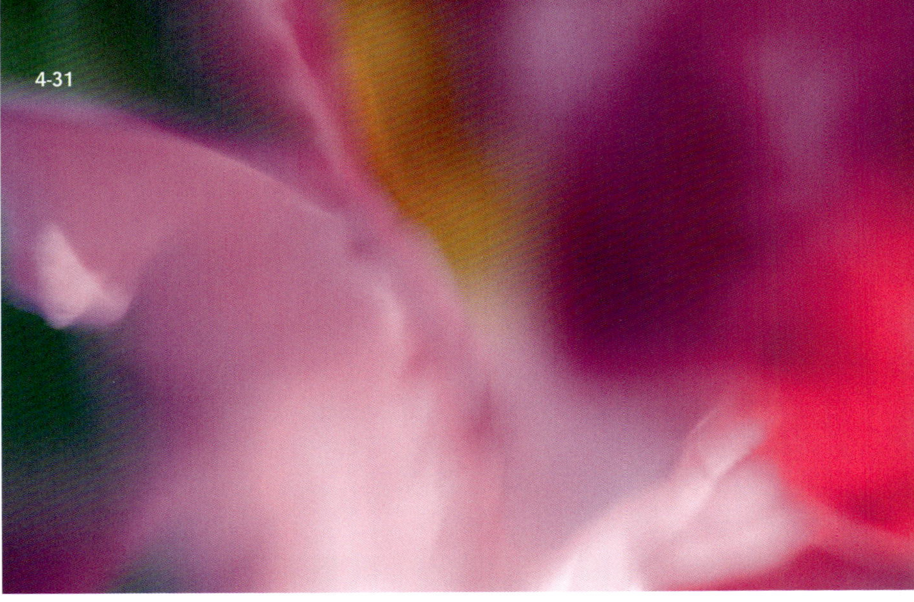

Image 4-31. To create this completely out-of-focus, abstract image of pink tulips in bright sunlight, I composed the picture first and then experimented with various focusing points and apertures. This was the most pleasing combination because it conveyed the sense of awe I was feeling as I peered through the lens. Even at f/11, defocusing the lens allowed for just enough detail to reveal itself. Micro-Nikkor 200mm.

vision for the viewer. With such shallow depth of field, this becomes necessary to render some sharpness. You can bracket for depth of field and focal points to create completely different images.

One way to really lose yourself in this process is to imagine you're a bug crawling along the edge of whatever object you're photographing. By literally "hunting" with your lens, you can discover all kinds of unique and pleasing compositions!

Each of the images on the facing page was created using the technique described above with a Canon 500D close-up lens attached to my 200mm macro lens.

Defocusing

This is a technique that involves moving the focusing ring of your lens slowly in and out to see how the image changes. It works best with subjects that have clearly defined edges, so that they are still somewhat recognizable even when they are only represented by circles and streaks of colors. Look for lighter-toned subjects set against darker-toned backgrounds, and be careful not to defocus too much, unless you

want to completely abstract your subject and make the image more about colors and shapes. The end result can be quite stunning, although nothing is pin-sharp, creating a dream-like feeling. (See **image 4-31**, as well as the bird-of-paradise series on pages 10 and 11.)

Defocusing works best with subjects that have clearly defined edges . . .

Another way to achieve subjectively pleasing out-of-focus areas is to make an image using a mirror lens in bright sunlight. Mirror lenses use a pair of mirrors to fold the light path in half, in addition to containing regular glass elements. They come in fixed focal lengths (e.g., 500mm or 1000mm) with fixed apertures (usually around f/8). What makes these lenses unique is that the smaller of the two internal mirrors blocks the light path somewhat, resulting in "rings" or "doughnuts" appearing around bright highlights in out-of-focus areas. Thus by deliberately throwing an entire image out of focus, you get some interesting circular patterns around highlight areas.

5. Tabletop Macro

enjoy photographing in my backyard "garden photography studio" as often as possible. It makes me feel like a kid in a candy store, since infinite creative possibilities abound there. In less than half an acre of sloped land, I've created a spectacular garden and waterfall in my backyard, along with numerous potted plants. (See **images 5-1** through **5-5.**)

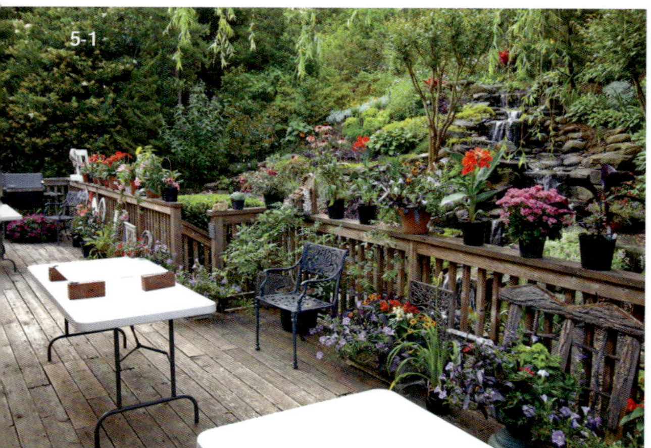

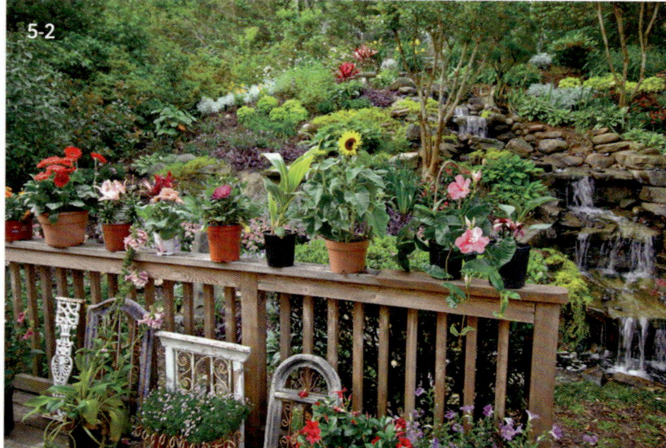

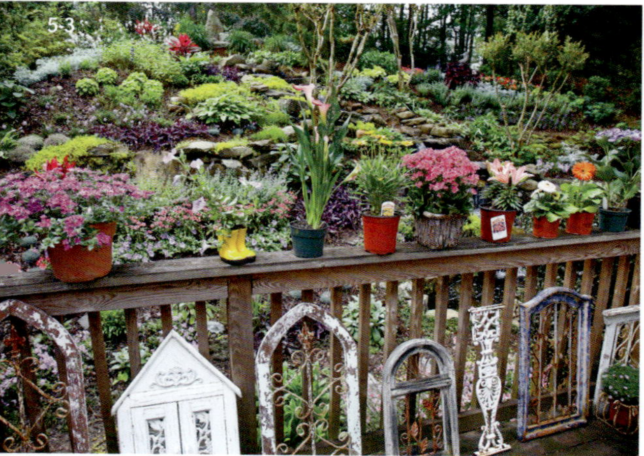

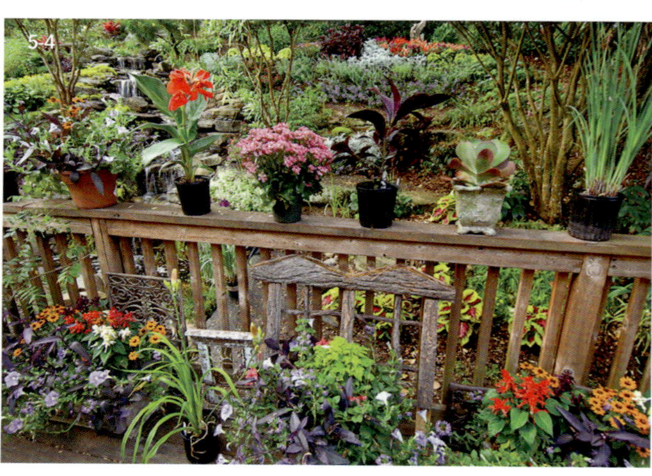

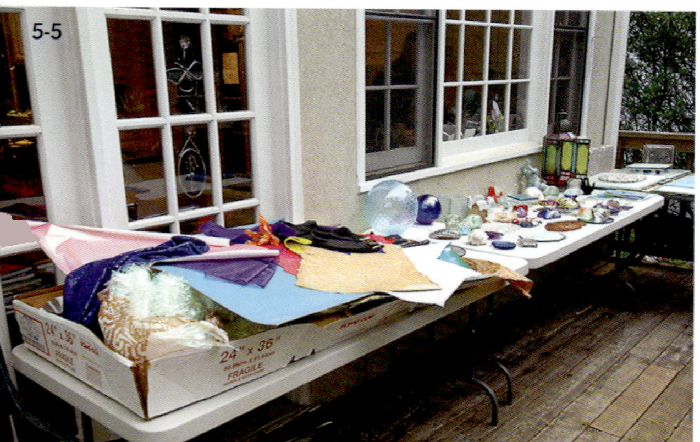

Images 5-1 through 5-5. My garden studio and healing sanctuary of creative possibilities.

When creating your own backyard "garden photo studio," it is important to have several flowers in pots, so you can move them around and create natural backgrounds for your subjects. If you plant too many flowers in the ground, you'll have a lot less control over your backgrounds.

In addition to potted plants, I've collected other various props, such as old window frames and textured wall hangings to enhance my image-making. Glass paperweights, feathers, geode slices, shells, cut flowers, and silk flowers are also among my favorite objects to photograph in my backyard. For backgrounds, I've also experimented with clear textured glass, iridescent glass, and colorful fabrics. (See **images 5-6** through **5-8**.)

Over the years, I've developed various techniques for making unusual, striking close-up images—mostly through my own experimentation. Looking through the viewfinder and making these images has been a joyous process of discovery and, indeed, a form of therapy. During my recovery from Chronic Fatigue Syndrome, when I didn't have the energy to travel to exotic destinations, I discovered literally, on my hands and knees, a whole new exciting world of miniature landscapes awaiting me in my own backyard nature sanctuary. Thus, the camera became a powerful tool for healing.

In this chapter, I'd like to share with you some ways to expand your vision and take your macro photography to the next level. These tips and techniques are meant to be a springboard for your own personal process of discovery. Purchasing the same props that I'll be demonstrating in this chapter in no way guarantees that you'll create great images.

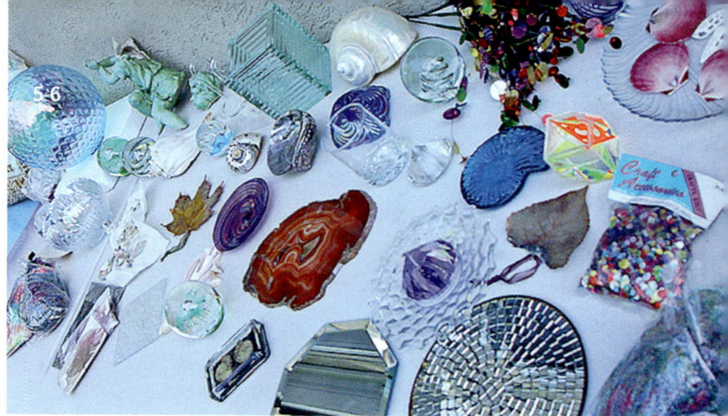

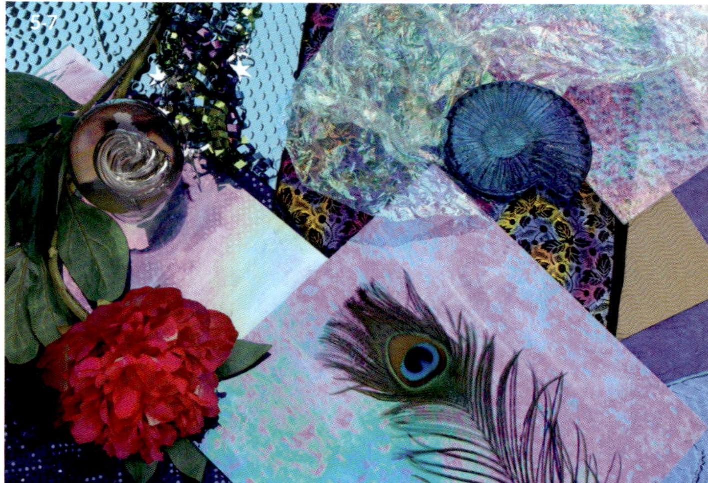

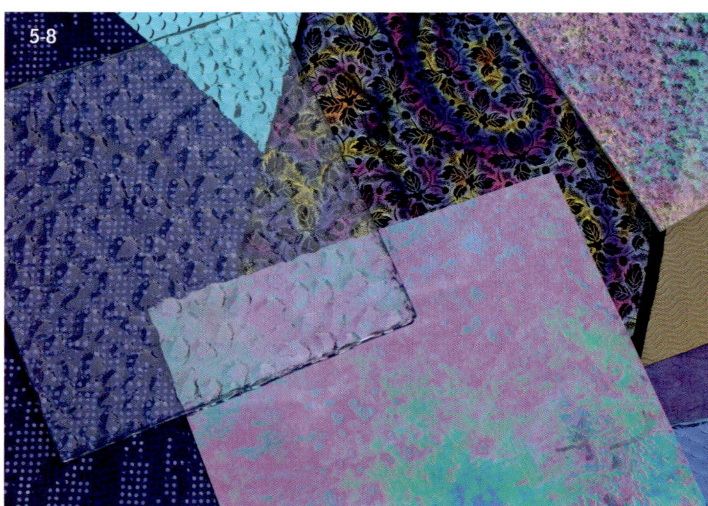

Images 5-6 through 5-8. Here's a sampling of the wide variety of props I've collected over the years. These tools can help you take your macro photography to the next level.

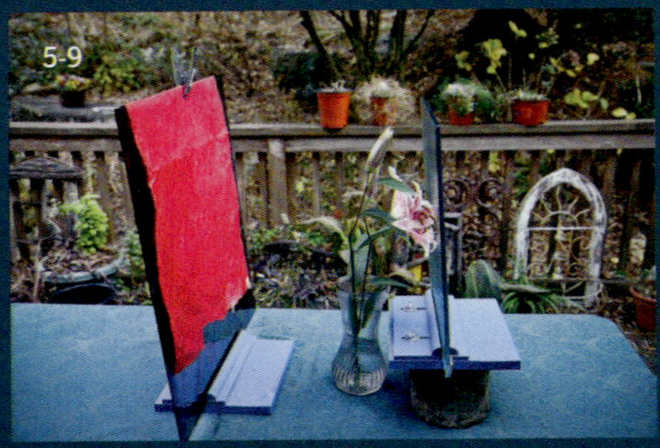
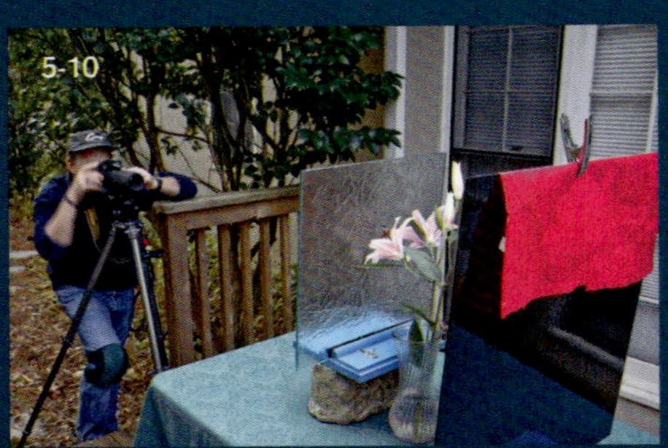
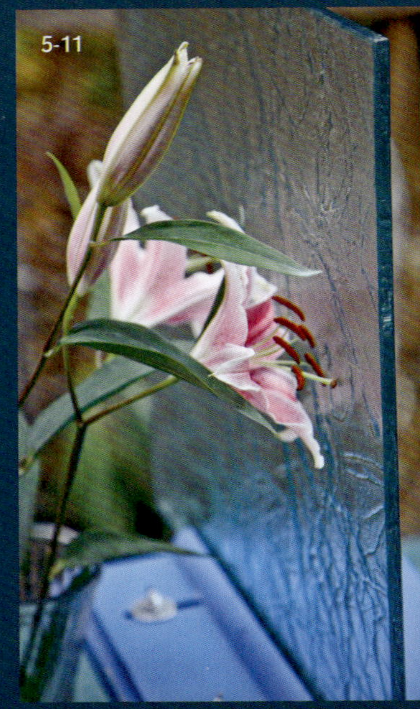

Image 5-9. Side view of textured glass setup with clear textured glass and pink paper background. **Image 5-10.** Rear view of textured glass setup. For maximum sharpness, it's important to keep the back of your camera as parallel to the surface of the clear glass as possible. **Image 5-11.** Notice how the flower petals touch the clear textured glass. The closer you place the flower to the glass, the more defined and less abstract the flower will appear in the final image. **Image 5-12.** The final image appears as if the flower was frozen in ice. Notice how I filled the frame and cropped some from the left side in-camera to avoid placing the flower directly in the center of the photograph.

These "props" are merely tools for translating your own unique creative vision. Ultimately, in order for the magic to happen, you will need to learn how to open your heart and mind to possibilities and trust in your own process.

Unlike some other forms of nature photography, macro photography affords the opportunity for developing intimacy with your subject. Often, when I'm in the creative flow, all time stops and I feel as if the subject finds me, rather than the other way around. The experience seems to transcend the image making itself, and I feel nothing short of sheer bliss. No matter how often I approach a subject, whether it's something I've seen repeatedly or never seen before, I try to see it with fresh eyes. This requires quieting yourself, getting rid of mental clutter, and being open and receptive to what the subject is trying to communicate to you as a visual artist.

Too often, especially in the digital era, photographers approach their subjects from mostly a technical or formulaic viewpoint. One way to move beyond this is to approach every subject with childlike wonder and curiosity as if you've never seen it before and may not ever see it again in exactly the same way. In doing so, you'll discover unimaginable ways of observing the world and begin to uncover the hidden beauty within the true essence of your subject.

Textured Glass

This setup involves using two pieces of glass, supported by two glass stands. By placing the subject, a vibrant lily in this case, between the two panes, you can control both the foreground and background easily. I used a textured piece of glass for the foreground and stained glass for the background. After shooting the subject with the stained glass background, I decided to try placing pink paper in the background (using a clamp) to complement the pink accent color of the lily. I could have also used cloth or any other material in the background, including other colorful flowers or plants. The key is placing the background far enough away

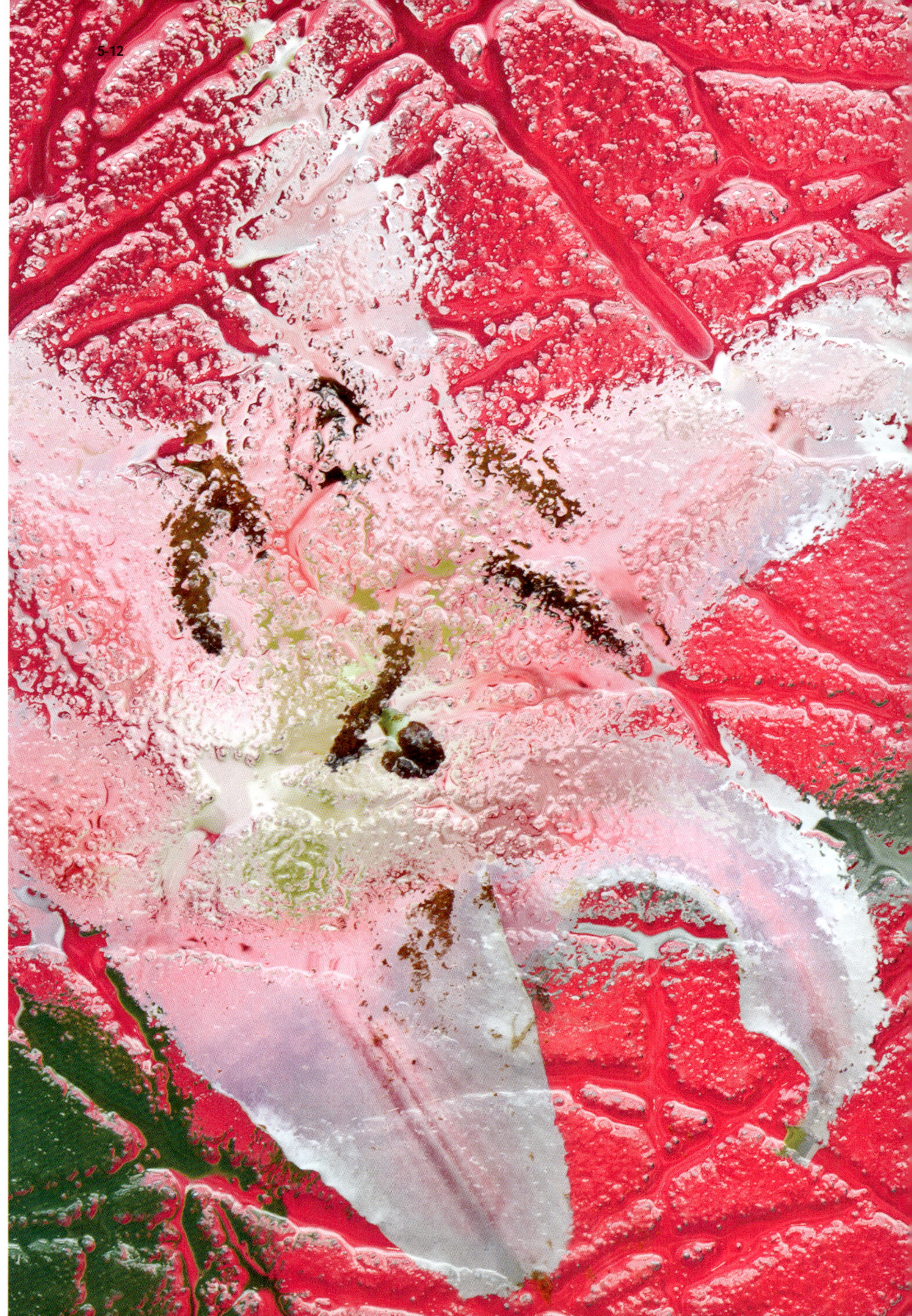

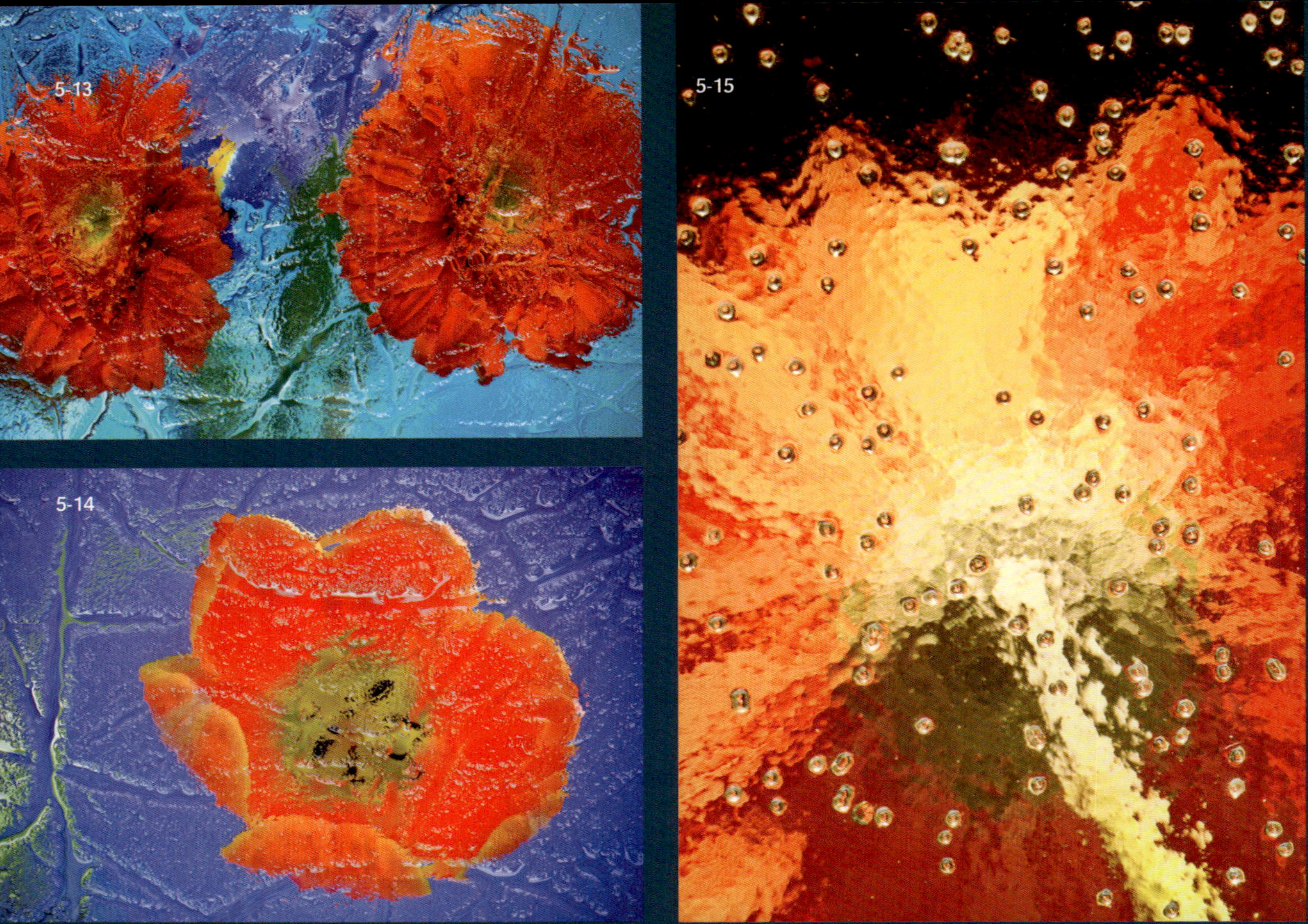

Image 5-13. Gerbera daisies and iris behind textured glass. Light-blue paper background. Nikon Micro-Nikkor 200mm f/4 lens. Exposure: f/8 at 1/100 second. **Image 5-14.** Tulip behind textured glass. Blue fabric background. Nikon Micro-Nikkor 200mm f/4 lens. Exposure: f/8 at 1/125 second. **Image 5-15.** Gerbera daisy behind bubbled textured glass. Black velvet background. Nikon Micro-Nikkor 200mm f/4 lens. Exposure: f/16 at 1/2 second.

from the subject so it falls out of focus. When shooting this type of subject, or any subject, behind textured glass, it's important to focus on the glass itself, not the flower behind the glass, and use a small enough aperture to achieve the desired depth of field. (See **images 5-9** through **5-11**.) In this case, I tried various apertures from f/4 to f/22 (keeping the point of focus on the glass) and ended up liking **image 5-12**, shot at f/14, the best because of the detail in the actual flower. This could not have been achieved had I placed the flower farther away from the textured glass, as the depth of field was very shallow.

Usually, if you place the flower 1–3 inches from the textured glass, you'll get some definition (even if fuzzy) around the edges of the petals.

Two additional tips: (1) Clean both sides of the glass well before shooting. You'd be amazed what your macro lens will pick up when it's closely focused on the glass, and you don't want to end up having to clean up your image unnecessarily in postproduction. (2) Since this technique involves focusing on the textured glass itself, you might consider using artificial silk flowers behind the glass, rather than fresh flowers, because the texture of the glass abstracts the flower to the point that it doesn't matter whether or not it's real!

Images **5-13** through **5-15** are some other examples of images taken behind textured glass in my backyard garden studio.

Iridescent Glass

For **images 5-16** through **5-18**, I placed a purple passionflower on a 20x24-inch sheet of iridescent glass under bright overcast skies and challenged myself to photograph it in three ways.

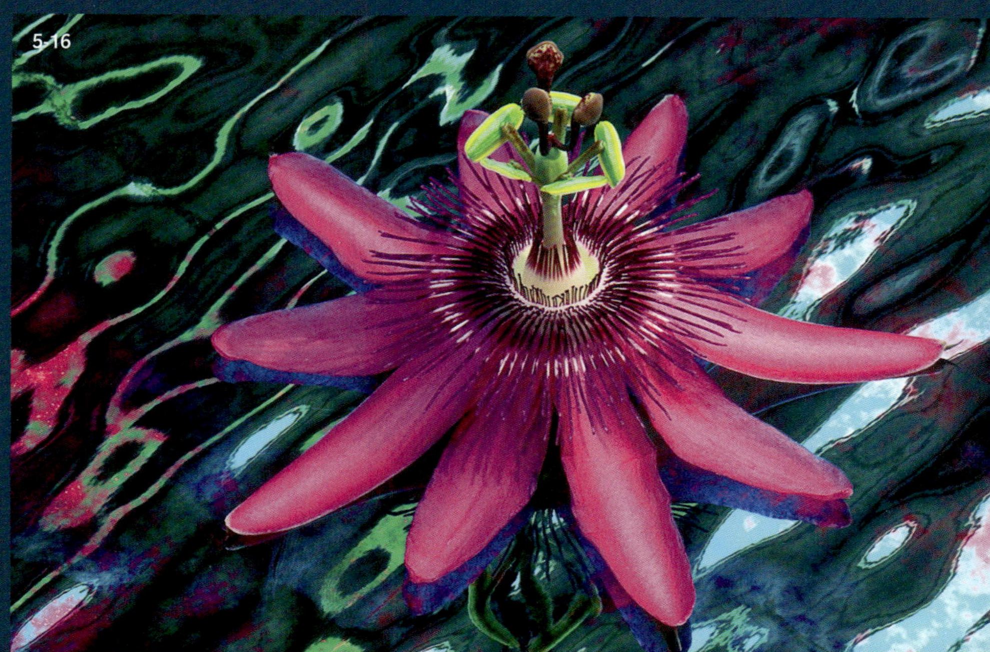

Image 5-16. The first of three renditions shows a passionflower reflected in iridescent glass. To achieve sharpness throughout, I stopped the lens all the way down to f/32. I was mesmerized with the various ripples on the surface of the glass and how the flower appeared to be floating on water.

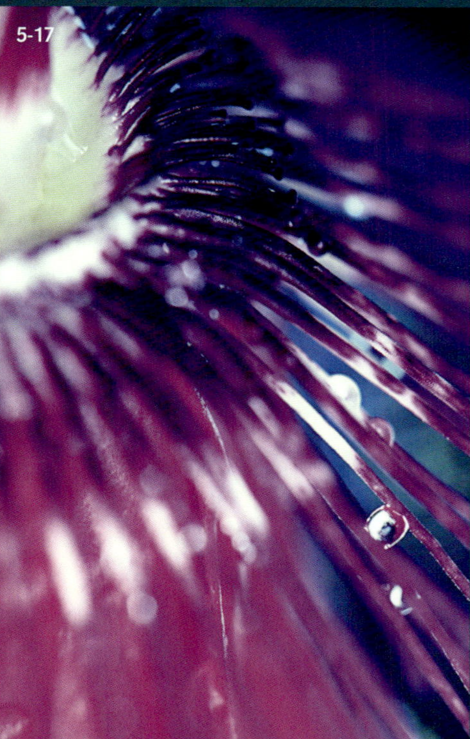

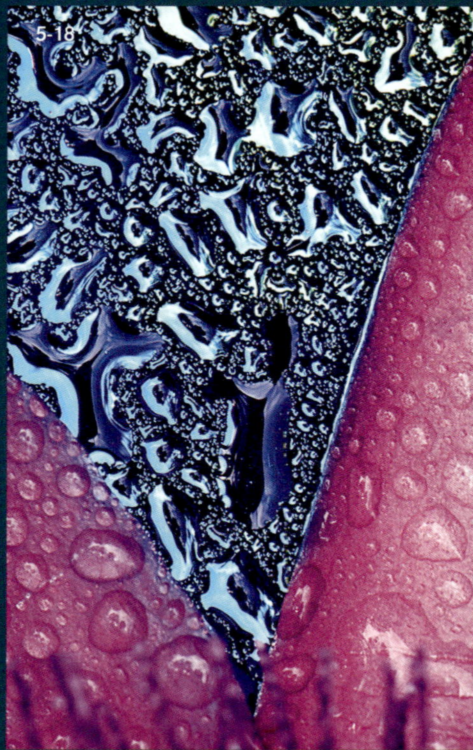

Image 5-17. In this example, I placed a 500D close-up filter on the end of my 200mm Nikon macro lens and repositioned the camera, focusing much closer to tightly fill the frame. What attracted me here were the oblique lines and complementary colors (purple and green). I shot this one at an aperture of f/5.6 to allow for some sharpness. I then sprayed the flower using a glycerin/water solution (see chapter 2) and noticed the single clinging drop. **Image 5-18.** After spraying the passionflower, I noticed how the water created interesting patterns on the glass. I quickly recomposed and made this image, which included a hint of petals, but is much more abstract.

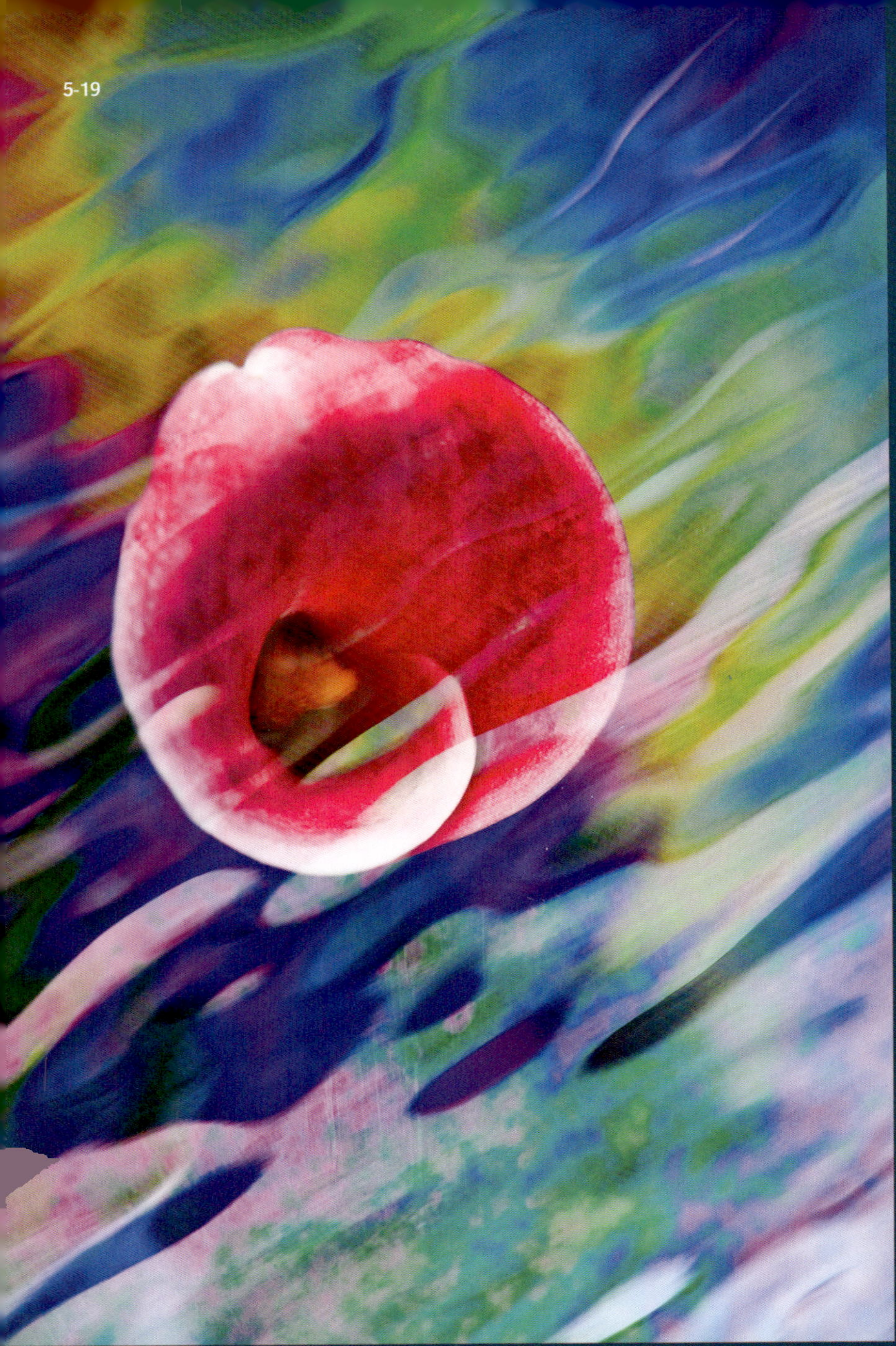

Image 5-19. Calla lily relected in iridescent glass. I stopped my lens down to f/16 to sharply define the flower.

Image 5-20. Black-eyed Susan positioned close to the iridescent glass (touching) with its reflection and a pink cloth held behind the flower at a 45 degree angle to the surface of the glass. **Image 5-21.** Sunflower positioned several inches away from the iridescent glass. Notice how its reflection is less defined, as the flower is not touching the glass.

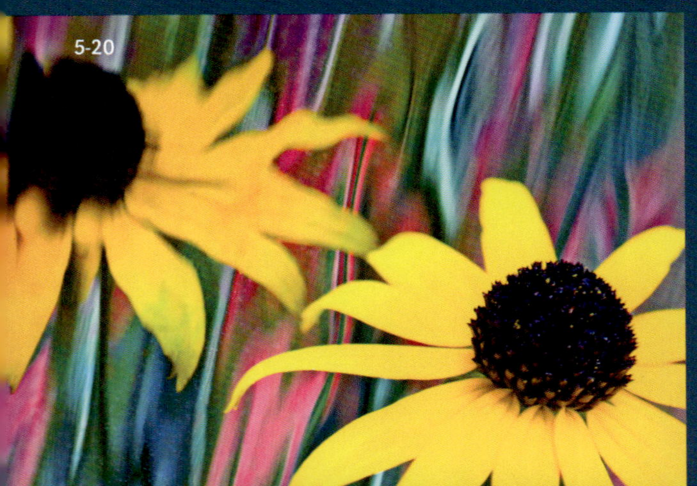

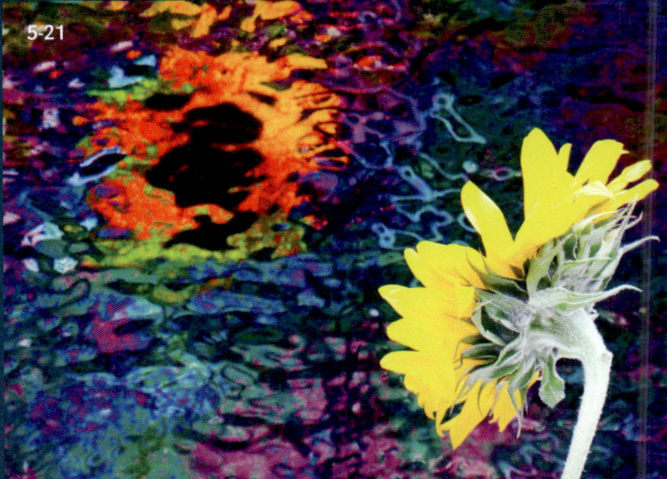

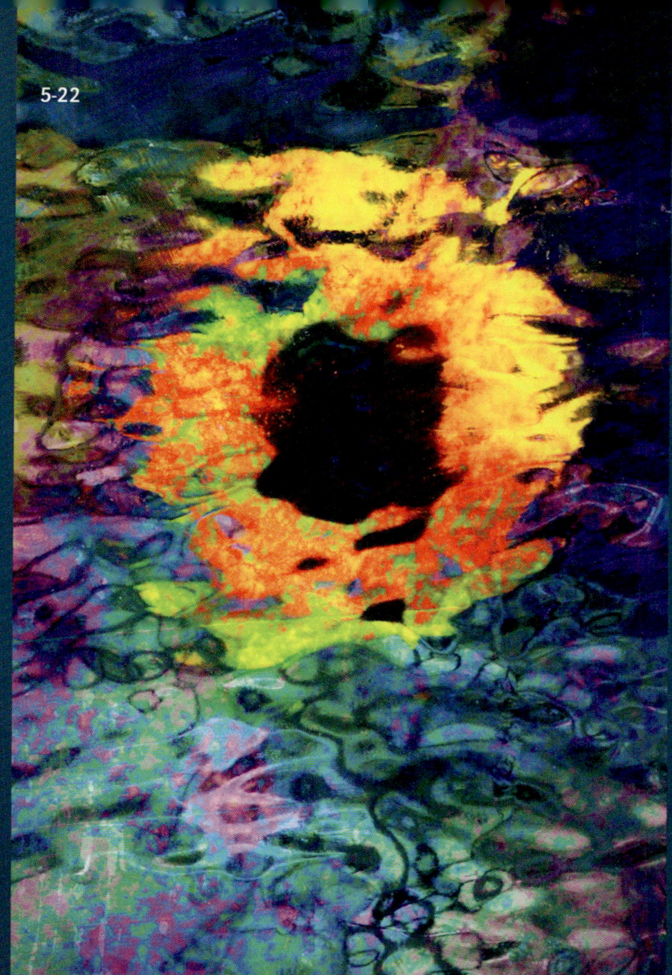

Image 5-22. Nikon Micro-Nikkor 200mm f/4 lens. Exposure: f/16 at 1/2 second.

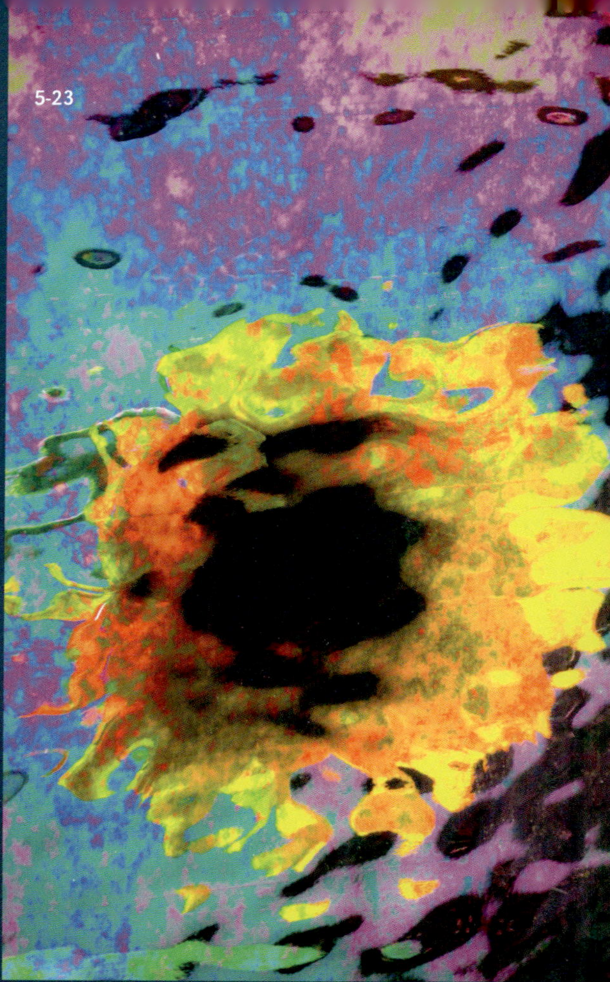

Image 5-23. Nikon Micro-Nikkor 200mm f/4 lens. Exposure: f/11 at 1/8 second.

Another favorite technique when shooting with iridescent glass is to capture the reflection of a flower in the glass itself, as in this calla lily. (See **image 5-19**.) I usually set up one large sheet of glass in a vertical position, stabilizing it with a glass stand. Then I position a vase with one flower or a grouping of flowers close to the glass.

Here is one example of the setup with a black-eyed Susan. (See **image 5-20**.) The pink background was created by holding a pink cloth behind the flower at a 45-degree angle to the surface of the glass. And here's a similar setup with a sunflower. (See **image 5-21**.)

Depending upon just how far away the flower is from the surface of the glass, you get more or less definition in its reflection. The closer to the glass, the more defined the reflection; the farther away, the less defined.

If you carefully observe and study the light as it's striking the iridescent glass, the overall look can drastically change with even the slightest perspective change, as in this pair of sunflower images taken from different vantage points at different apertures. (See **images 5-22** and **5-23**.)

Unlike shooting flowers behind textured glass, when shooting flowers reflecting on iridescent glass, you'll need to focus *beyond* the surface of the glass, not on the glass, to achieve the desired effect. You could also use artificial flowers, since the flower itself won't be in the picture. Again, be sure the glass is clean before photographing to prevent dirt and dust from appearing in your photos.

When shooting reflections of flowers on stained glass, you can also get completely different results depending upon where you focus the lens and what aperture you decide to use. (See **images 5-24** through **5-26**.) You'll want to be sure to use your depth-of-field preview button (shown in image 3-15

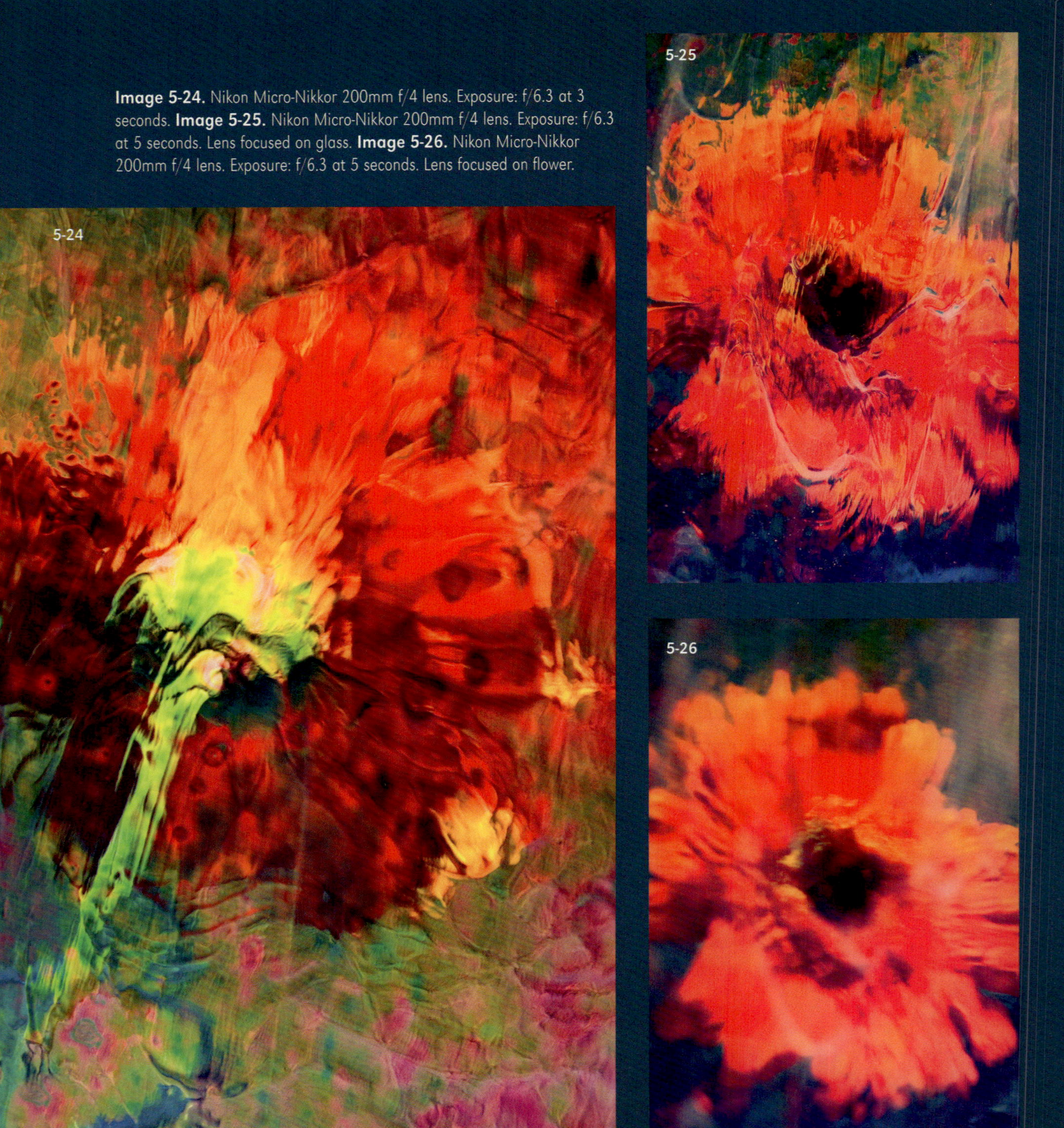

Image 5-24. Nikon Micro-Nikkor 200mm f/4 lens. Exposure: f/6.3 at 3 seconds. **Image 5-25.** Nikon Micro-Nikkor 200mm f/4 lens. Exposure: f/6.3 at 5 seconds. Lens focused on glass. **Image 5-26.** Nikon Micro-Nikkor 200mm f/4 lens. Exposure: f/6.3 at 5 seconds. Lens focused on flower.

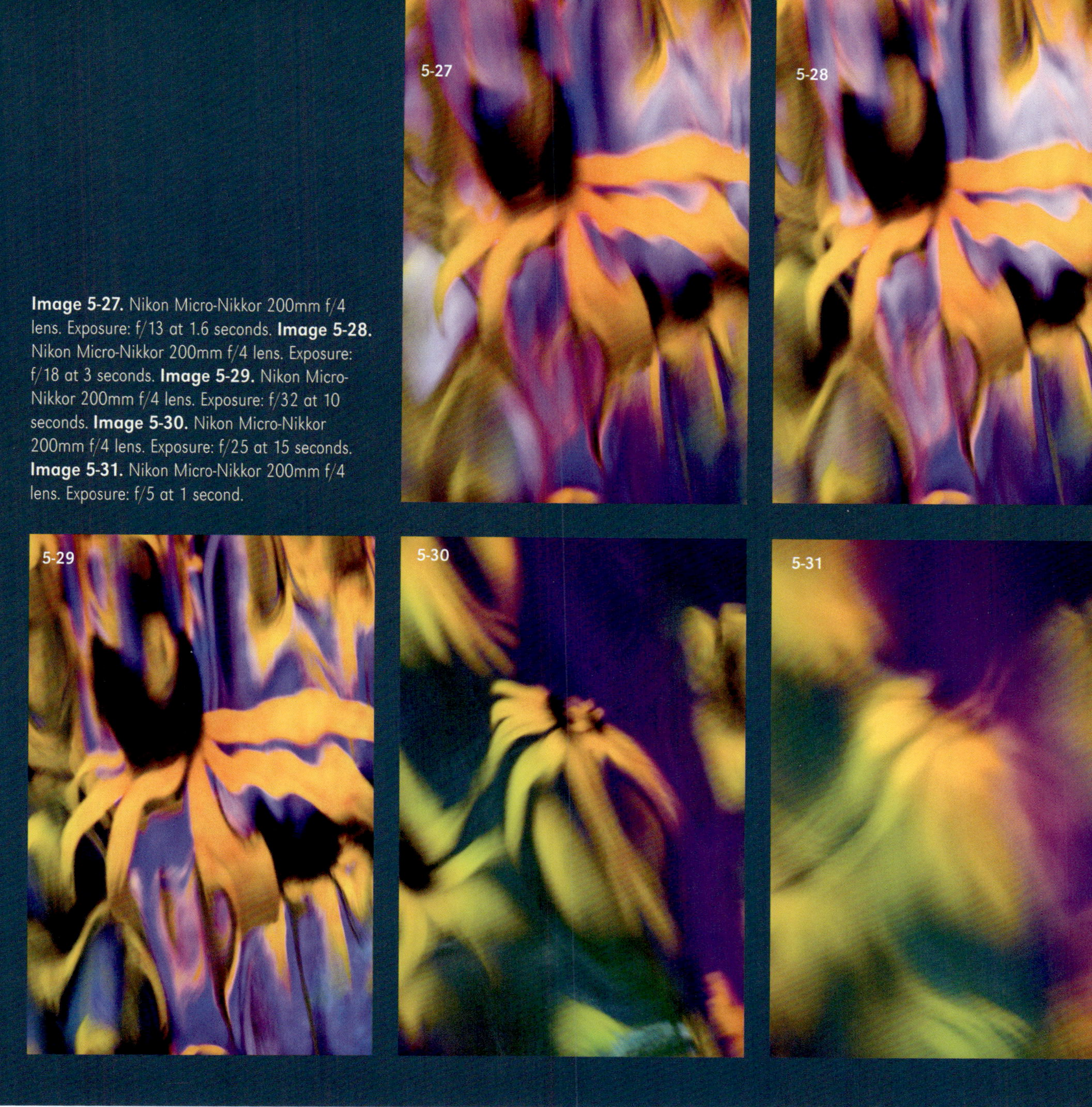

Image 5-27. Nikon Micro-Nikkor 200mm f/4 lens. Exposure: f/13 at 1.6 seconds. Image 5-28. Nikon Micro-Nikkor 200mm f/4 lens. Exposure: f/18 at 3 seconds. Image 5-29. Nikon Micro-Nikkor 200mm f/4 lens. Exposure: f/32 at 10 seconds. Image 5-30. Nikon Micro-Nikkor 200mm f/4 lens. Exposure: f/25 at 15 seconds. Image 5-31. Nikon Micro-Nikkor 200mm f/4 lens. Exposure: f/5 at 1 second.

in chapter 3) to preview exactly what will be sharply defined and what will be more blurred. I usually take a series of images at various apertures, bracketing to see which photograph I like best. **Images 5-27** through **5-31** illustrate the reflection of a black-eyed Susan taken at various apertures.

I usually take a series of images at various apertures, bracketing to see which I like best.

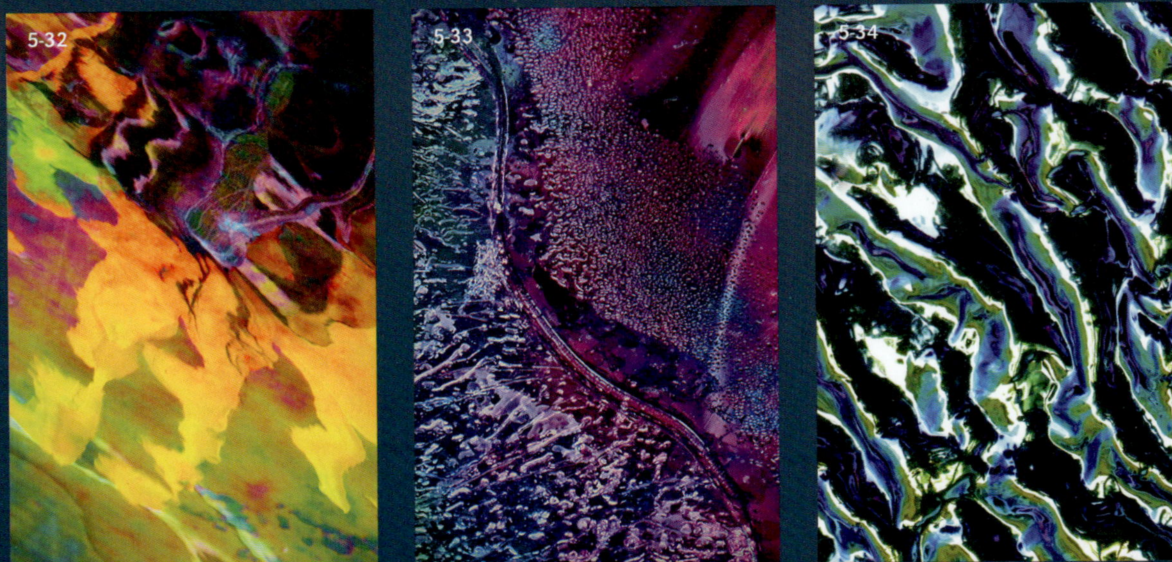

Image 5-32. Iridescent glass itself as the subject can reveal rainbows of color. **Image 5-33.** Ice frozen on a piece of iridescent glass. **Image 5-34.** Macro image of dichroic glass.

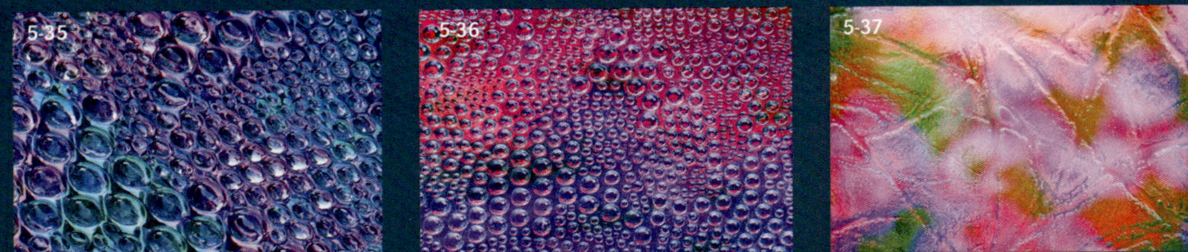

Image 5-35. Close-up of clear bubble glass placed on top of a sheet of iridescent glass. **Image 5-36.** Close-up of clear bubble glass with a pink gerbera daisy on a blue background positioned below the glass. **Image 5-37.** Flowers behind textured glass. These flowers appear out of focus because they were held four feet away from the glass. I focused on the surface of the glass in this image and did not stop my lens down to more than f/5.6 to achieve this effect.

Glass as the Main Subject

Iridescent glass (**image 5-32**), in particular, is so interesting that oftentimes you don't even need flowers to create an interesting image. Each of the images in this series was made using iridescent glass or iridescent glass combined with textured glass. **Image 5-33** was made one chilly morning when I noticed water had frozen on the glass. **Image 5-34** is a close-up of a small piece of dichroic glass, which causes an array of striking, brilliant color to be displayed.

(*Note:* Originally created by NASA for the aerospace industry, dichroic glass or "dichro" is available online from Artisan Dichroic [www.artisandichroic.com], Delphi Glass [www.delphiglass.com], or your local stained-glass supply store.) **Image 5-35** and **5-36** were made by placing textured bubble glass on top of a sheet of iridescent glass. **Image 5-37** is a composite montage combining out-of-focus flowers with clear textured glass.

Water Droplets on Glass

The next time you find yourself stuck indoors on a rainy or snowy day, think about trying this very cool technique, inspired by my dear friend and mentor, Nancy Rotenberg, who wrote the foreword of this book before passing away in 2011. To borrow Nancy's jubilant phrase, it's a "macro party" you certainly won't want to miss!

Take an ordinary sheet of clear glass and raise it about 12 inches off the floor using sturdy supports such as bricks at each corner. Then coat the glass with Rain-X (available at any hardware or automotive supply store) and spray with water from a fine-mist water bottle. Place a flower (and complementary-colored background cloth or colored background paper) under the sheet of glass so that it's about 5 or 6 inches below the surface of the glass and aim your macro lens above the glass, keeping the camera back as parallel to the surface of the glass as possible. (Of course, you can also try this technique outdoors—as illustrated in **images 5-38** through **5-40**—but keep in mind you might have to place a large black cloth over your head and the entire setup to eliminate reflections from above.)

You won't believe your eyes! Bingo . . . a flower repeats itself and appears inside each water droplet. (See **image 5-41**, page 92.) The trick here for success is making sure you keep your camera as parallel as possible to the surface of the glass and also focusing the lens on the water droplets, not the flower below. Like shooting reflections in iridescent glass, I also recommend that you bracket aperture settings to see which ones yield the best results.

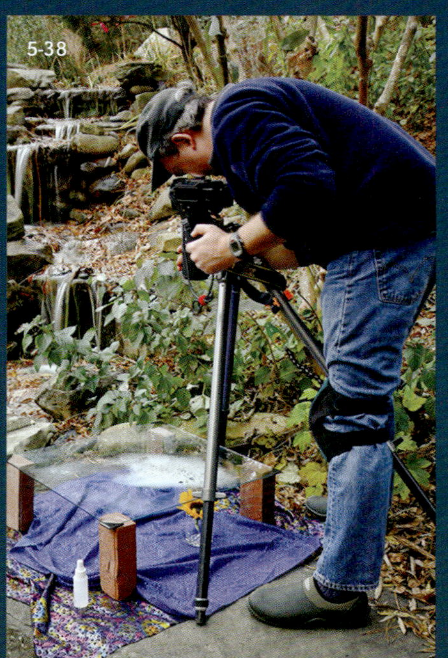

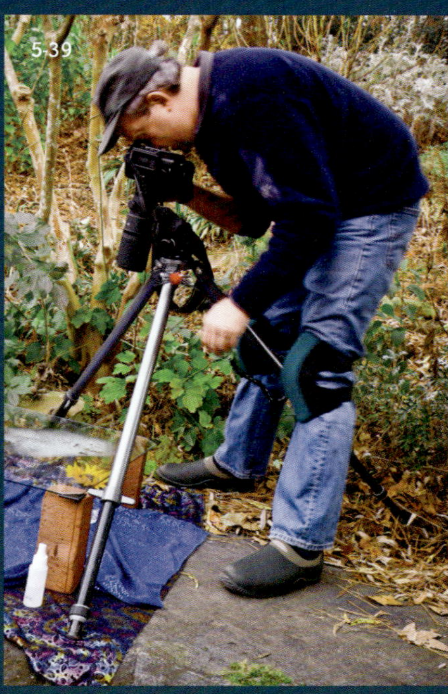

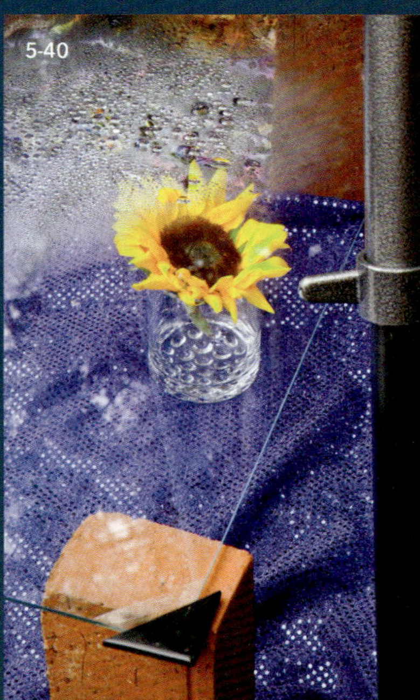

Image 5-38. Here's the setup I used for shooting a sunflower reflected in water droplets on glass. When trying this technique, it's important to keep your camera back parallel to the surface of the glass and focus on the flower inside the drops for maximum sharpness. Experiment with various aperture settings (while also changing shutter speeds, if you are working in manual exposure mode) and see which image produces the most pleasing effect. **Image 5-39.** Sometimes, lowering your camera closer to the glass produces an image with greater impact. This allows you to fill the frame with larger water droplets. Just be sure not to bump the glass when lowering your tripod! (A tripod with a removable center column also might help when trying this technique.) **Image 5-40.** I cut the stem of the sunflower and placed it in a drinking glass, which was smaller in diameter than the flower (so that the glass would not show in the final image). This also allowed me to position the flower parallel to the surface of the glass above, which was important for maximum sharpness.

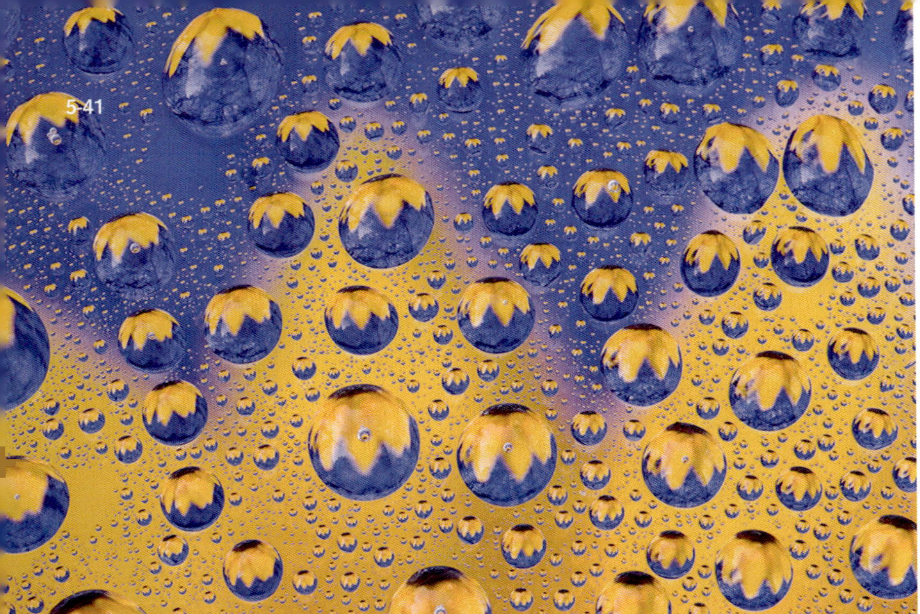

Image 5-41. Nikon Micro-Nikkor 200mm f/4 lens. Exposure: f/8 at 1/2 second.

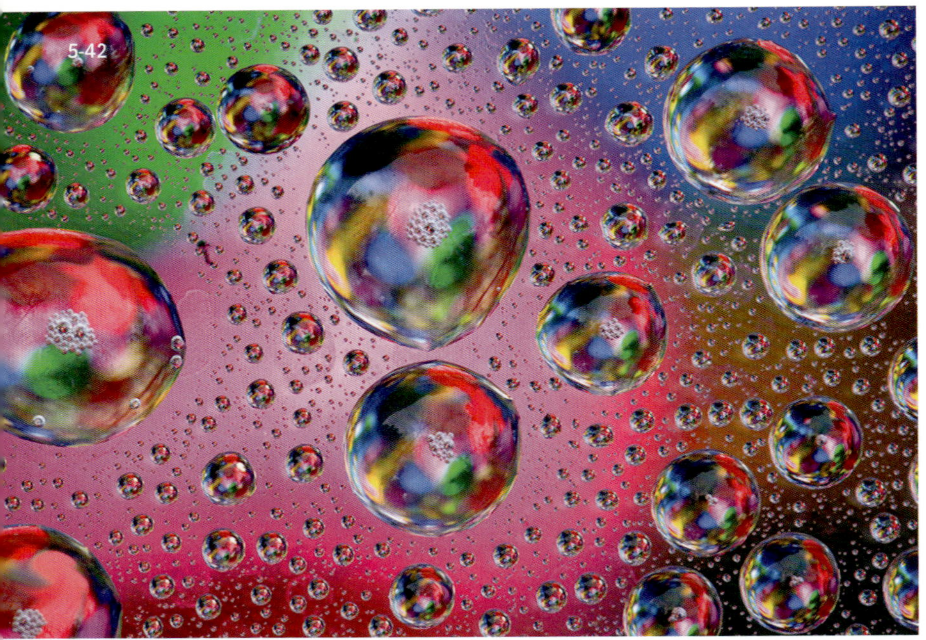

Image 5-42. Nikon Micro-Nikkor 200mm f/4 lens. Exposure: f/8 at 1 second.

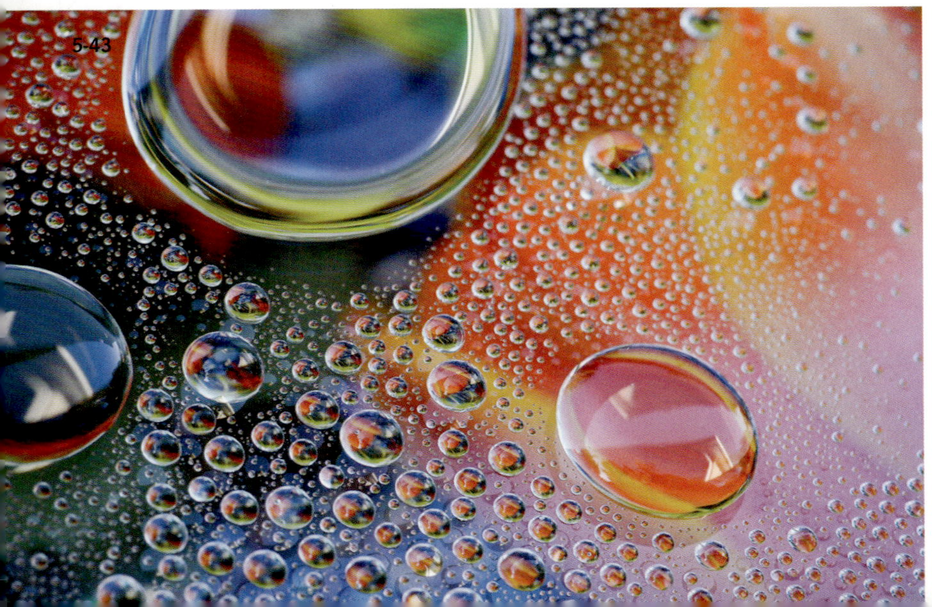

Image 5-43. Nikon Micro-Nikkor 200mm f/4 lens. Exposure: f/5.6 at 1/5 second.

You'll soon discover that you need a fairly wide aperture (e.g., f/5.6 or f/8) to achieve sharpness in the water droplets but not in the flower below. For best results, be sure to experiment with various compositions.

You can also try this technique by placing other colorful objects besides flowers—such as colored ribbons, wrapping paper, colored tinsel, feathers, or even an American flag or old family photo—below the surface of the glass. **Images 5-42** and **5-43** were created by placing colored ribbons and tinsel below the glass.

Food Coloring, Water, and Three Vases

This technique will challenge you to see the world in unimaginable ways. Start by filling three flower vases with water and placing them together on a table. I suggest using at least two vases with some texture or pattern along the sides (as illustrated in **image 5-44**). Drop red, blue, and green food coloring into each of the respective containers and then begin shooting close-ups with your macro lens, aiming straight into the sides of the vases so as to pick up the colors reflecting and mixing with each other. At first, you probably won't be able to "see" anything. But after some patience and determination, you'll soon discover a whole new visually exciting universe of abstract patterns, colors, lines, shapes and textures. See **images 5-45** through **5-51**. (This is a good exercise to repeat on a regular basis, since you'll never see things the exact same way more than once.)

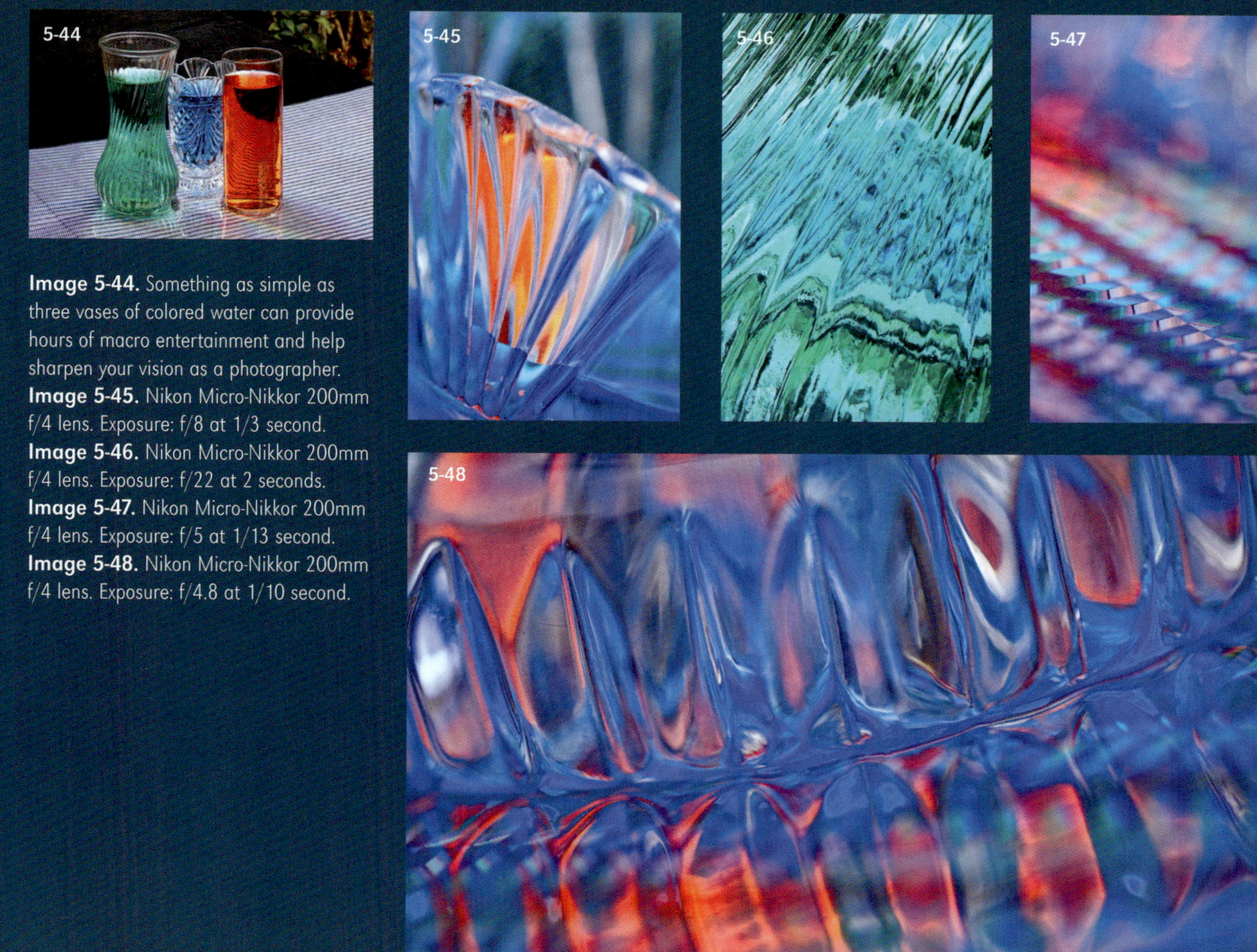

Image 5-44. Something as simple as three vases of colored water can provide hours of macro entertainment and help sharpen your vision as a photographer.
Image 5-45. Nikon Micro-Nikkor 200mm f/4 lens. Exposure: f/8 at 1/3 second.
Image 5-46. Nikon Micro-Nikkor 200mm f/4 lens. Exposure: f/22 at 2 seconds.
Image 5-47. Nikon Micro-Nikkor 200mm f/4 lens. Exposure: f/5 at 1/13 second.
Image 5-48. Nikon Micro-Nikkor 200mm f/4 lens. Exposure: f/4.8 at 1/10 second.

For added fun, place the three vases on a sheet of holographic paper (as illustrated in **image 5-47**) and shoot the vases in direct sunlight. The paper displays a multi-color prismatic effect that bounces light into the colored water. Another macro party, for sure!

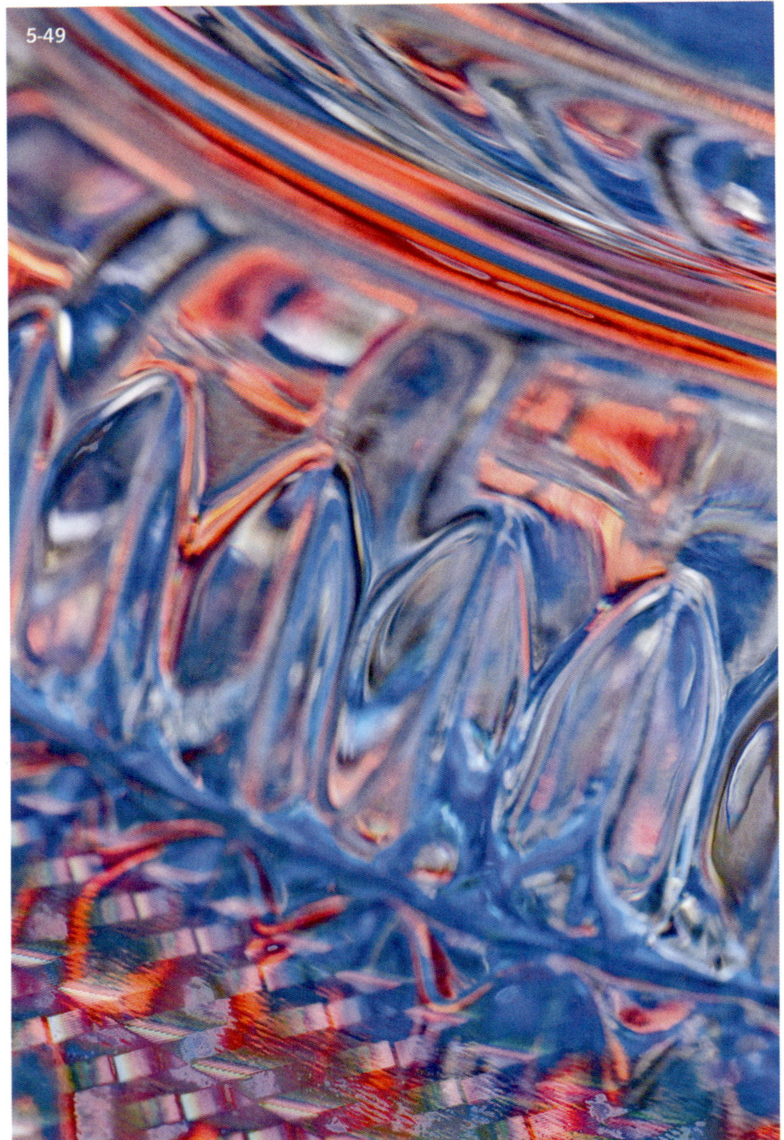

Image 5-49. Nikon Micro-Nikkor 200mm f/4 lens. Exposure: f/22 at 2.5 second.

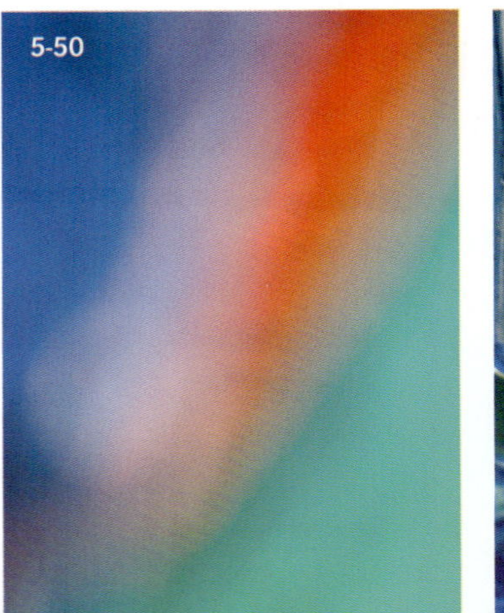

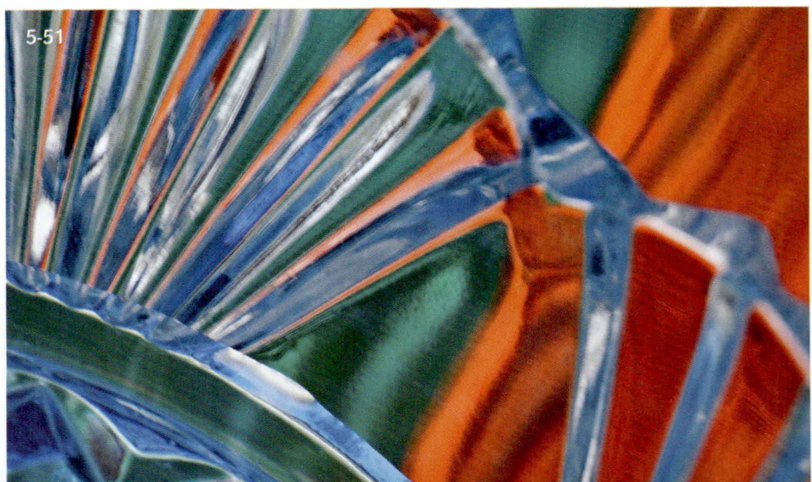

Image 5-50. Nikon Micro-Nikkor 200mm f/4 lens manually defocused at f/4.
Image 5-51. Nikon Micro-Nikkor 200mm f/4 lens. Exposure: f/16 at 2.5 seconds.

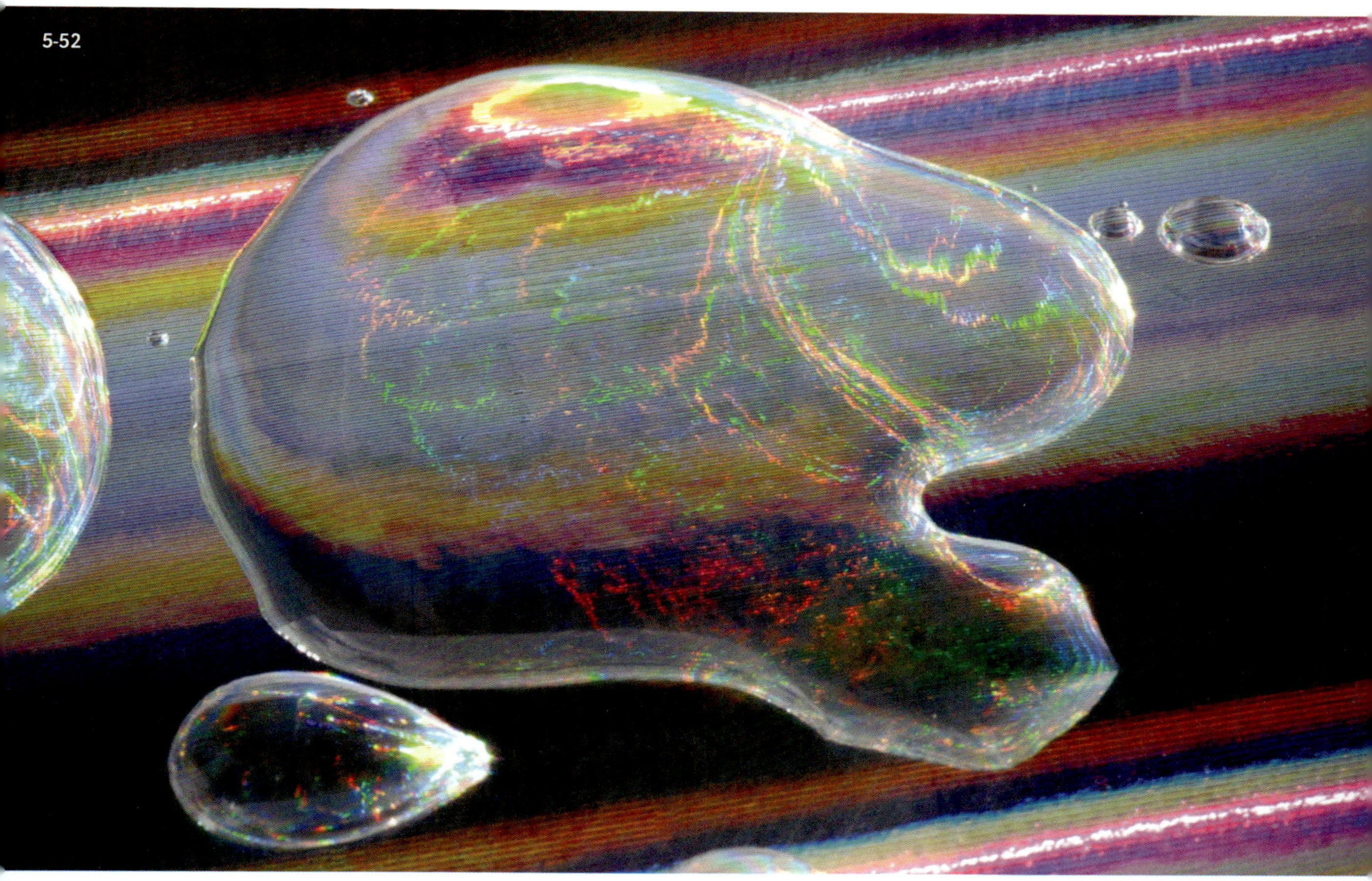

Glycerin on Prismatic Bulletin Board

I've discovered another fun and creative use for holographic paper (actually, a bulletin board covered with holographic paper, which caught my eye while I was shopping at Wal-Mart one day!) By placing drops of glycerin directly onto the bulletin board, you can get wonderful abstract patterns. The prism effect is enhanced when shooting this setup in direct sunlight. (If you're indoors, then try shining a flashlight or other direct light source onto the glycerin drops.) For this image, I used a toothpick to move the glycerin around and shape the drops exactly as I wanted them. (See **images 5-52** and **5-53**.)

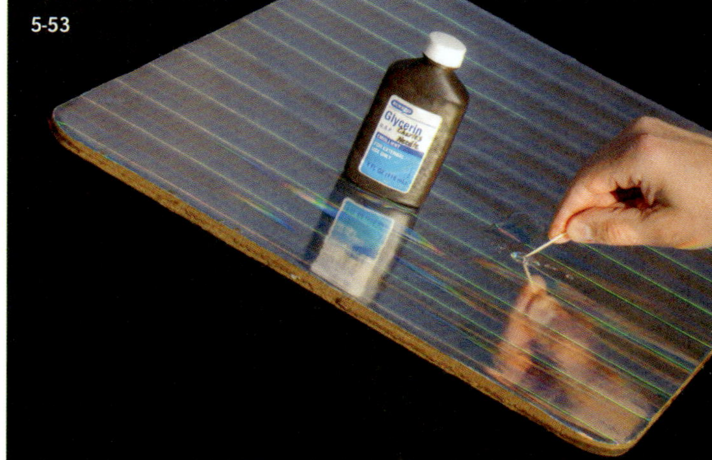

Images 5-52 and 5-53. You can pour drops of liquid glycerin on iridescent, reflective surfaces, such as this bulletin board covered with holographic paper. Here, I'm using a toothpick to help shape the glycerin droplets.

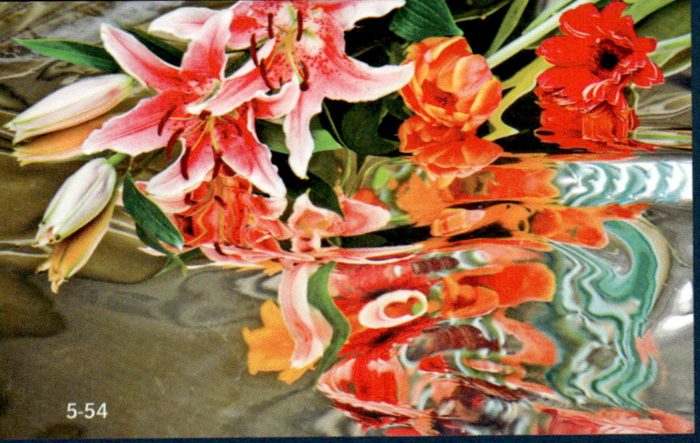

5-54

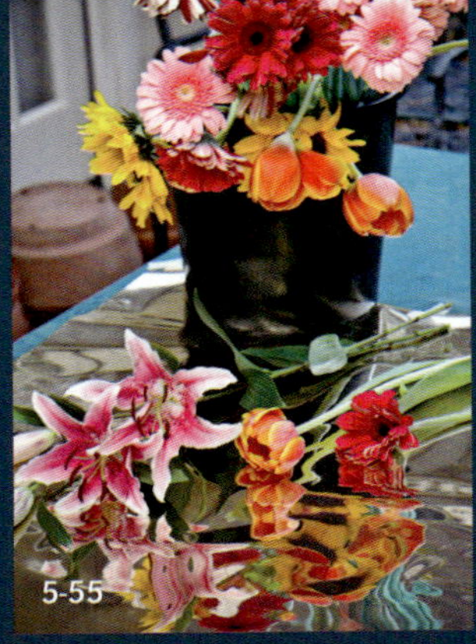

5-55

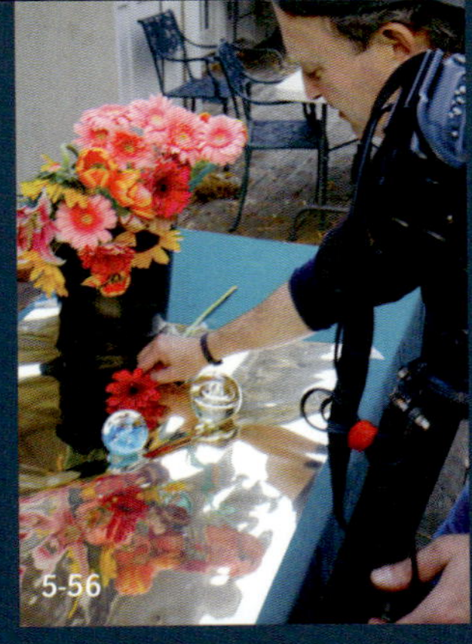

5-56

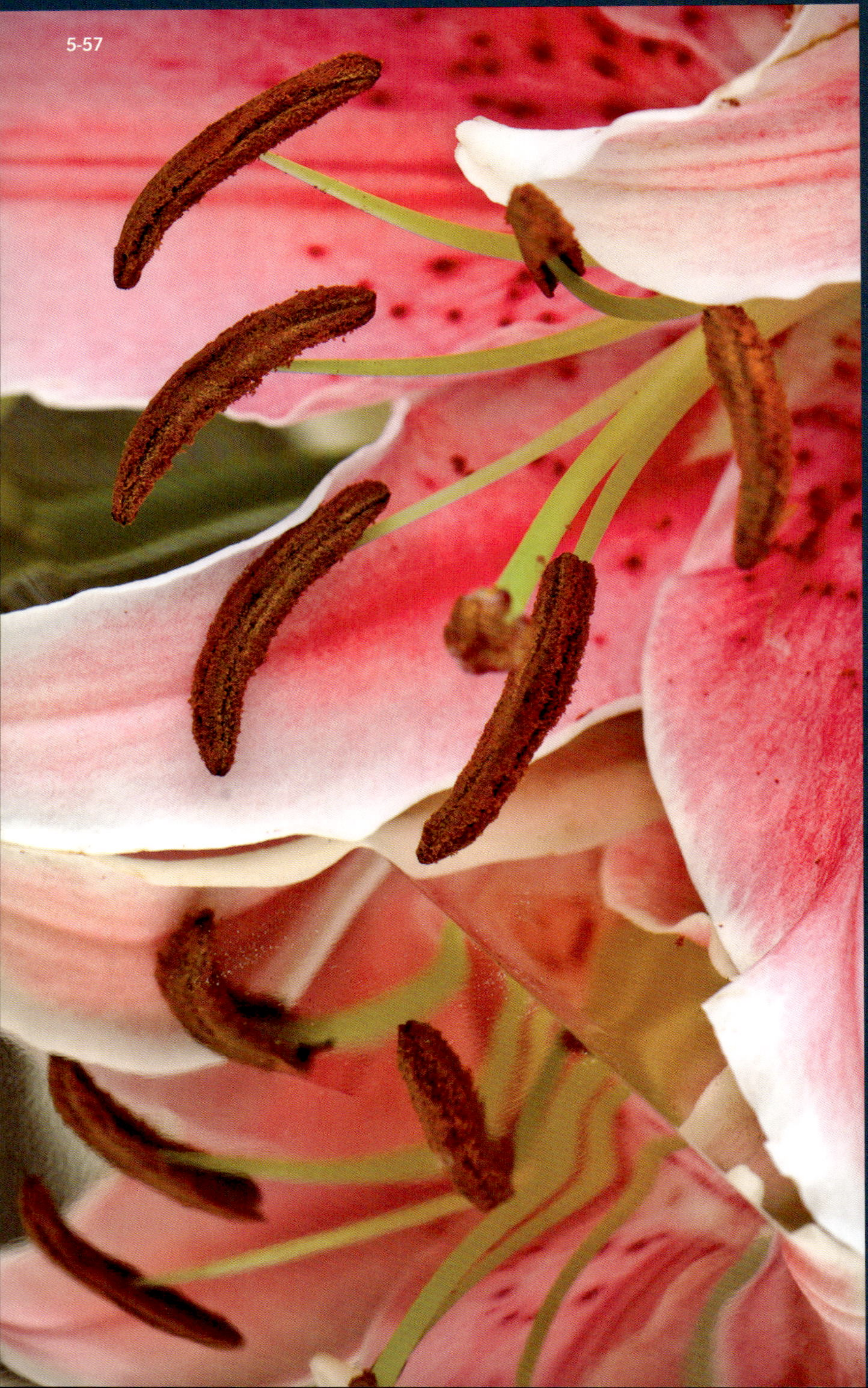

5-57

Image 5-54. To perfect this technique, you can start by placing flowers directly on top of the Mylar, as shown here. This composition is a bit too busy, so I would move in closer to simplify or just place a single flower on top of the Mylar, as in image 5-57. **Image 5-55.** The flowers in this bucket, when positioned correctly, can serve as a colorful backdrop to the flowers laying on top of the Mylar sheet. For best results and a clearer composition, aim your macro lens at the reflection and/or the flowers on the Mylar sheet itself while excluding the reflection of the flower vase (or black bucket, in this case). **Image 5-56.** To create wrinkles in the Mylar, I placed glass paperweights on top of the Mylar. Oftentimes, laying the Mylar perfectly flat isn't nearly as interesting as purposefully wrinkling it, which distorts the reflection further. **Image 5-57.** Nikon Micro-Nikkor 200mm f/4 lens. Exposure: f/32 at 1/30 second.

Magical Mylar

Mylar is a highly reflective metallic foil that you can buy at specialty paper stores and high-end art supply stores, such as Sam Flax. (It is often referred to as Dura Lar in the graphic arts industry.) I prefer the gold Mylar for this macro project (as opposed to silver) because of the warm tones it produces. You can purchase small gold Mylar sheets online (www.shopatron.com/index/527.0.20226.5335.0.0.0). I sell individual 12-foot rolls of gold Mylar in my macro workshops.

Don't be afraid to defocus your lens to abstract your subject further . . .

In the setup, you can place single flowers or groups of flowers directly on top of the Mylar to start (**image 5-54**), and then add a vase of colorful flowers above (as shown in **images 5-55** and **5-56**) to add more color and alter the mini landscape. Before you position your camera, get down so you're at eye level with the table and study the Mylar reflections from several different angles. You may see several different compositions from several different viewpoints. One helpful tip is to bend the Mylar slightly with your hands to change the reflections and then place paperweights (or other small, heavy objects) on the Mylar to hold it in place. Experiment and don't be afraid to defocus your lens to abstract your subject further, as shown in **images 5-58** and **5-59**.

Image 5-58. Out-of-focus flower reflections on gold Mylar. Nikon Micro-Nikkor 200mm f/4 lens. Exposure: f/8 at 1/3 second.
Image 5-59. Out-of-focus flower reflections on gold Mylar. Nikon Micro-Nikkor 200mm f/4 lens. Exposure: f/8 at 1/3 second.

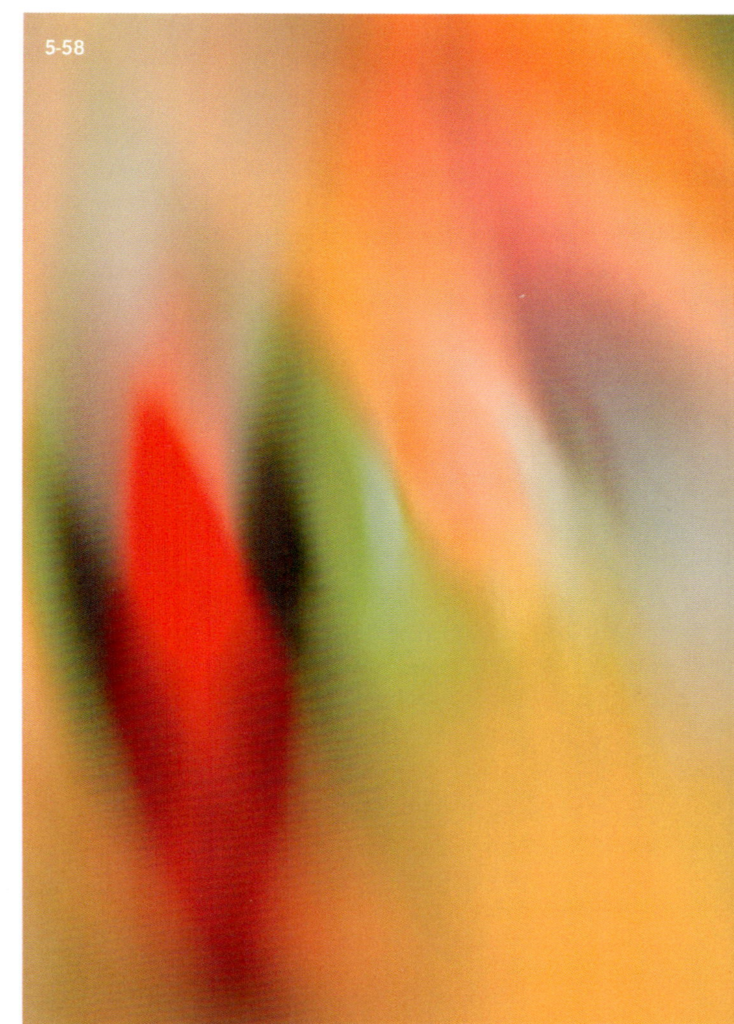

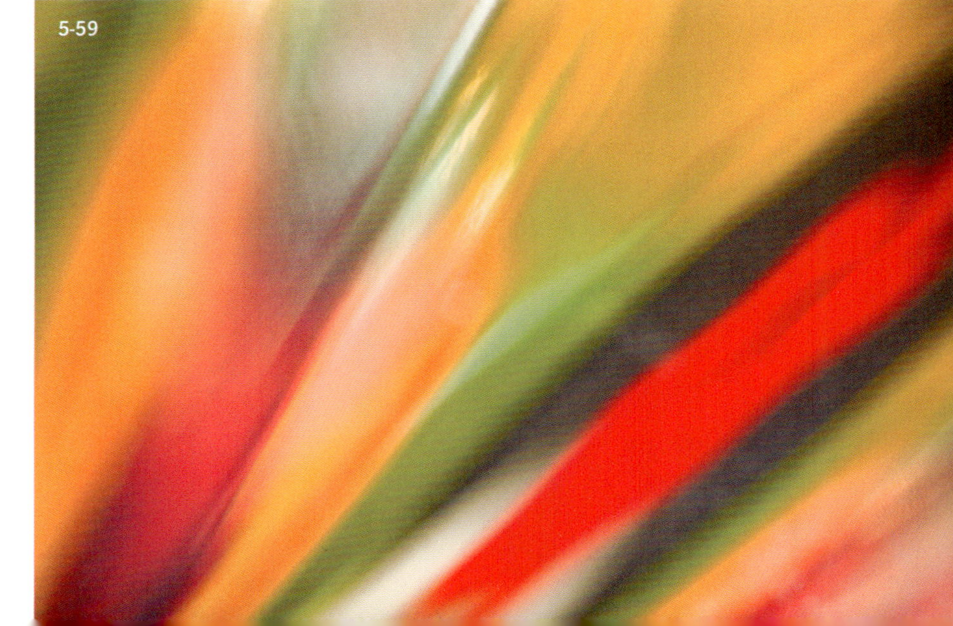

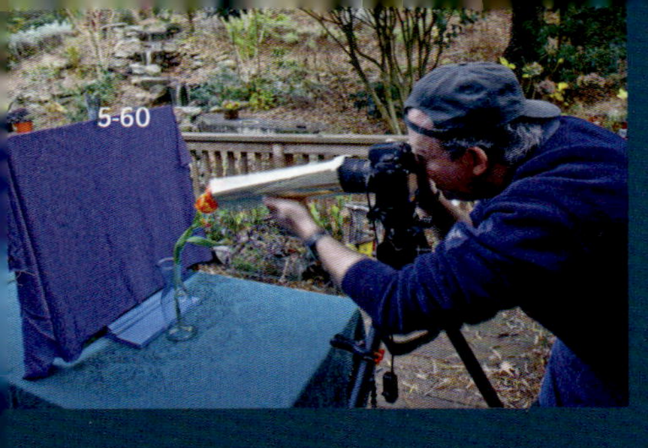

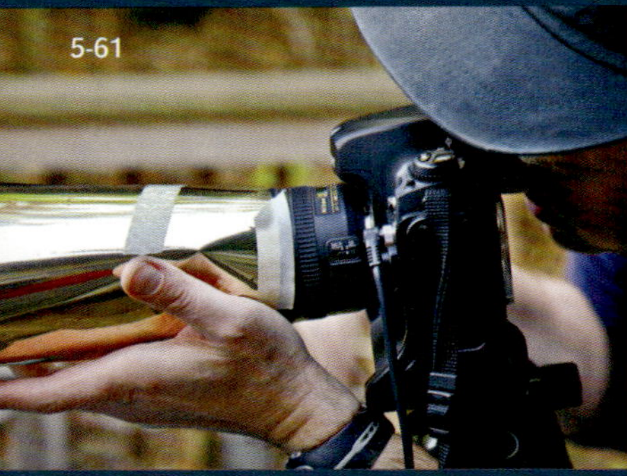

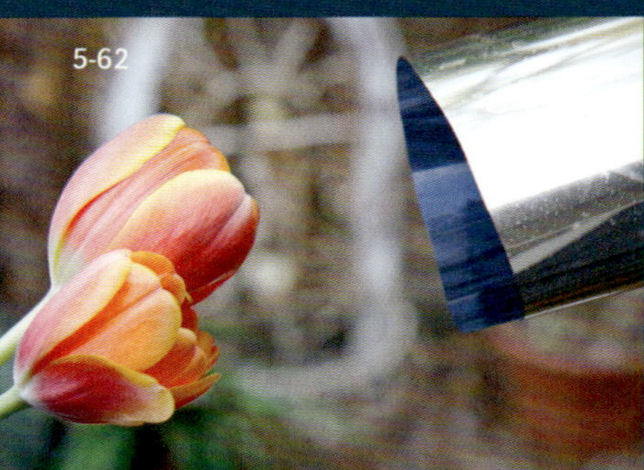

Images 5-60 through 5-62. The setup for the final images. Use masking tape to secure the Mylar to your wide-angle lens, then crinkle the Mylar tube with your hand while looking through the viewfinder.

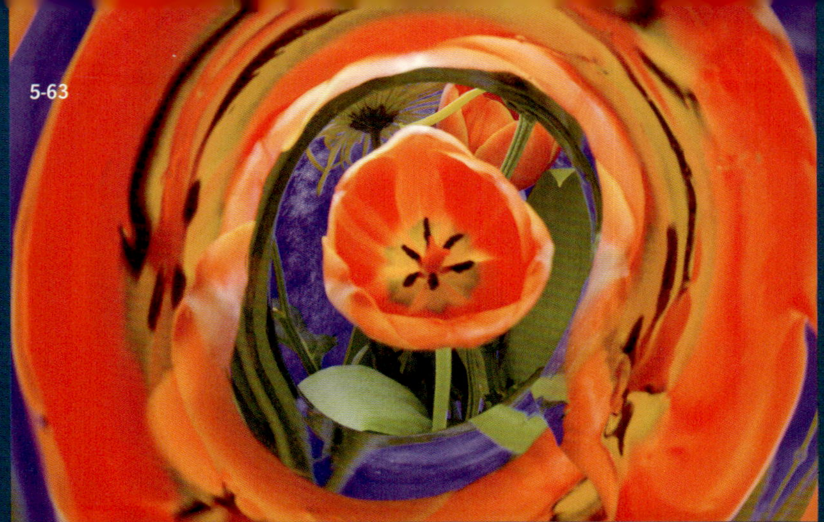

Image 5-63. Nikon Micro-Nikkor 200mm f/4 lens. Exposure: f/22 at 1.3 seconds.

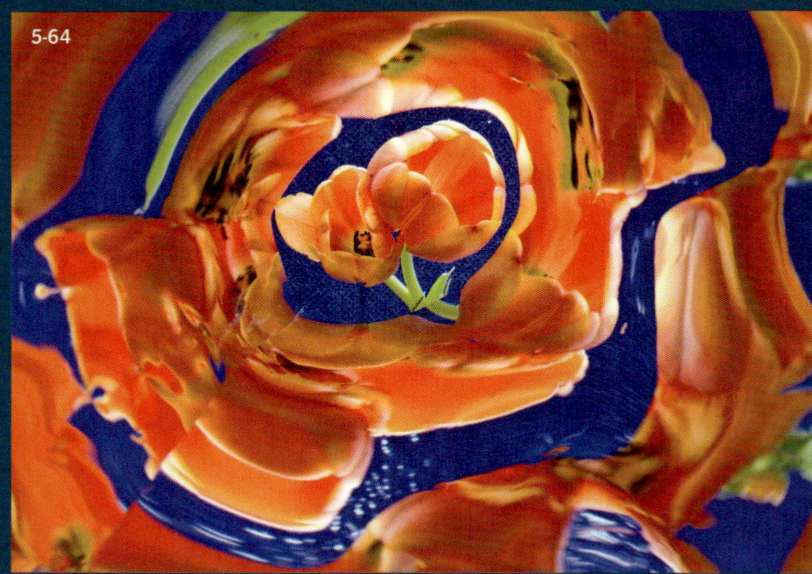

Image 5-64. Nikon Micro-Nikkor 200mm f/4 lens. Exposure: f/22 at 1.3 seconds.

Another fun way to photograph flowers using Mylar is to construct a tube with masking tape around a wide-angle lens and aim the Mylar tube at a flower or group of flowers. (See **images 5-60** through **5-62**.) In this case, I set up a blue background to complement the orange tulip and used my hand to crinkle the Mylar while looking through the viewfinder. (See **images 5-63** and **5-64**.)

I set up a blue background to complement the orange tulip and used my hand to encircle the mlyar.

Feather Boa Fun

This idea came to me while I was shopping at a party supply store. A brightly colored rainbow feather boa caught my attention on one aisle of the store, and I wondered what would happen if I were to shake the feather boa behind a flower (or any subject) and make a photograph using a slow shutter speed. (See **image 5-65**.) After some trial and error, I was pleased with the results. (See **images 5-66** through **5-68**.) The trick was holding the boa far enough away from the flower (about a foot or more) and keeping it held so that there were no apparent gaps between the rows of feathers. I stopped down my macro lens to f/36 in order to decrease my shutter speed to 1 second. All three of these examples were shot at 1 second shutter speeds, but you can see a noticeable difference since the boa was moving around at variable speeds. Have fun with this one and experiment! There are probably a multitude of other creative macro ideas you could come up with using a boa, so feel free to contact me to share ideas and images.

Image 5-65. By shaking something colorful, such as a colorful boa, behind your subject (any subject) and making a photograph using a shutter of about 1 second, you can create some interesting backgrounds. **Image 5-66.** Nikon Micro-Nikkor 200mm f/4 lens. Exposure: f/36 at 1 second. **Image 5-67.** Nikon Micro-Nikkor 200mm f/4 lens. Exposure: f/36 at 1 second. **Image 5-68.** Nikon Micro-Nikkor 200mm f/4 lens. Exposure: f/36 at 1 second.

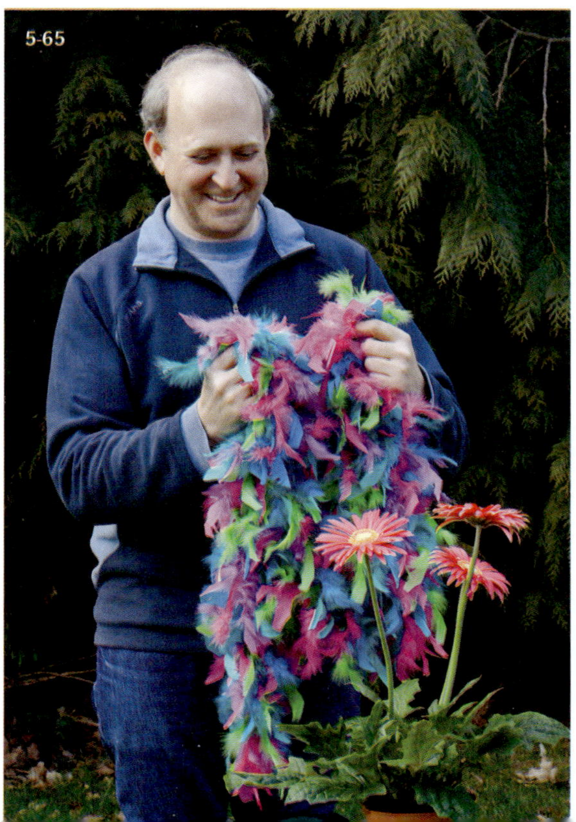

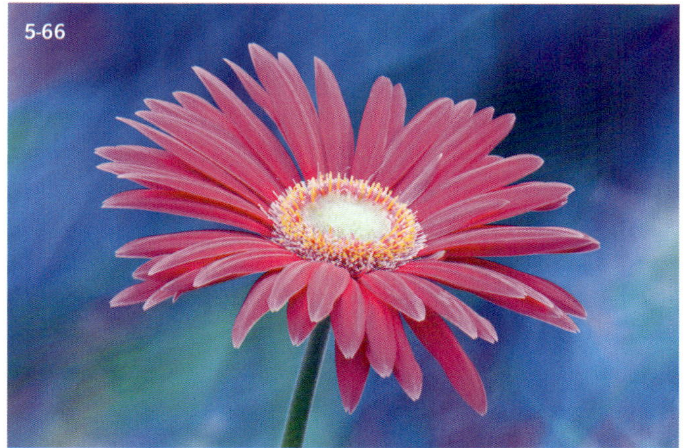

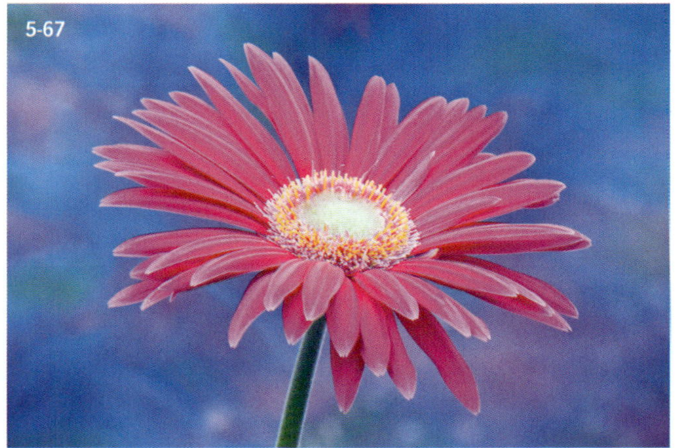

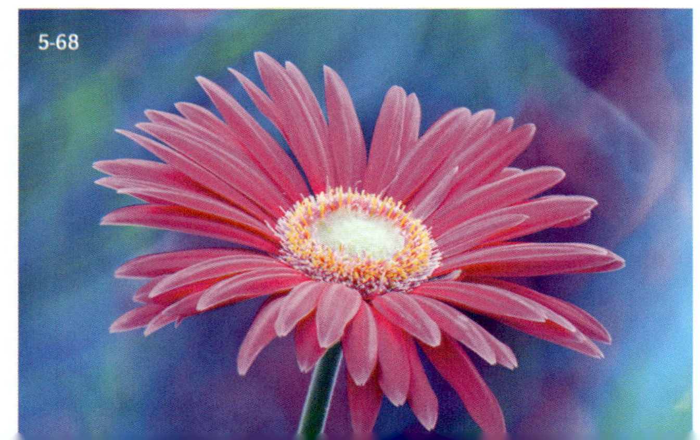

Copper Leaf Ornament

Another shopping adventure—this one during the Christmas holidays—caused my creative juices to flow again. I purchased an iridescent plated real sugar maple leaf ornament (available online at www.naturesleaf.com/catalog_details.php?ID=343) and set it up in my backyard garden studio one afternoon with the idea of shooting the leaf with green foliage in the background. After trying this method for a while, I experimented with various colored paper and colorful cloth backgrounds, making sure my camera back was parallel to the maple leaf.

Suddenly, the lightbulb went on! I saw a piece of holographic paper lying on the table next to me and quickly set it up as a background, making sure it was far enough

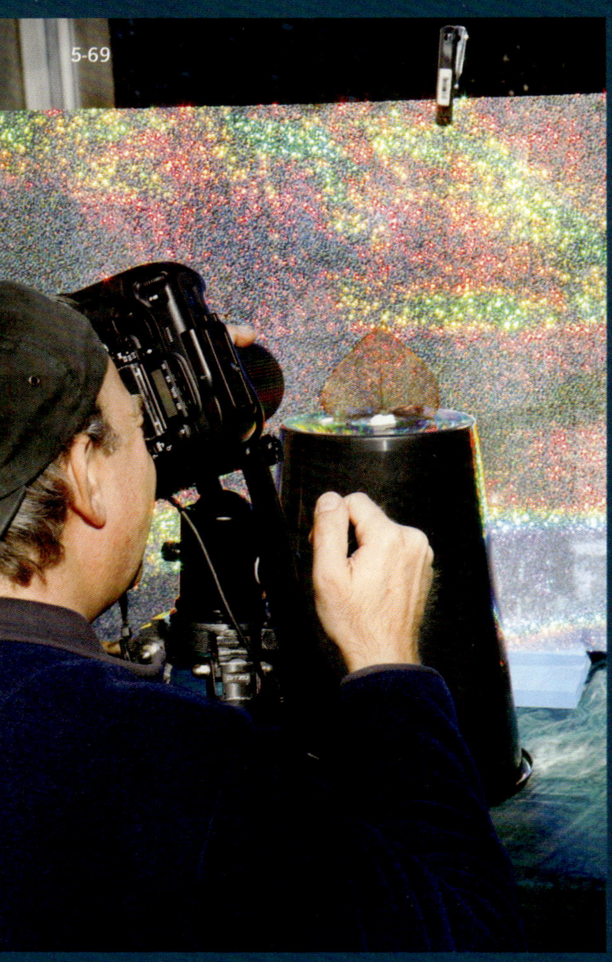

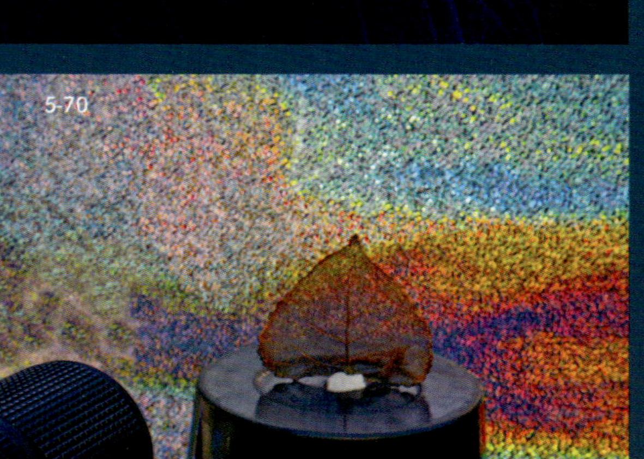

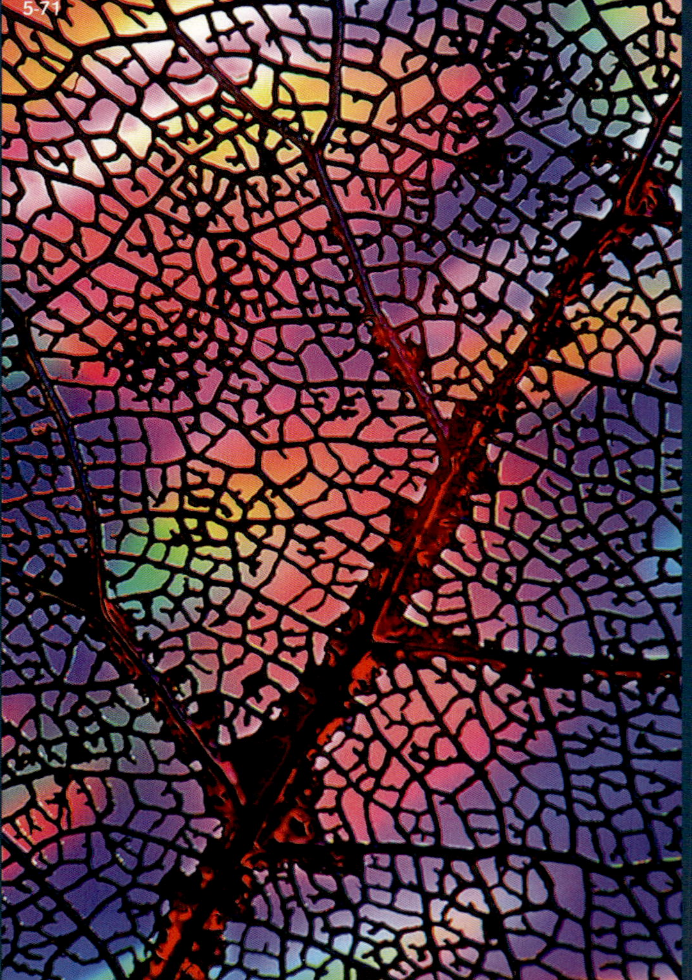

Image 5-69. This was the setup for shooting the copper leaf ornament. The key to success here is to use holographic paper as your background, with a direct light source shining on the paper. In this case, the sun was my main light, as I was photographing in my garden studio. **Image 5-70.** Using putty, I positioned the leaf on an upside-down bucket, making sure it was at a 90-degree angle and parallel to the image sensor plane. **Image 5-71.** Nikon Micro-Nikkor 200mm f/4 lens. Exposure: f/5.6 at 1/2 second.

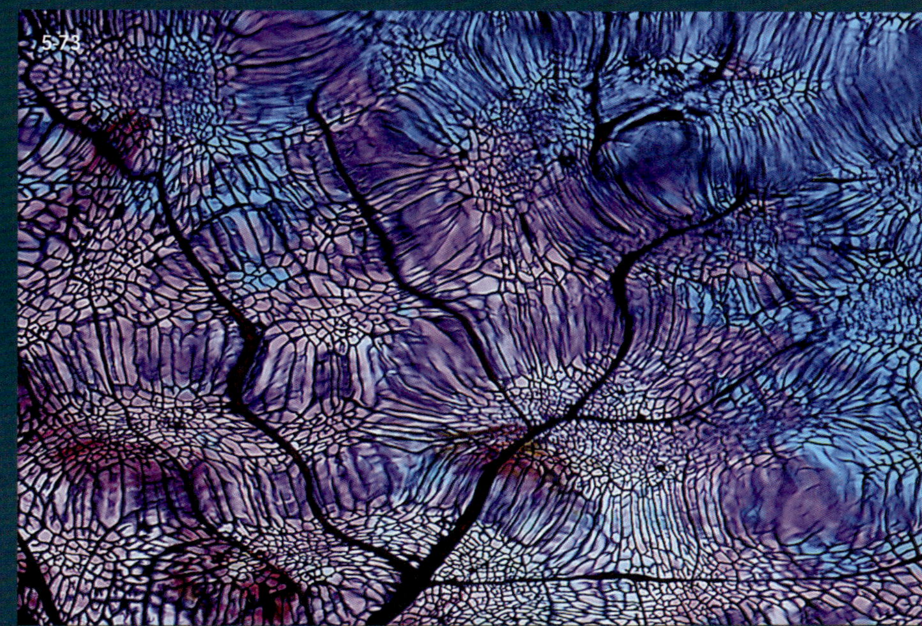

Image 5-72. Using putty, I positioned the copper leaf ornament at a 45-degree angle on top of a sheet of iridescent glass and photographed the reflection of the leaf, not the leaf itself. **Image 5-73.** The result of aiming my lens at the reflection of the copper leaf in the iridescent glass. Nikon Micro-Nikkor 200mm f/4 lens. Exposure: f/16 at 2 seconds.

away from the leaf to blur since I was going to shoot at a fairly wide aperture setting (f/5.6). As fate would have it, the sun was shining that day from behind my setup and cast a bright glow on the holographic paper and the leaf. (See **images 5-69** and **5-70**.) When I peered through my macro lens, I could not believe my eyes! I saw a dance of color unlike any other. It was as if I were looking at a beautiful stained-glass window in a church. (See **image 5-71**.) The muses had come to visit me that day, for sure, and I had fun photographing this one sugar maple leaf for several hours on end.

Following all that excitement, I asked myself, "What if I were to place iridescent glass behind the leaf?" That was interesting, but then I realized that the reflection in the glass was what was really attracting me. So, I laid the glass down flat on the table, got some putty and braced the leaf at a 45-degree angle to the glass. (See **image 5-72**.) Nearly two hours had passed before I realized I had been lost in the beautiful reflection of the leaf for that long of a time period, making some beautiful and unusual images highlighting lines, colors, shape, and texture. **Image 5-73** was the most pleasing result for me.

The muses had come to visit me that day, for sure . . .

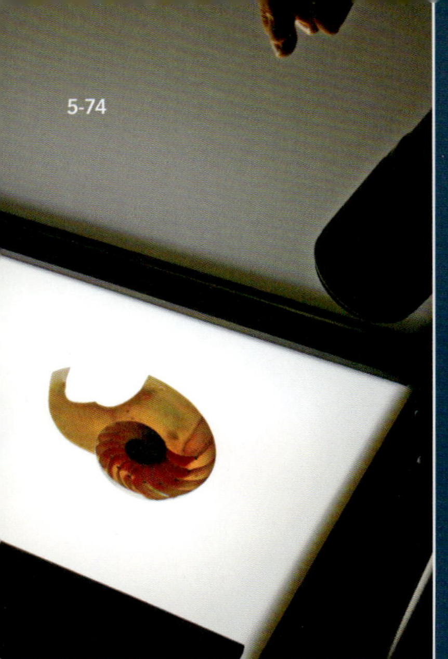

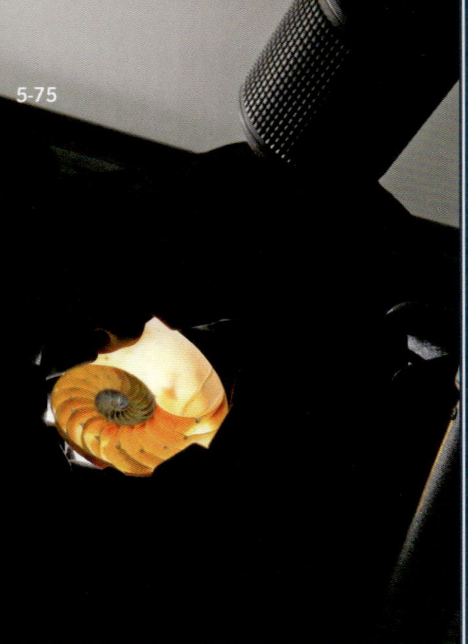

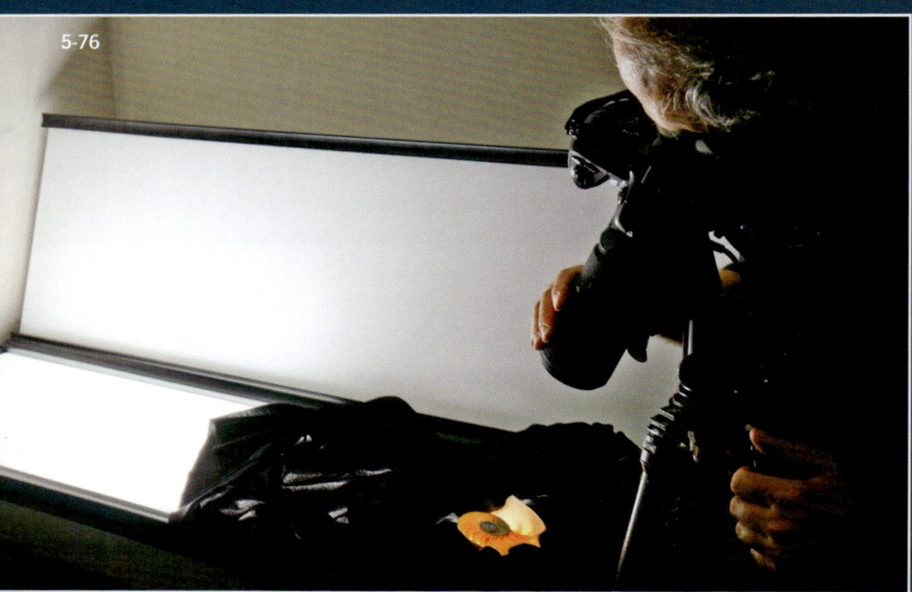

Image 5-74. At first, I tried photographing this nautilus shell slice on a light table without a black cloth. The resulting image was underexposed severely, due to an abundance of light spilling around the shell. **Image 5-75.** In order to outsmart my camera's meter, I placed a black cloth around the shell and aimed my 200mm macro lens at the center, making sure the camera back was as parallel to the top edge of the nautilus slice as possible for maximum sharpness. **Image 5-76.** Here's a close-up of how the shell looked when surrounded by the black cloth. **Image 5-77.** This was the final result of the backlit nautilus shell with some blue LED flashlight color added in the center during the exposure to enhance shadow detail. Nikon Micro-Nikkor 200mm f/4 lens. Exposure: f/4.5 at 1/30 second.

Nautilus Shell

I have always been attracted to spirals, and particularly the shell of the chambered nautilus because of its beauty and proportional perfection. To capture this beauty, I placed the shell on a color-balanced light table and placed a black cloth around the shell to prevent light from spilling out and fooling the camera meter. I then aimed my 200mm macro lens at the shell, making sure to fill the frame and to keep the camera back as parallel as possible to the shell in order to maximize sharpness. (See **images 5-74** through **5-76**.) Keep in mind that, with a backlit subject like this, you'll probably need to overexpose the image by 1 to 2 stops to maintain shadow detail. **Image 5-77** was my favorite macro image in this series, by far.

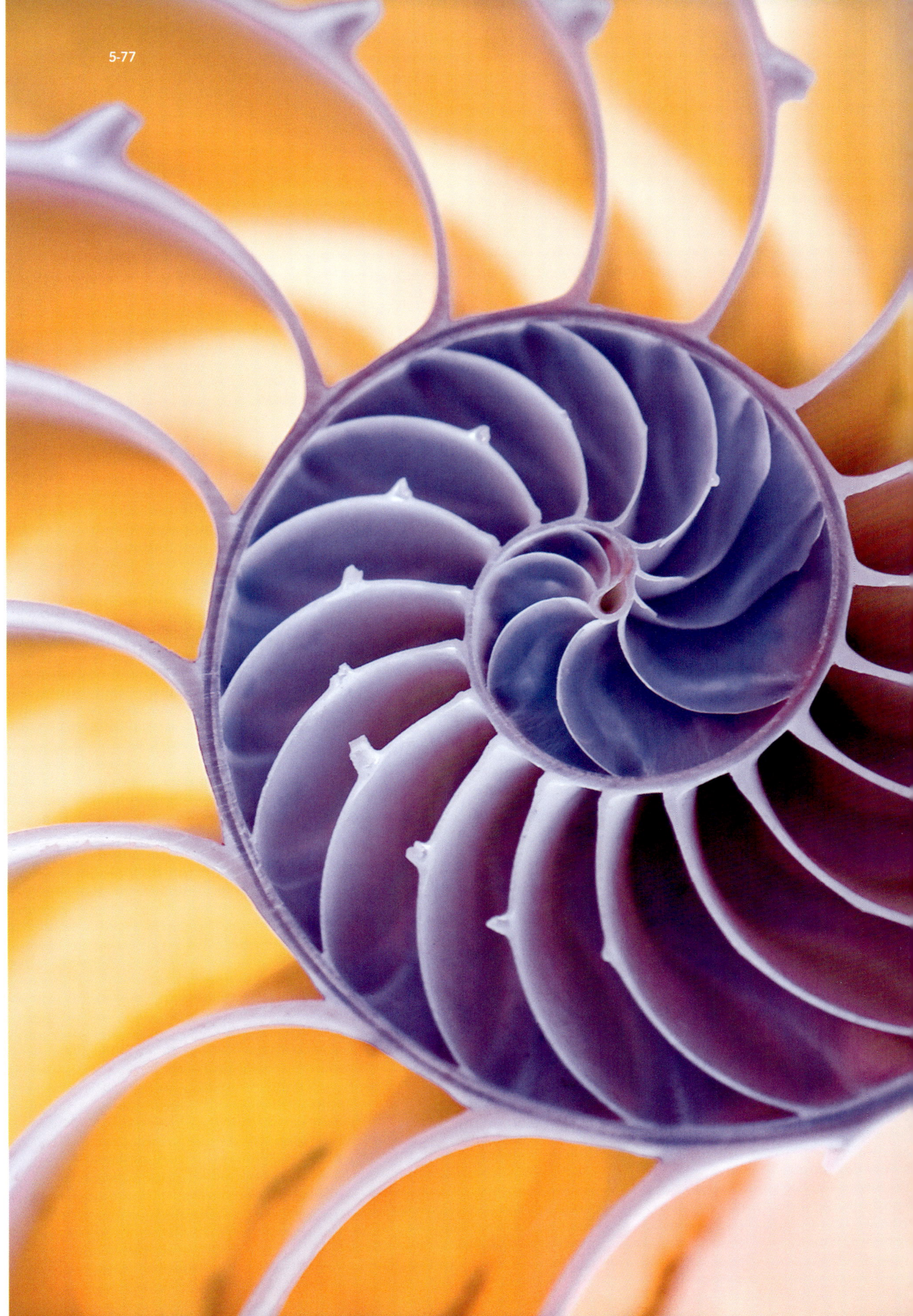
5-77

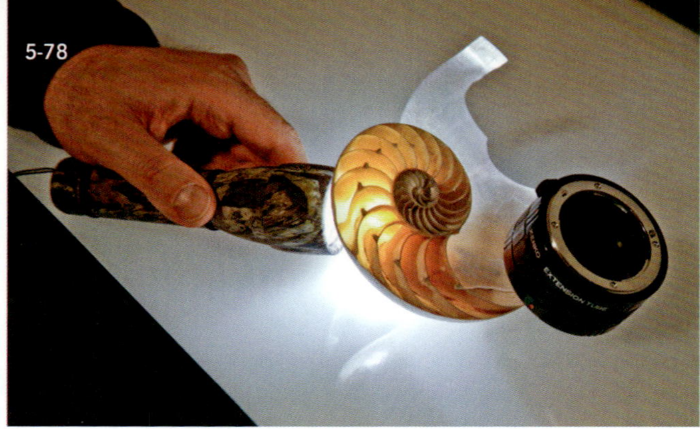

Then, I experimented with removing the black cloth and adding the red flashlight from underneath the shell, this time turning off the light table's light and making the flashlight the sole light source. To help position the nautilus shell and allow room for the flashlight to shine from underneath, I used an extension tube to hold the shell in place. (See **image 5-78**.) This created an added dimension to the shell, as you can see in **images 5-79** and **5-80**. I tried blue flashlight as well but found the red light to be more pleasing. Besides shells, you could also photograph other transparent objects backlit on a light table, such as sliced fruit (kiwis, oranges, limes, strawberries, etc.), flowers, plants, and glass objects. Keep in mind that other types of shells, such as abalone and conch shells, can make interesting macro subjects. If shells are transparent enough, try backlighting them on a light table using the same technique outlined above. See **images 5-81** through **5-83**.

I tried blue flashlight as well but found the red light to be more pleasing.

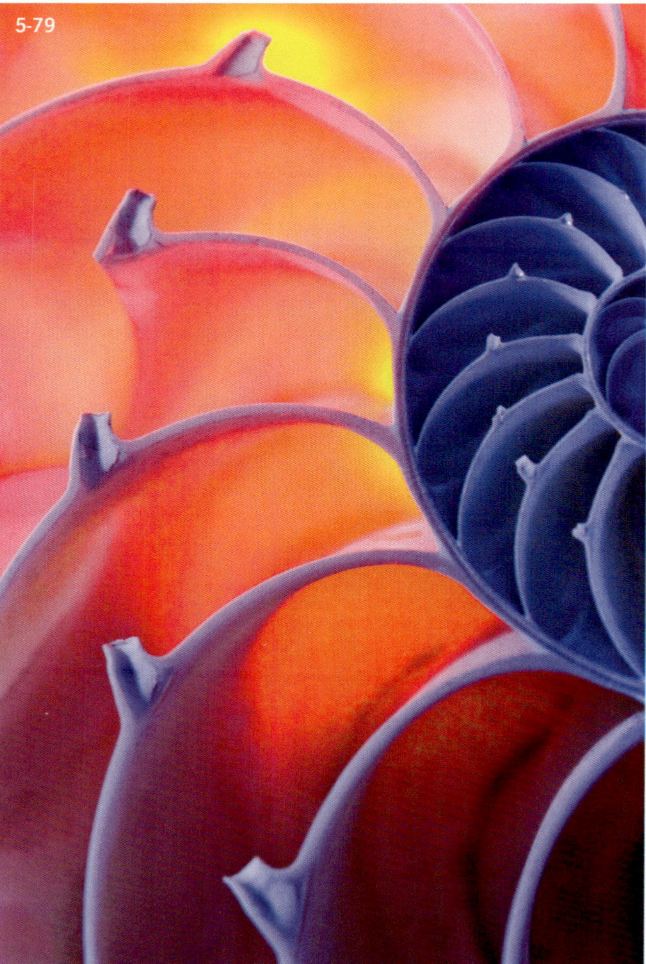

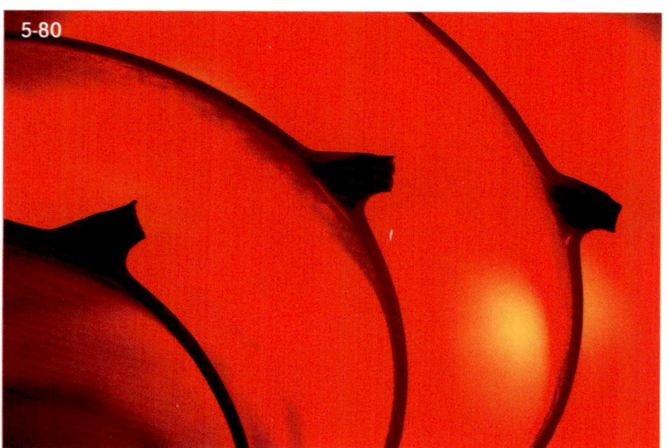

Image 5-78. For a completely different look, I experimented with adding the red colored LED flashlight from underneath the shell, this time turning off the light table light and making the flashlight the sole light source. This created an added dimension to the shell, as you can see in images 5-79 and 5-80. I tried blue as well but found the red light to be more pleasing. **Image 5-79.** Nikon Micro-Nikkor 200mm f/4 lens. Exposure: f/5.6 at 1/6 second. **Image 5-80.** Nikon Micro-Nikkor 200mm f/4 lens. Exposure: f/8 at 1/5 second.

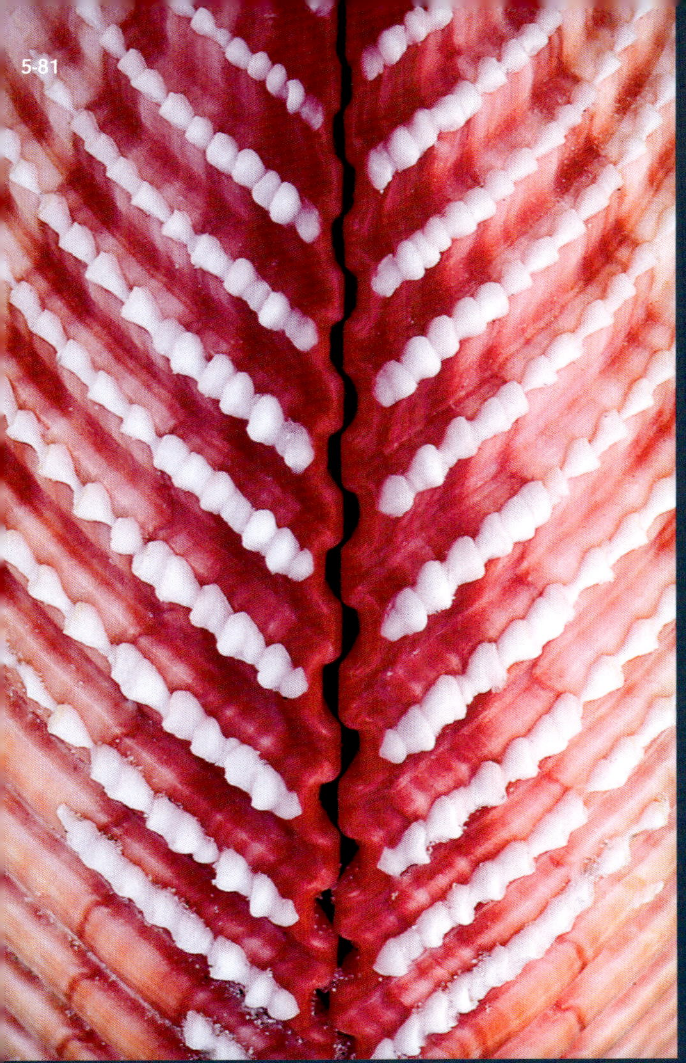

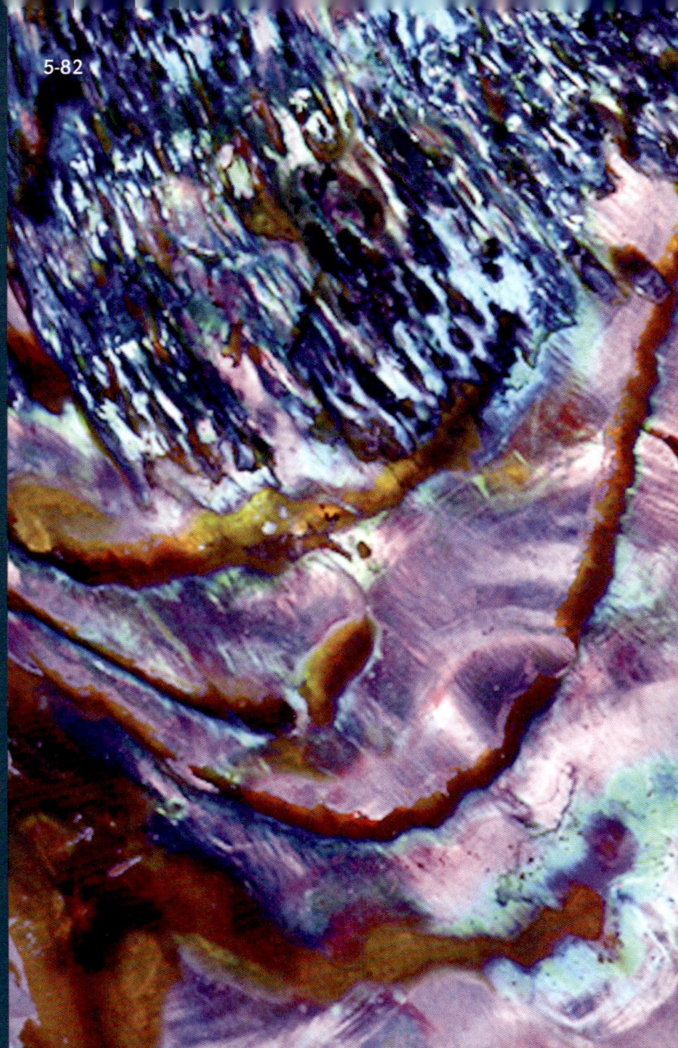

Images 5-81 through 5-83. Macro images of other shells. Each of these was photographed outdoors under overcast light (no flash) using my Nikkor 200mm f/4 lens.

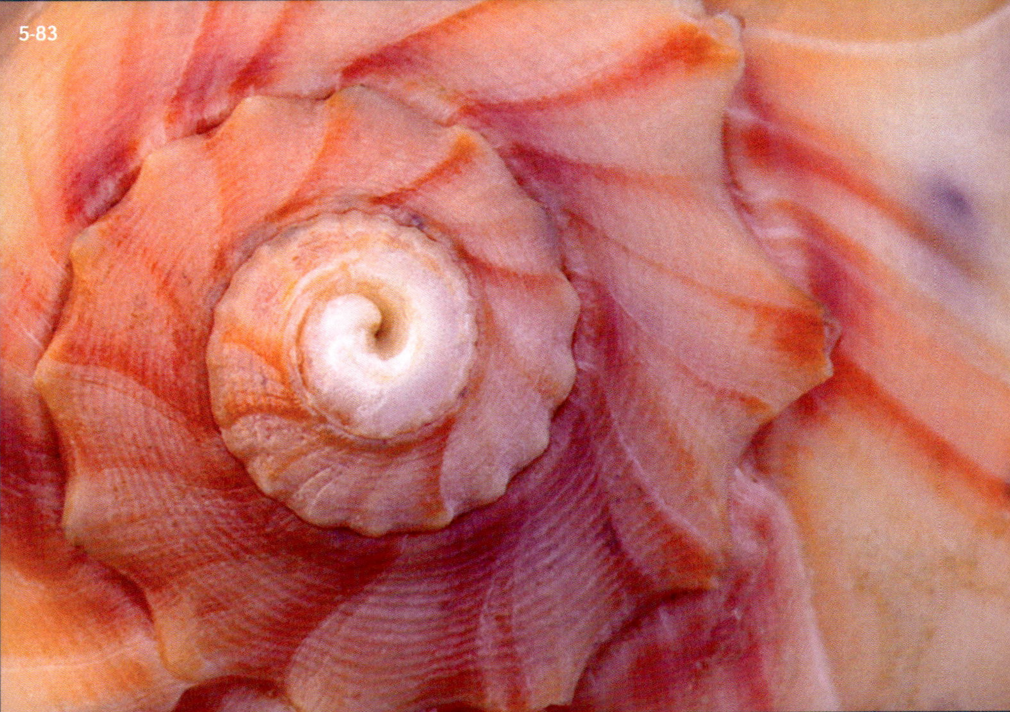

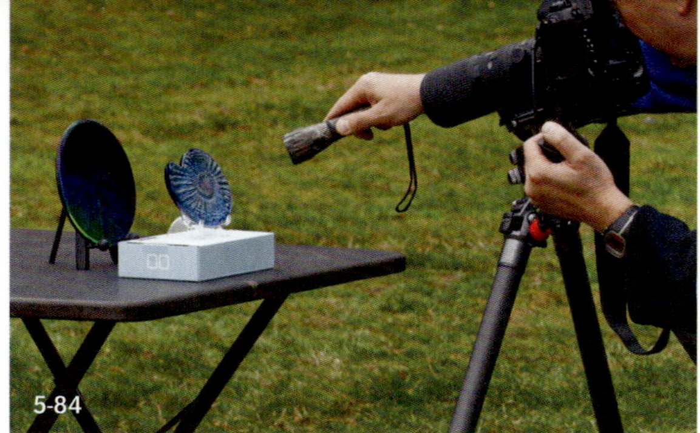

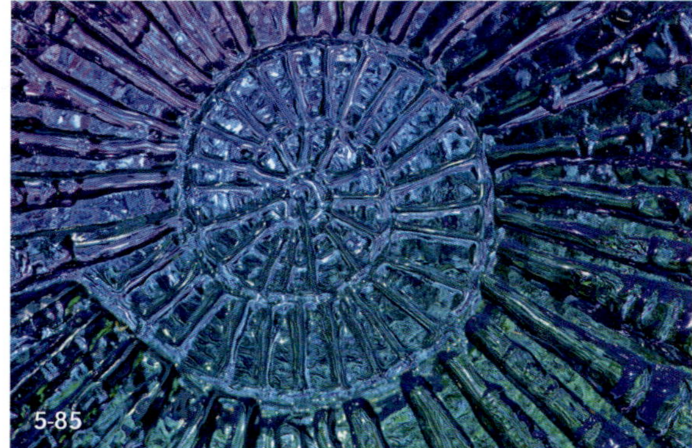

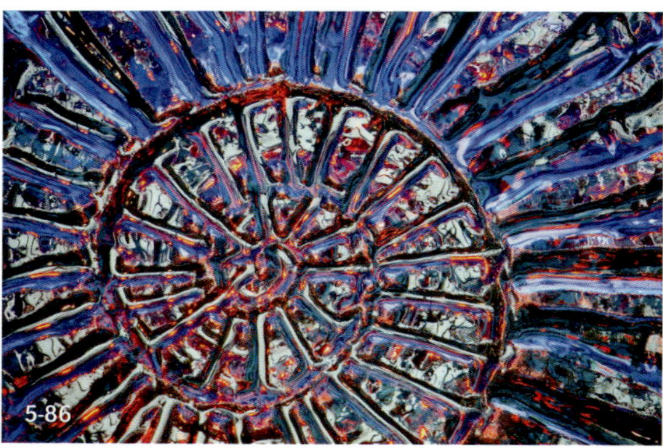

Image 5-84. Here's my setup for photographing a glass nautilus paperweight with a colored dichroic glass disc from behind. **Image 5-85.** Nikon Micro-Nikkor 200mm f/4 lens. Exposure: f/5.6 at 1/1000 second with no flashlight. **Image 5-86.** Nikon Micro-Nikkor 200mm f/4 lens. Exposure: f/32 at 6 seconds with red flashlight.

Because I am drawn to nautilus shells, in particular, one day I decided to photograph a glass paperweight nautilus by placing it on a plastic stand with a colored dichroic glass disc behind it. (See **image 5-84**.) Both of these objects were purchased at a local antique store. Again, the success of this image depended on using the correct camera angle to ensure sharpness throughout. It was crucial that the camera back was parallel to the subject plane, as was the case when photographing the actual nautilus shell on the light table. Because of the varied height of the two objects (once placed on supporting stands), it was necessary to elevate the nautilus paperweight to get the purple and green colors to shine through. (See **image 5-85**.) **Image 5-86** is the same shell paperweight with a slightly different composition and the addition of the red LED flashlight for color accent.

Cross-Polarization Technique

One method for making colorful abstract images involves using clear plastic objects, such as bowls, plates, cups, or cutlery. Often, these clear plastic objects (typically found at a party supply store) are made using an injection-molded process, which means the plastic takes on some ability to polarize light itself and contains hidden stress lines.

Objects with distinct patterns that mimic cut crystal work especially well. When light waves of different polarizations are passed through these plastics, the material refracts each of them differently, which creates interesting rainbow patterns. (For more on the science behind this effect, Google the word "birefringence.")

Objects with distinct patterns that mimic cut crystal work especially well.

The technique, called cross-polarization, involves placing the clear plastic object between two polarized filters. You can do this on a bright, sunny day outdoors, or indoors using a direct light source such as a flashlight or tungsten lamp aimed directly at the plastic object. I've discovered it works equally well on a bright, overcast day.

Here's the setup (as illustrated in **image 5-87**): Find a dark-colored surface (black velvet will work, or anything else that's close to black). Place the stressed-plastic object (or objects) on a sheet of polarizing paper and lay it on the dark surface. In this case, I worked with a plastic bowl and focused on the lines along the side. (See **image 5-88**.) You should be able to see some of the rainbow effect immediately without even looking through the lens. Put a circular polarizer filter on the end of your macro lens and aim it directly at the plastic object. The effect will be magnified even more! Try different camera positions (higher or lower, and also move your tripod 360 degrees around the object) to vary your composition and capture differing degrees of polarization. Also, bracket your aperture settings and vary where you place your focus to make strikingly abstract images.

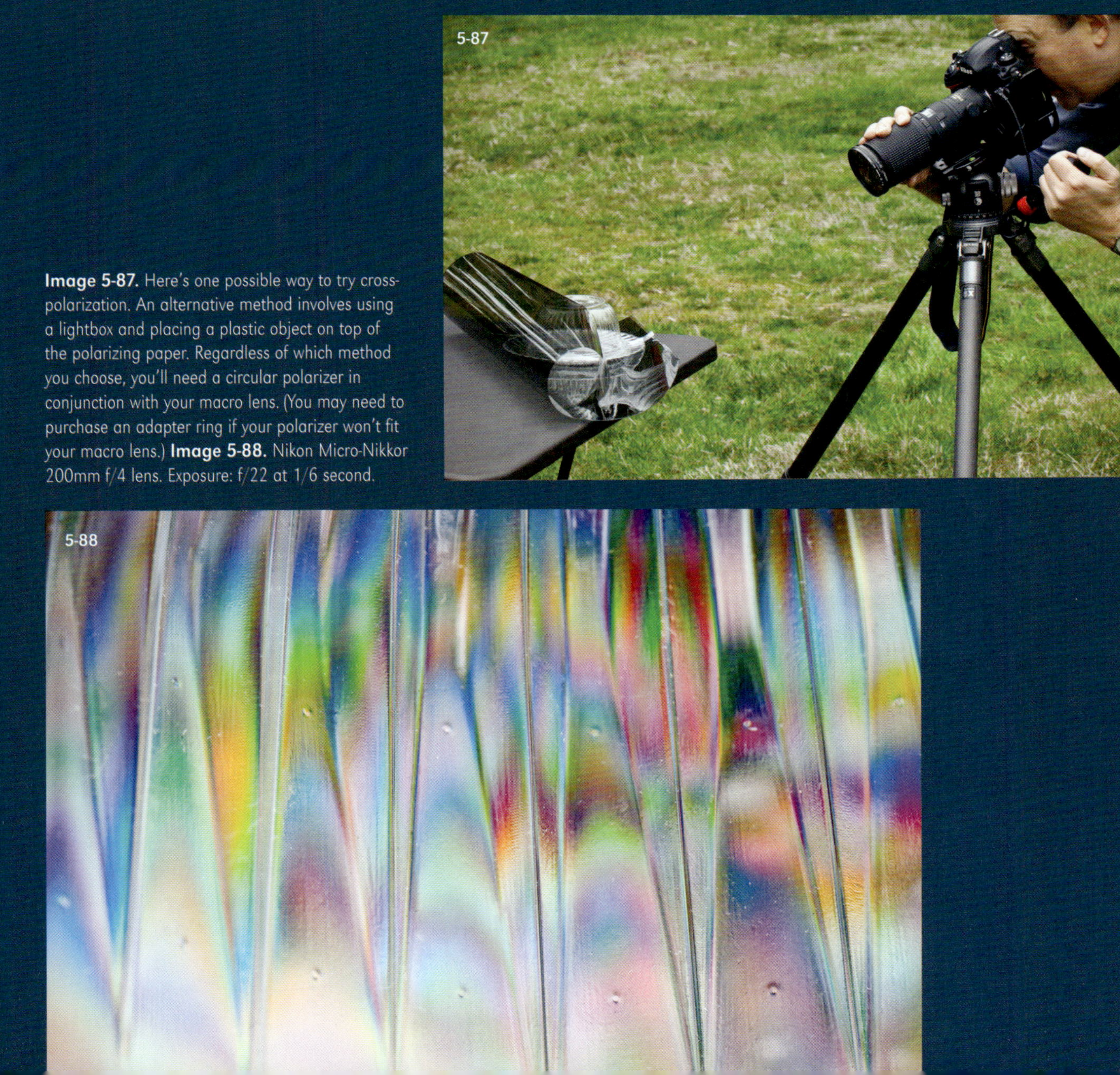

Image 5-87. Here's one possible way to try cross-polarization. An alternative method involves using a lightbox and placing a plastic object on top of the polarizing paper. Regardless of which method you choose, you'll need a circular polarizer in conjunction with your macro lens. (You may need to purchase an adapter ring if your polarizer won't fit your macro lens.) **Image 5-88.** Nikon Micro-Nikkor 200mm f/4 lens. Exposure: f/22 at 1/6 second.

You might even wish to experiment with what I call "double cross-polarization" by covering the object with polarizing paper from the top as well as on the bottom, wrapping it between two layers of polarizing paper. (See **images 5-89** and **5-90**.) This method helps intensify the colors even more and adds excitement to the party! **Images 5-93** through 5-96 were all created by wrapping a scallop-edged plastic plate between two layers of polarizing paper and then aiming my macro lens at tightly composed sections of the plate.

Whether you're trying straight cross-polarization or double cross-polarization, a polarizer filter is needed. (See **images 5-91** and **5-92** to see the effect with and without a polarizer.)

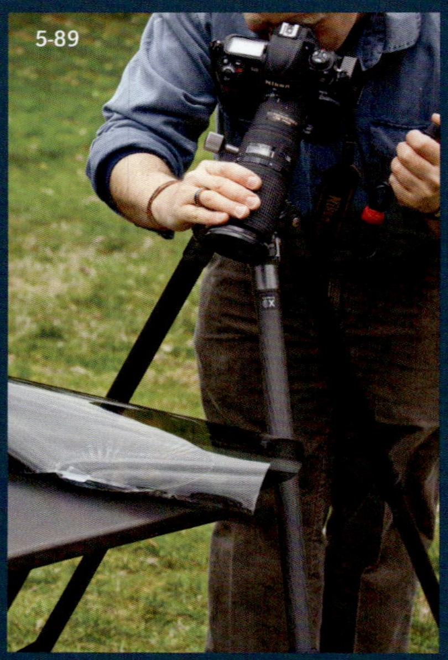

Image 5-89. For *double* cross-polarization, try wrapping a plastic object with polarizing paper on the top and bottom. This will intensify colors even more.

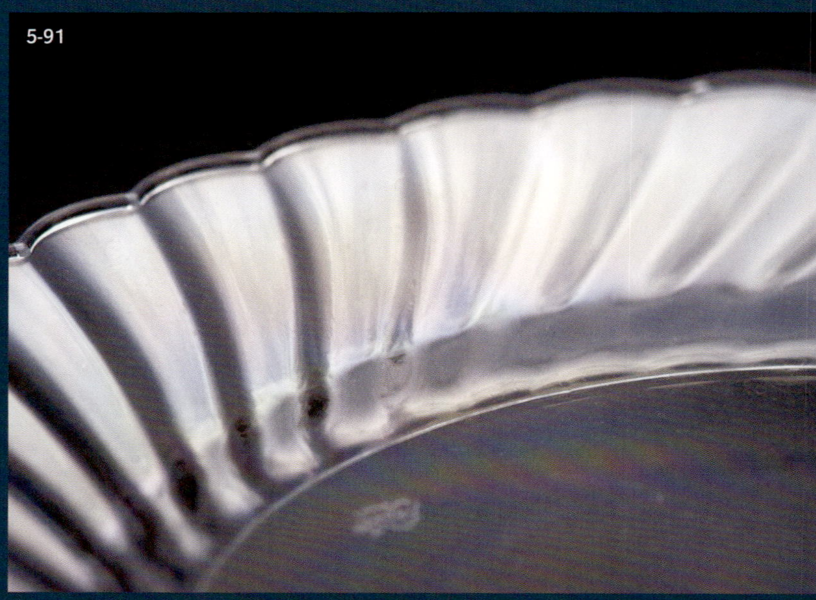

Image 5-91. Without circular polarizing filter.

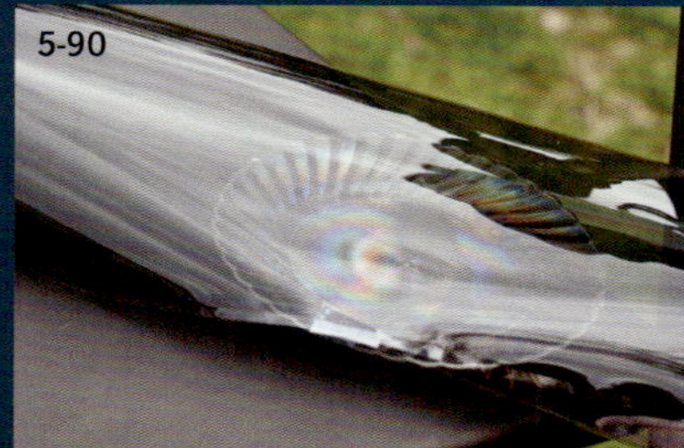

Image 5-90. When you wrap a plastic object in polarizing paper, you can almost see the effect of cross-polarization through the thin film, as shown here.

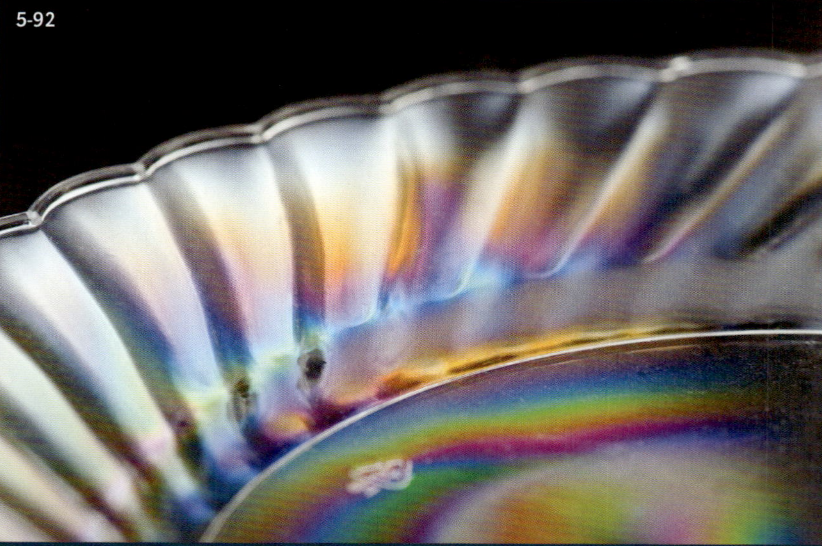

Image 5-92. With circular polarizing filter.

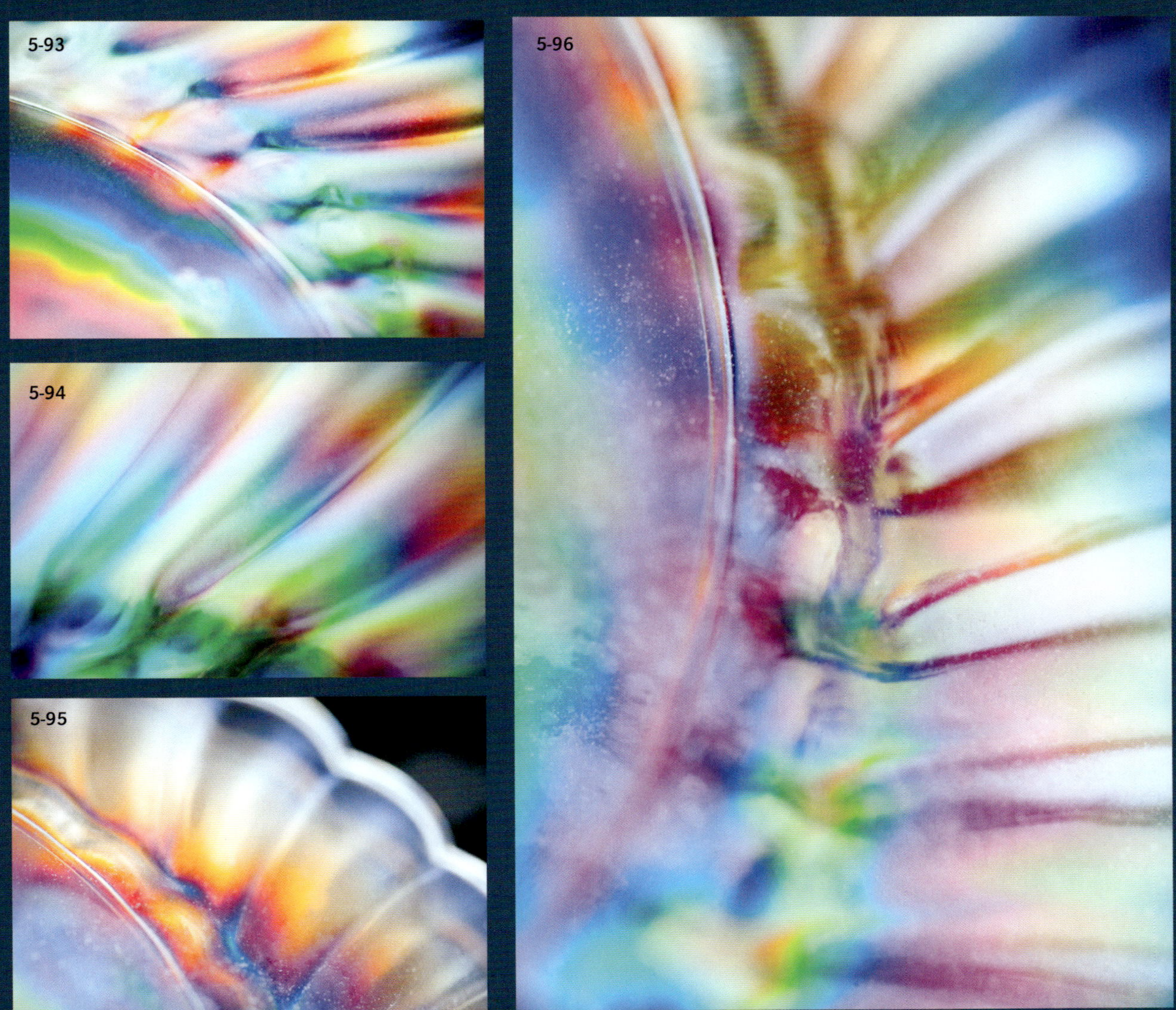

Image 5-93. Nikon Micro-Nikkor 200mm f/4 lens. Circular polarizing filter. Exposure: f/5 at 1/15 second. **Image 5-94.** Nikon Micro-Nikkor 200mm f/4 lens. Circular polarizing filter. Exposure: f/5.3 at 1/15 second. **Image 5-95.** Nikon Micro-Nikkor 200mm f/4 lens. Circular polarizing filter. Exposure: f/11 at 1/2 second. **Image 5-96.** Nikon Micro-Nikkor 200mm f/4 lens. Circular polarizing filter. Exposure: f/11 at 1/2 second.

Sheets of polarizing material are available at prices ranging from $19 for a 5x8 ½-inch piece up to $132 for a 17x30-inch size from Edmund Industrial Optics (www.edmundoptics.com/onlinecatalog/displayproduct.cfm?productID=1912) or in 17x20-inch sheets for $44.50 from B&H Photo (www.bhphotovideo.com/c/product/45130-REG/Rosco_101073001720_Polarizing_7300_Filter_.html). If you do decide to purchase the B&H version, then be forewarned; it has a tendency to curl since it is shipped rolled in plastic tubing. You'll need to stretch the piece out and place paperweights or other heavy objects on the four corners for a couple of days to flatten it.

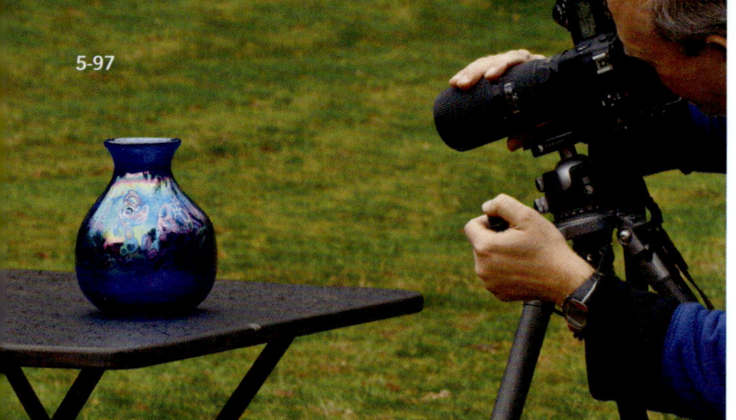

Iridescent Flower Vase

As you can likely tell by now, I'm drawn to all things iridescent not only because they make colorful macro subjects but because they appear to change colors depending on the angle at which they are viewed. I spent the majority of an afternoon making abstract images from an iridescent flower vase. (See **image 5-97**.) By changing my angle of view (aiming my 200mm macro lens parallel to whatever section of the curved surface I was trying to capture, which meant raising and lowering my tripod), I was able to create these three striking and unusual abstract images. (See **images 5-98** through **5-100**.)

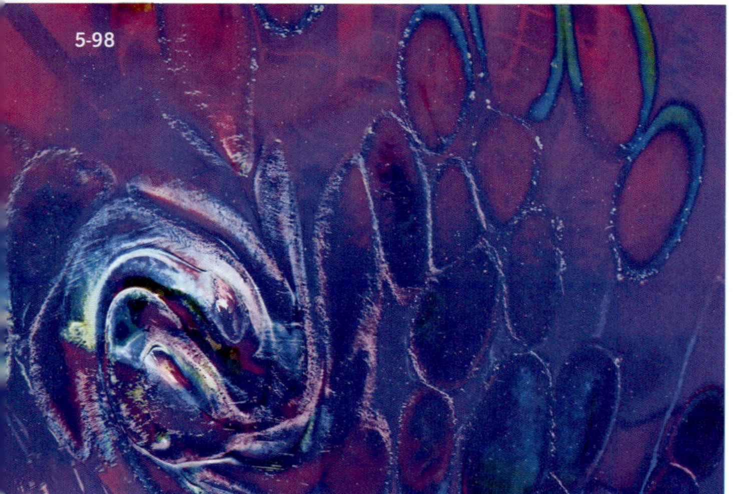

Each photo communicates a slightly different feeling and visual message.

In this case, I placed my focus on the surface of the glass (and not beyond or past the surface) because I wanted to capture the design on the surface of the vase. In addition, I experimented with various aperture settings—from wide-open to completely closed-down. The first two photos, images **5-98 and 5-99** were photographed at f/40, but the last (**image 5-100**) was taken at f/4. Each photo communicates a slightly different feeling and visual message. Bracket your aperture settings in 1-stop increments. Don't forget to use your depth-of-field preview button to help you previsualize the final result. If you're shooting under bright, sunny conditions outdoors, you might want to use a diffuser and/or a polarizer filter to eliminate any unwanted reflections.

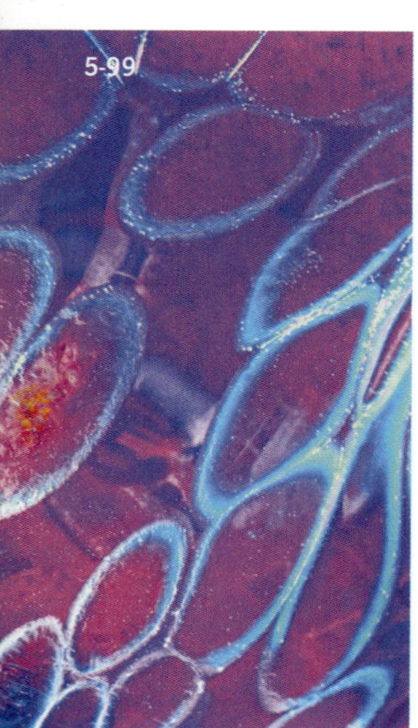

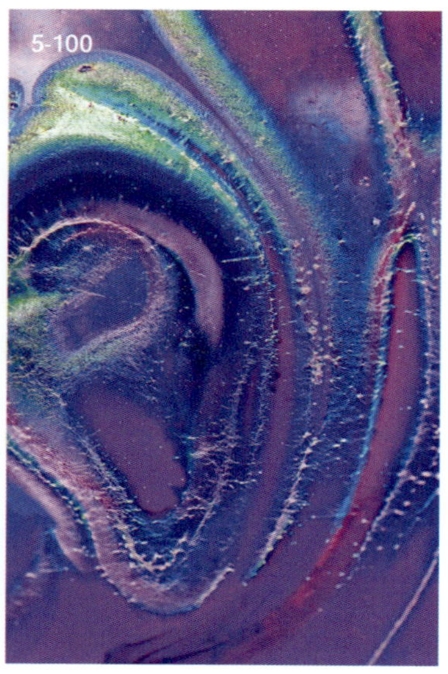

Image 5-97. Here's the setup for photographing an iridescent flower vase. No matter what object you're shooting close up, it's important to remember to keep your camera's back as close to parallel as possible to the surface of your subject to maximize depth of field and sharpness. Here, I focused on the top portion of the vase so the end of my 200mm macro lens was parallel to that part of the vase. **Image 5-98.** Nikon Micro-Nikkor 200mm f/4 lens. Exposure: f/40 at 2 seconds. **Image 5-99.** Nikon Micro-Nikkor 200mm f/4 lens. Exposure: f/40 at 5 seconds. **Image 5-100.** Nikon Micro-Nikkor 200mm f/4 lens. Exposure: f/4 at 1/8 second.

Magic's Water Bowl

My adorable Maltese, Magic, is spoiled rotten! He eats and drinks from cut-glass "crystal." One day, when standing at my kitchen sink washing Magic's bowl, I was struck by the unusual pattern and design on the bowl and decided to photograph his bowl while placing a variety of different colorful backgrounds under the glass bowl—everything from colored and holographic papers to stained glass and colored ribbons. (See **image 5-101**.)

One of my favorite images was made when placing a colored tinsel garland (purchased at a local party supply store) under the bowl, as illustrated in **images 5-102** and **5-103**. The first (**image 5-104**) was photographed at a smaller aperture (f/22), while the second (**image 5-105**) was photographed at f/8.

Image 5-101. Here's my setup for photographing a crystal-cut bowl. Notice that the back of my camera was parallel to the bottom surface of the bowl because that's the area I chose in my composition. **Image 5-102.** You can experiment with various backgrounds while shooting through glass. Here, I placed a colored tinsel garland under the crystal bowl, which has turned upside-down. **Image 5-103.** Detail of the colored tinsel garland under the crystal bowl, which has been turned upside-down. **Image 5-104.** Nikon Micro-Nikkor 200mm f/4 lens. Exposure: f/22 at 1/13 second. **Image 5-105.** Nikon Micro-Nikkor 200mm f/4 lens. Exposure: f/8 at 1/80 second.

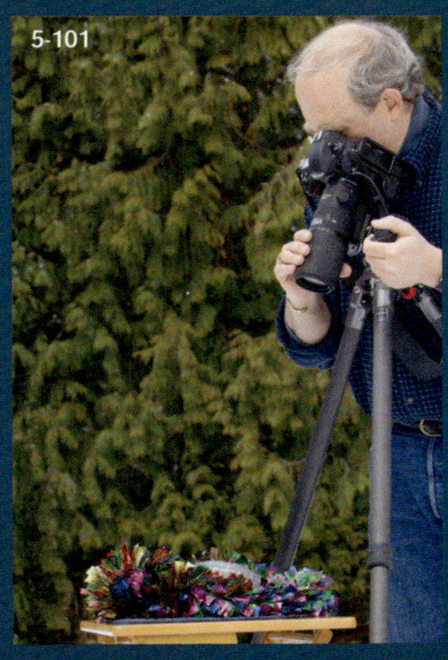

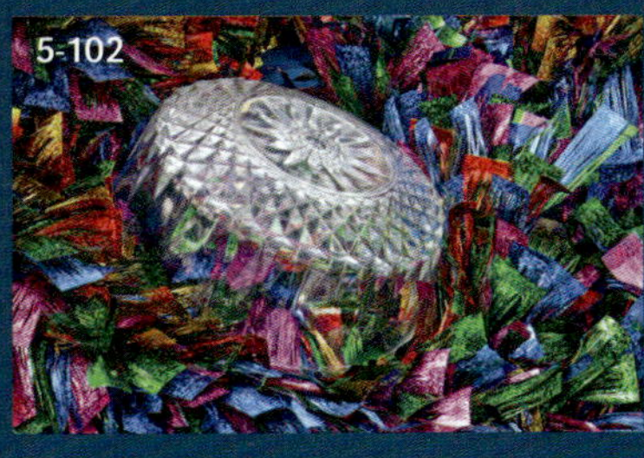

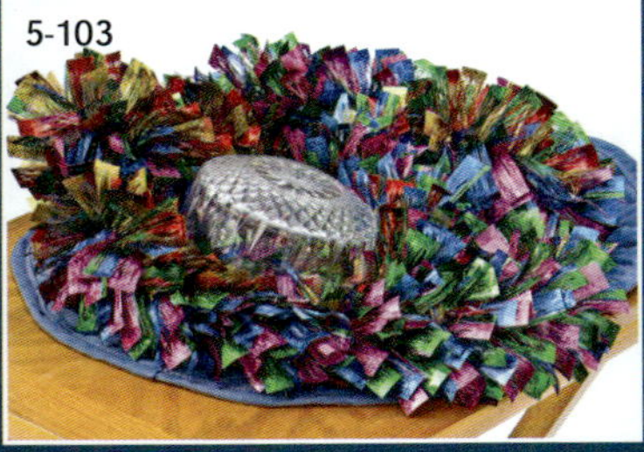

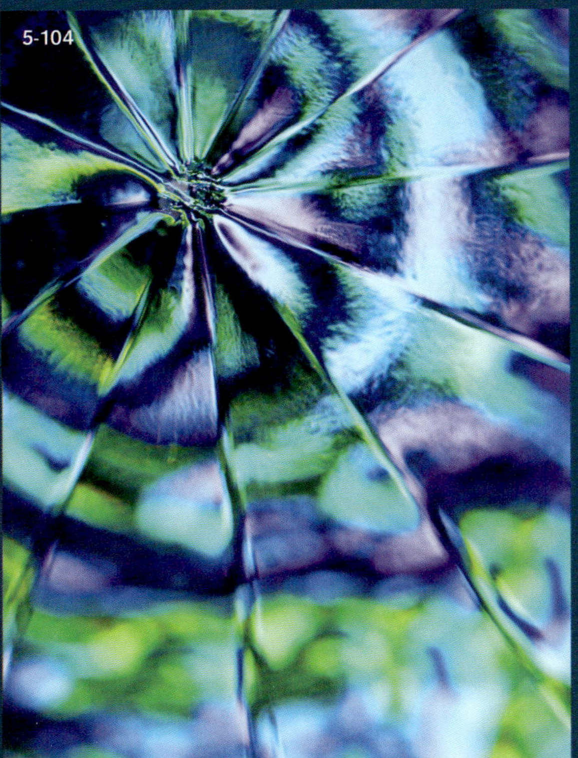

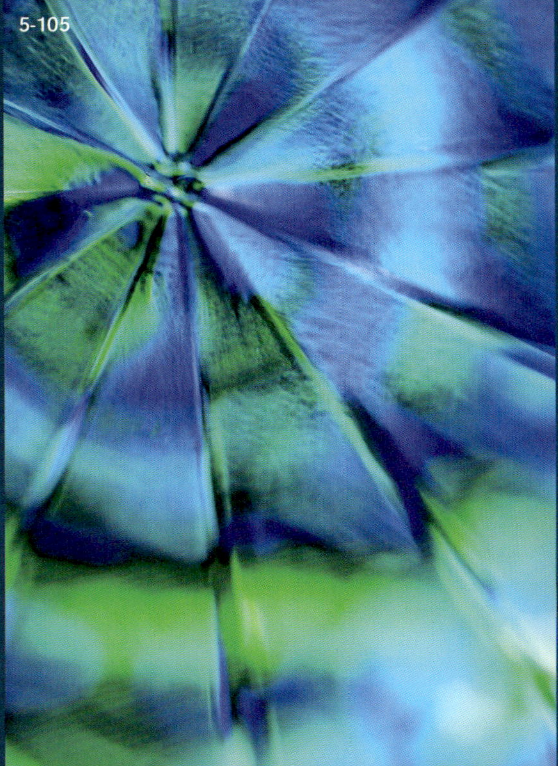

Architectural Glass Block

Another mesmerizing object you can shoot through is an architectural glass block, available at The Home Depot, Lowe's, or a craft supply store such as Michael's. In this setup, I placed a pink dahlia and purple poppy directly behind the glass block and used a large sheet of light-green paper as a background to complement the pink and purple flowers. The part of the glass showing the most distortion was near the center, so I elevated the flowers on a book and covered the book with blue paper to mix hues and avoid having part of the book reflecting in the glass. (See **image 5-106**.) Notice in **image 5-107** that I attached a Plamp with a Plamp extension to the edge of the table to help position the flowers.

To shoot the flowers behind the glass, you'll want to use the same technique as when photographing flowers behind textured glass: focus your lens on the surface of the glass, use your depth-of-field preview button to bracket the depth of field, and experiment with different backgrounds and compositions. **Images 5-108** through **5-110** were each made at different aperture settings. The final result depends upon just how much detail you want sharply focused in the image. **Image 5-111** shows a slightly different composition with the pink daisy filling the frame.

To take this image one step further, I sprayed the glass block with Crystal Frost (available at most craft supply stores) as shown in **image 5-112** and photographed the pink daisy through the frosty glass. The result appears even more abstract. (See **image 5-113**.)

Image 5-106. Most of the distortion in this architectural glass block occurred near the center, so I elevated the flowers on a book and covered the book with blue paper to mix hues and avoid having part of the book reflecting in the glass. **Image 5-107.** To help position the flowers behind the architectural glass block, I used a Plamp with a Plamp extension, clamping one end to the flowers and the other end to the table. Plamps can be extremely useful for tabletop macro photography.

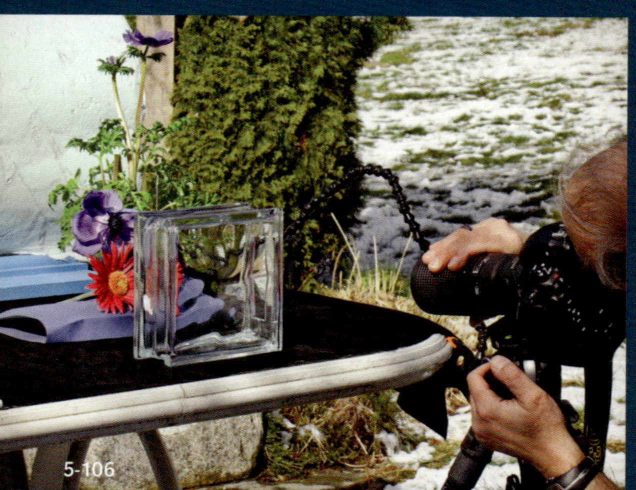

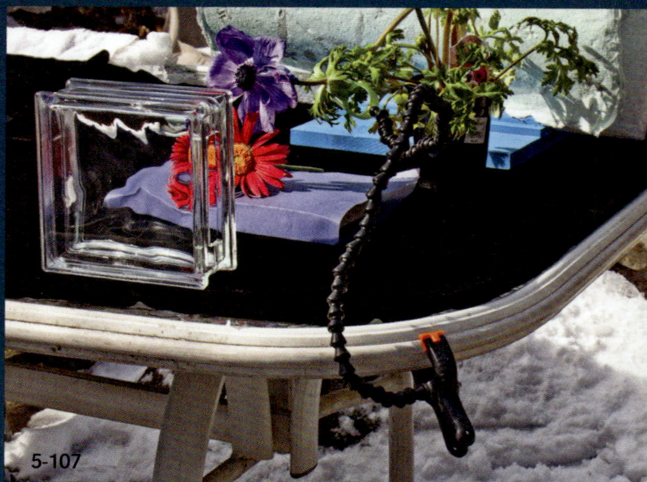

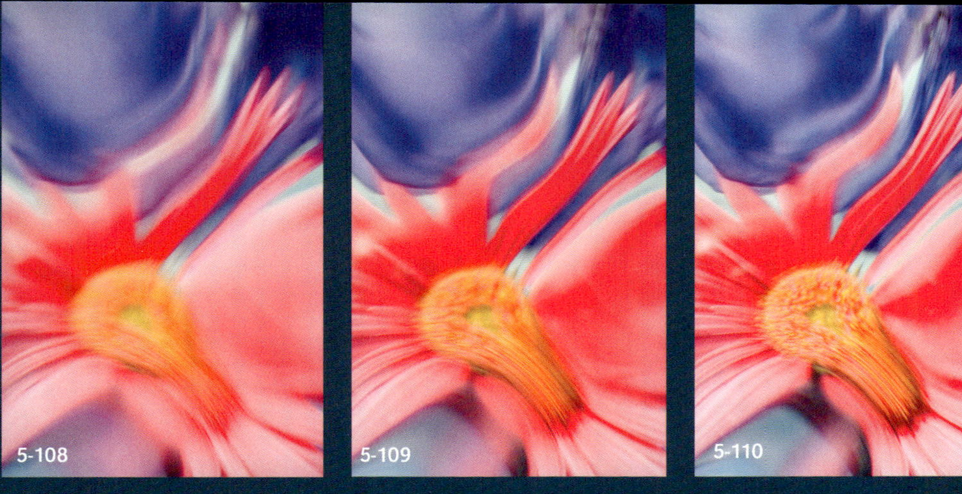

Image 5-108. Nikon Micro-Nikkor 200mm f/4 lens. Exposure: f/5.6 at 1/60 second. **Image 5-109.** Nikon Micro-Nikkor 200mm f/4 lens. Exposure: f/11 at 1/40 second. **Image 5-110.** Nikon Micro-Nikkor 200mm f/4 lens. Exposure: f/22 at 1/10 second. **Image 5-111.** Nikon Micro-Nikkor 200mm f/4 lens. Exposure: f/5 at 1/250 second.

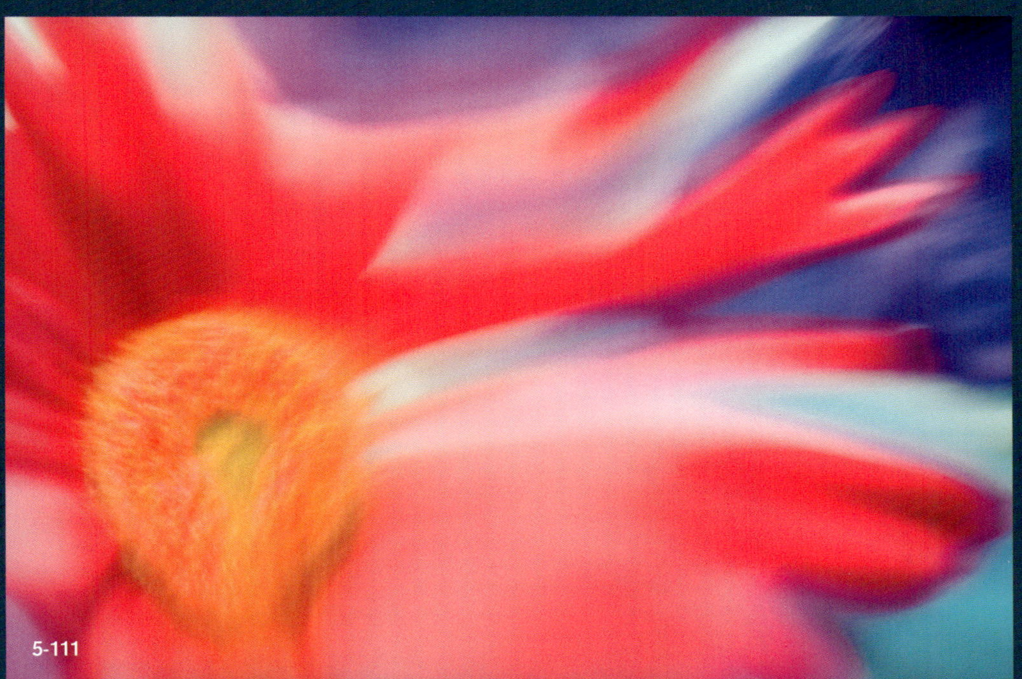

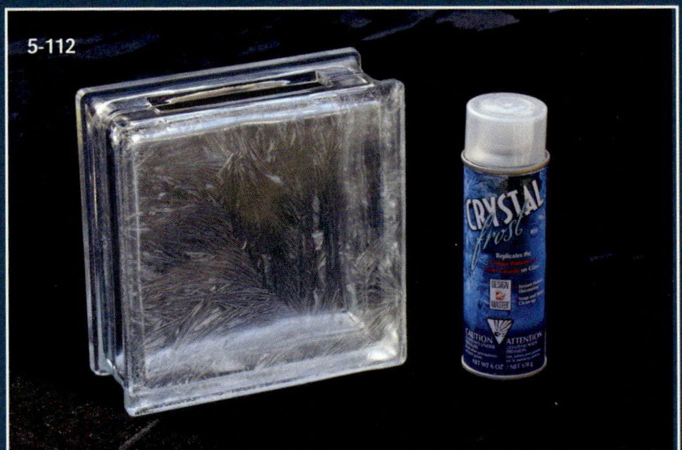

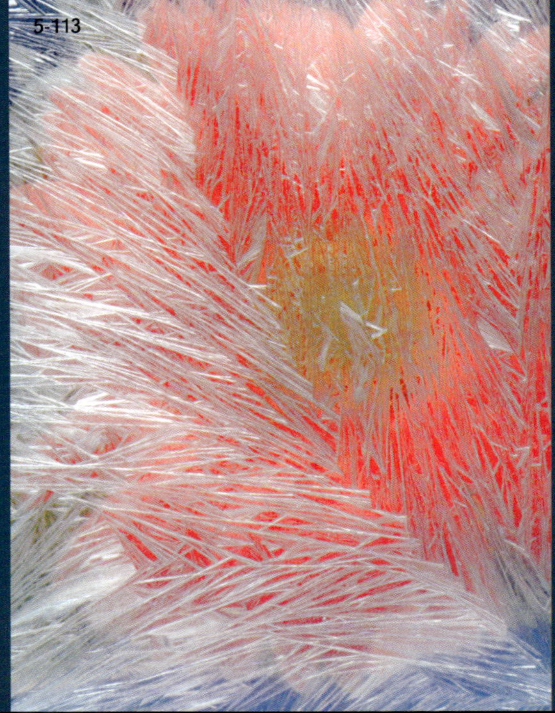

Image 5-112. To create the illusion that the pink daisy was behind a frosty window, I sprayed the architectural glass with Crystal Frost, which is available at most craft supply stores. **Image 5-113.** Nikon Micro-Nikkor 200mm f/4 lens. Exposure: f/11 at 1/8 second.

Bubble-Bottomed Drinking Glass

In this setup, I placed a bubble-bottomed drinking glass on its side, bracing it with one stone on either side and then placed a pink gerbera daisy inside the glass, resting it on the lip. (See **images 5-114** and **5-115**.) For background color, I used a green bubble mailer and held it far enough away that it would fall out of focus. (You wouldn't have to use a bubble mailer necessarily. I just wanted something green, since red and green are complementary colors.) Large flowers with symmetry, such as daisies or sunflowers, work best when trying this technique.

As has been the case when shooting other glass objects and stained/textured glass, the final image will vary, depending upon where you place your focus and what aperture setting you use. Again, use your depth-of-field preview button to previsualize the final look.

To start, I suggest that you first focus your macro lens on the bubbles at the end of the glass and use the widest possible aperture. Then stop the lens aperture down in 1-stop increments and compare each of the images on your computer monitor once you have downloaded them from the camera. In my case, **image 5-116**, which was photographed at f/22, was the most visually appealing.

To prevent bright reflections off the glass from appearing in your viewfinder, use a black cloth, as illustrated in **image 5-117**. Be sure to cover the entire glass as well as your camera,

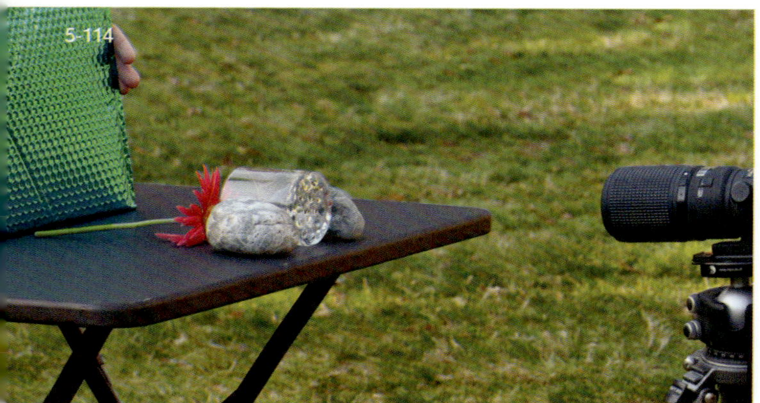

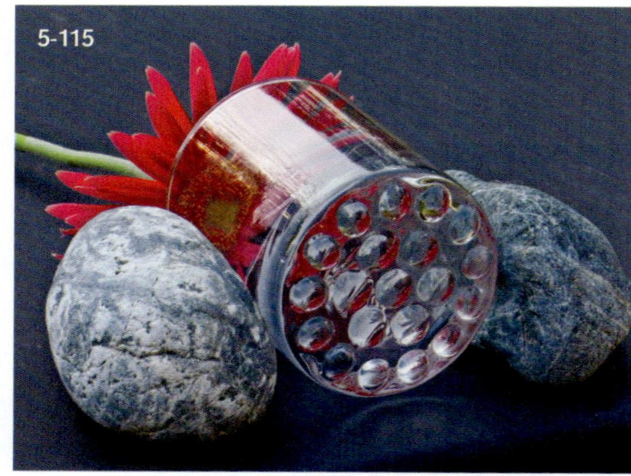

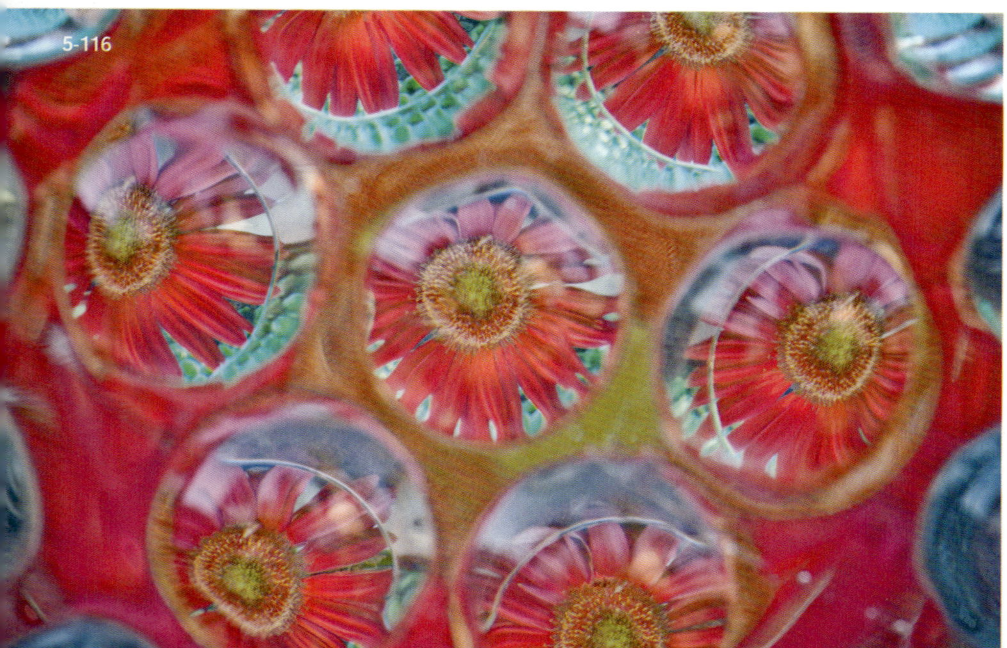

Image **5-114.** Here's my setup for the bubble-bottomed drinking glass. I filled the frame with nothing but the bubbles. To maximize sharpness and depth of field, I stopped my lens down to f/22 and was certain to keep the back of my camera parallel to the bottom surface of the drinking glass. Image **5-115.** To keep the drinking glass from rolling, I placed a stone on either side. When composing, I was careful to make sure the stones did not appear in the final image. **Image 5-116.** Nikon Micro-Nikkor 200mm f/4 lens. Exposure: f/22 at 1 second.

or you'll still get bright areas. By covering the entire area, you get much more pleasing results with more deeply saturated colors. Using this setup, **images 5-118** and **5-119** show how you'll get completely different results when choosing two different f-stops.

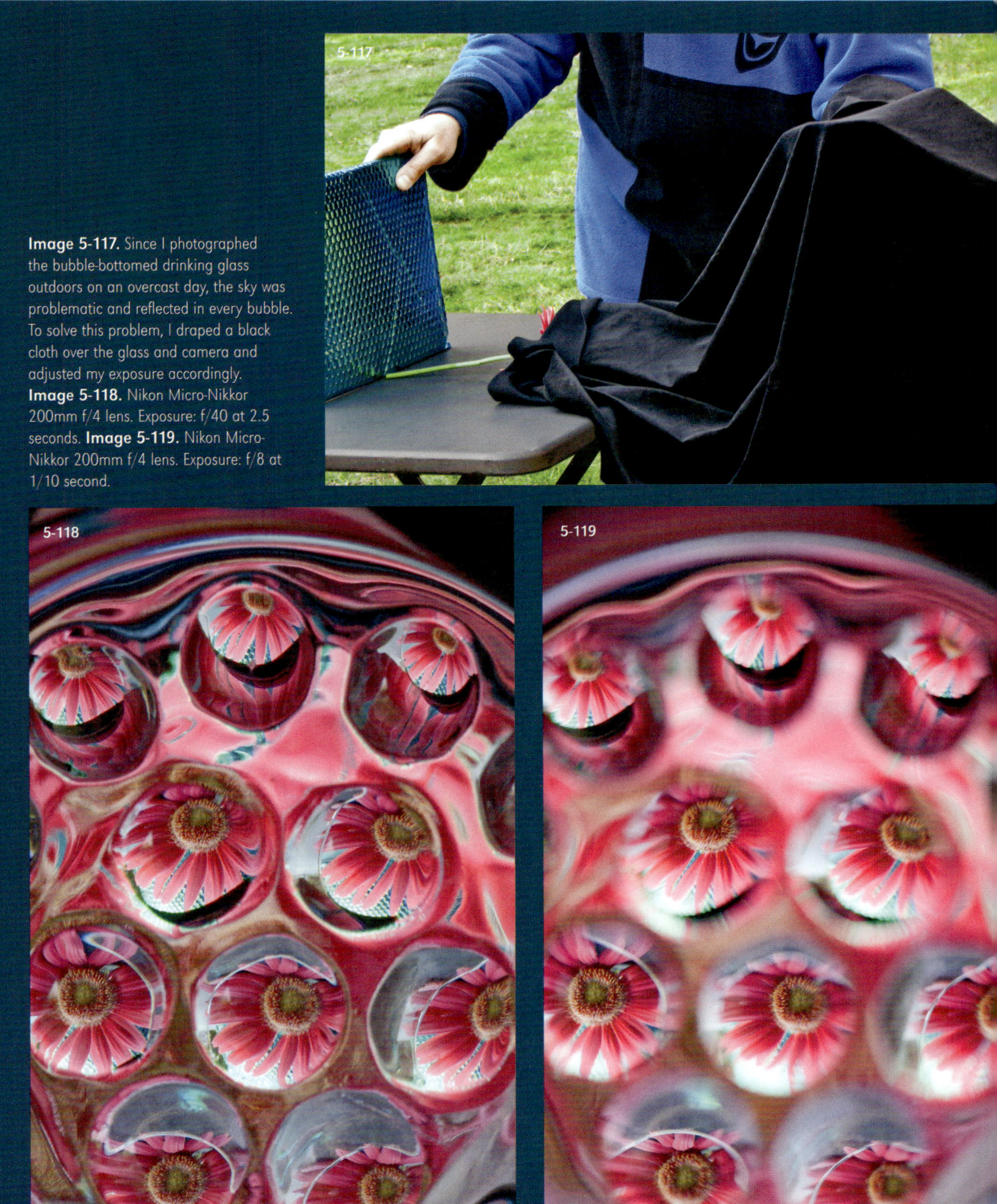

Image 5-117. Since I photographed the bubble-bottomed drinking glass outdoors on an overcast day, the sky was problematic and reflected in every bubble. To solve this problem, I draped a black cloth over the glass and camera and adjusted my exposure accordingly. **Image 5-118.** Nikon Micro-Nikkor 200mm f/4 lens. Exposure: f/40 at 2.5 seconds. **Image 5-119.** Nikon Micro-Nikkor 200mm f/4 lens. Exposure: f/8 at 1/10 second.

Copper Pot

Everyday household items often make for ideal close-up photography subjects. One day while waiting for a pot of soup to come to a boil, I noticed several interesting reflections off the sides and lid. I could hardly wait for the soup to be fully cooked. Once the liquid concoction was done, I waited for it to cool, transferred it into another container, immediately cleaned the pot (which I had purchased at Williams-Sonoma), and headed outside on my patio to play.

For me, what made this pot especially visually exciting was the fact that it was made of hammered copper. I braced the pot on its side using a small stick and pebble and laid some colorful potted flowers around it. (See **images 5-120** through **5-122**.) When trying this yourself, be sure to position the flowers high enough so their reflection will be revealed in the greatest amount of surface area. Notice here in this setup that I placed the red poppy above the purple and blue morning glories. You could use bricks or other support mechanisms to elevate the flowerpots lying on their sides, but keep in mind that everything will be reflected in the pot.

This type of setup works best in bright sunlight, but bright overcast lighting works well also. Keep in mind, you'll need to minimize reflections from the sky above if you're shooting outdoors.

The camera technique for this setup is similar to when you're shooting glass. The two factors that contribute most to the success of your final image are where you place your focus and how much depth of field you want. Because there are so many possible combinations of these two

Image 5-120. Here's my setup for photographing abstract flower reflections in the outside surface of a hammered copper pot. You could use a bouquet of fresh or silk flowers, but here I used some potted flowers and laid them on their side. **Image 5-121.** To keep the copper pot from moving on the table, I used a small stick and pebble. **Image 5-122.** Be sure to position the flowers high enough off the table so their reflection will be revealed in the greatest amount of surface area, as shown here.

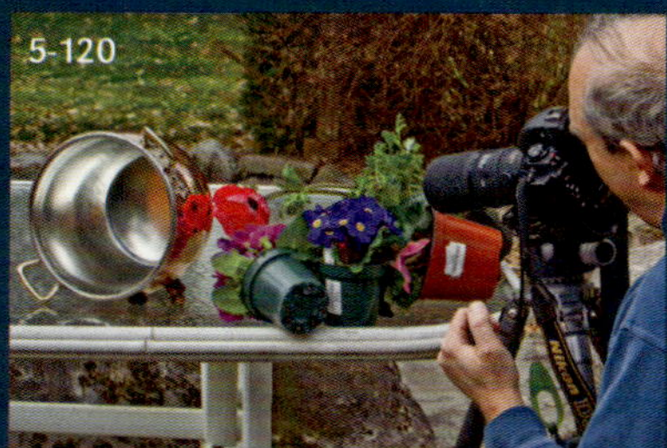
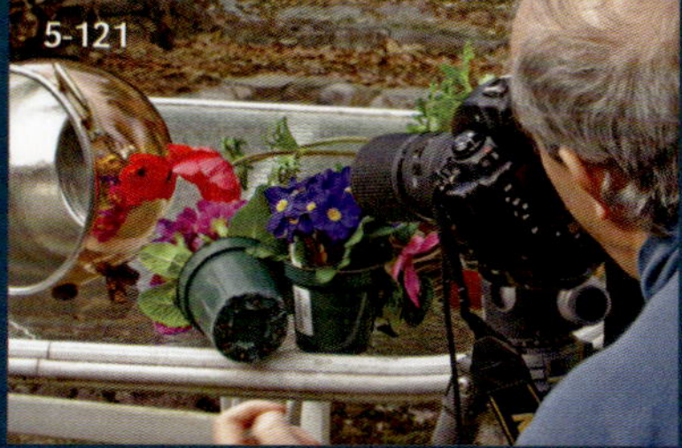
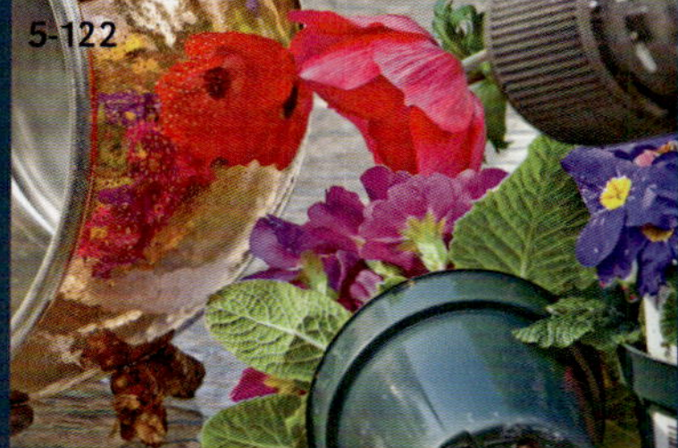

Image 5-123. Nikon Micro-Nikkor 200mm f/4 lens. Exposure: f/8 at 1/500 second. **Image 5-124.** Nikon Micro-Nikkor 200mm f/4 lens. Exposure: f/25 at 1/10 second.

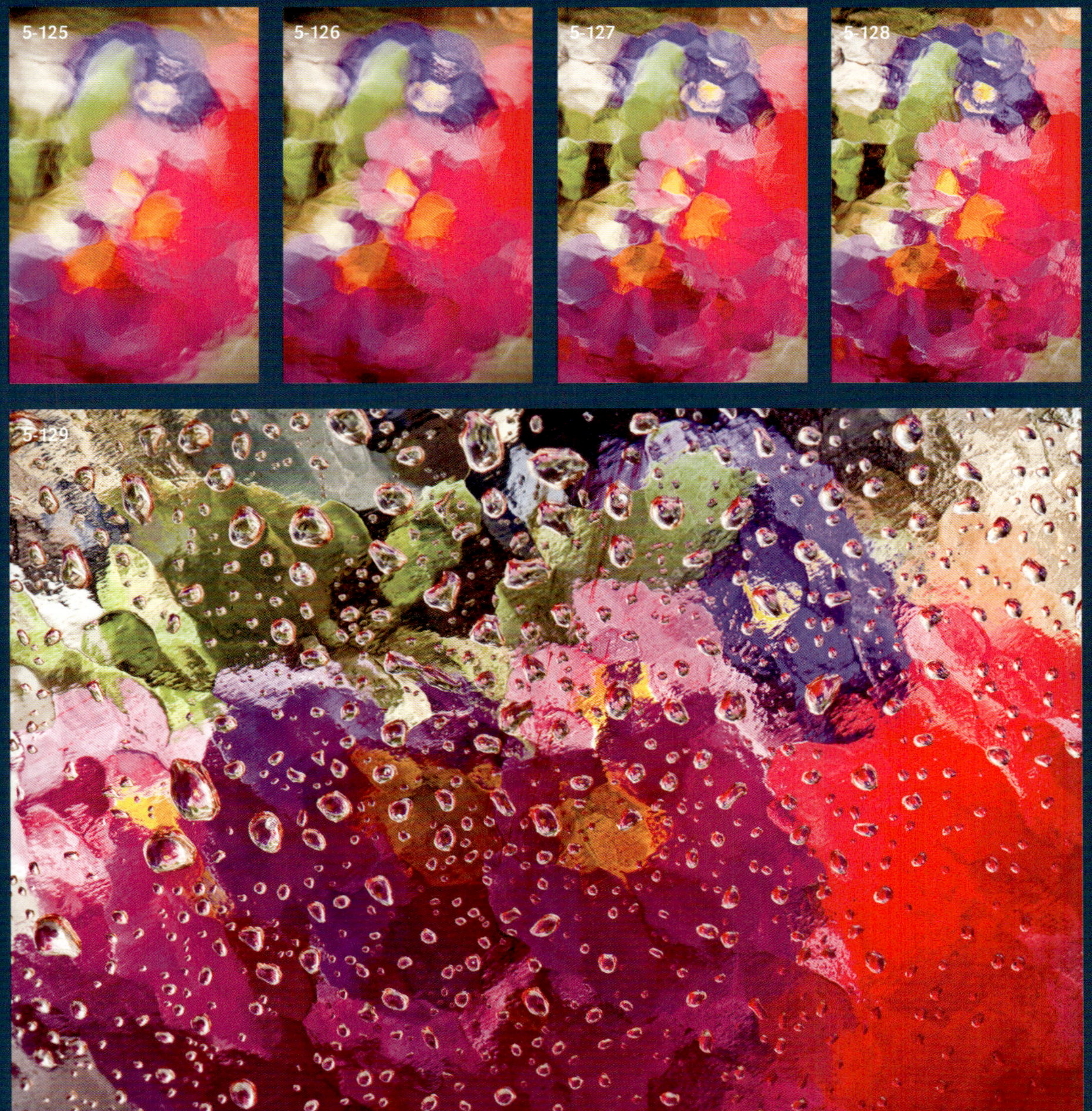

Image **5-125.** Nikon Micro-Nikkor 200mm f/4 lens. Exposure: f/5.6 at 1/100 second. Image **5-126.** Nikon Micro-Nikkor 200mm f/4 lens. Exposure: f/8 at 1/60 second. Image **5-127.** Nikon Micro-Nikkor 200mm f/4 lens. Exposure: f/16 at 1/15 second. Image **5-128.** Nikon Micro-Nikkor 200mm f/4 lens. Exposure: f/32 at 1/4 second. Image **5-129.** Copper pot reflection with sprayed water droplets. Nikon Micro-Nikkor 200mm f/4 lens. Exposure: f/40 at 1/3 second.

factors, it's a good idea to bracket both focus and depth of field. The more shallow the depth of field, the softer the overall image will be. The greater the depth of field, the sharper and crisper everything appears. One tip is to change the focus of your lens while you're stopped down using the depth-of-field preview button. (See **images 5-123** through **5-129**.)

Several months later, while in France visiting a small church, I noticed the stained-glass windows reflecting in a baptismal bowl that was also made of hammered copper. My adrenaline started flowing again, and I immediately set up my tripod. The abstract patterns in this bowl were truly amazing. (See **images 5-130** through **5-132**.) Depending on the angle of view, whether I raised or lowered the tripod (even in small increments), my composition changed dramatically. Again, I bracketed where I placed my focus as well as aperture settings to create different effects.

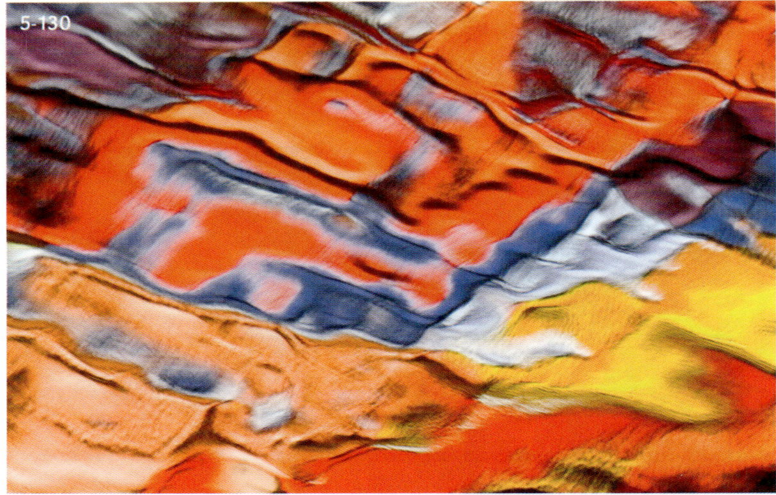

Image 5-130. Nikon Micro-Nikkor 200mm f/4 lens. Exposure: f/22 at 1/2 second.

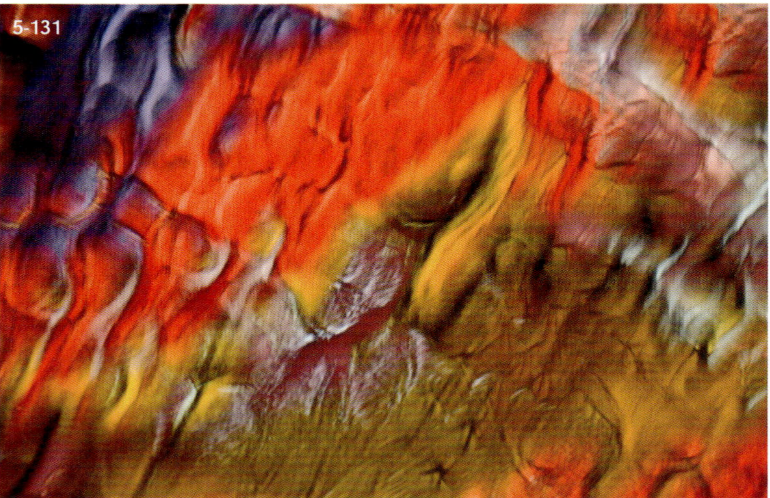

Image 5-131. Nikon Micro-Nikkor 200mm f/4 lens. Exposure: f/16 at 1/50 second.

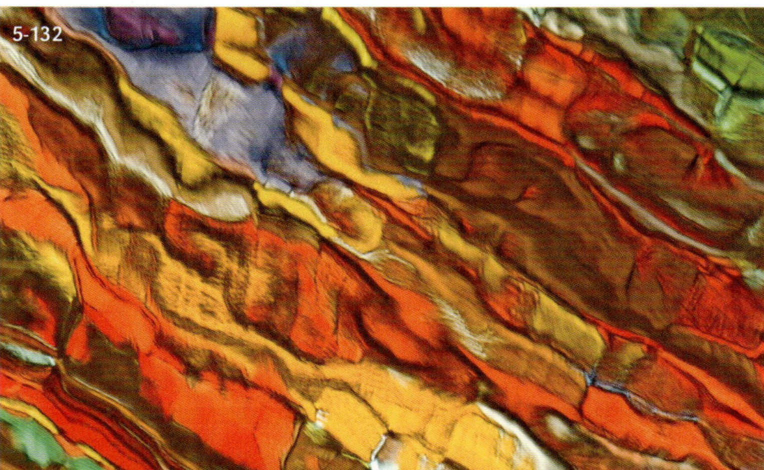

Image 5-132. Nikon Micro-Nikkor 200mm f/4 lens. Exposure: f/36 at 1.3 seconds.

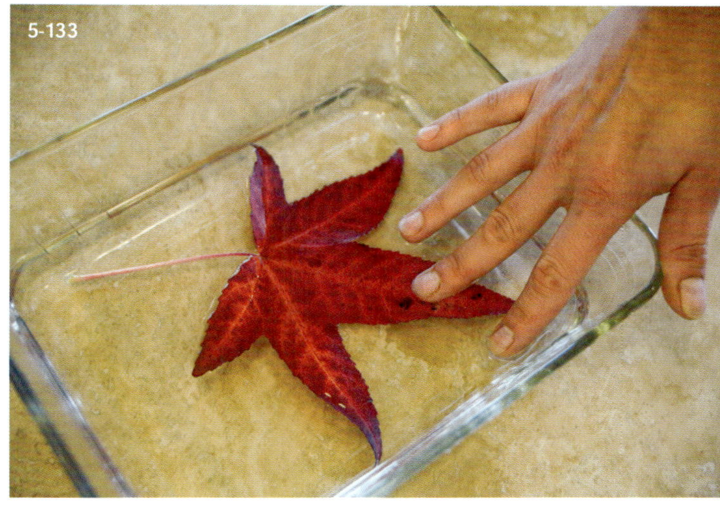

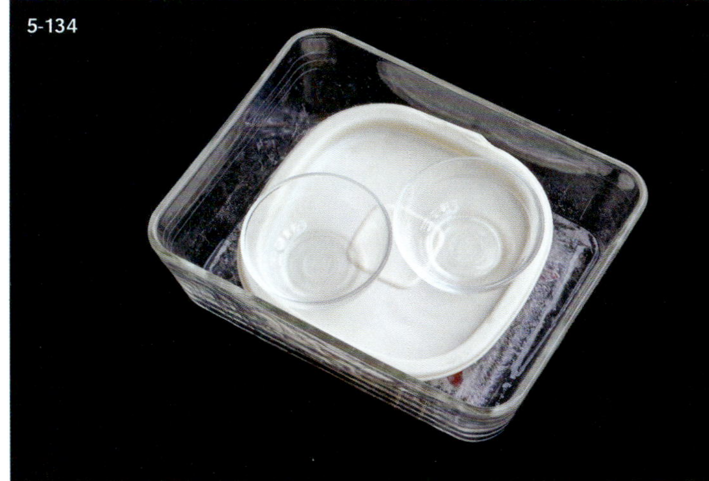

Image 5-133. First, I placed a leaf in a Pyrex baking dish and poured about 1/4 inch of water on top. Be sure to use only just enough water to cover the surface of the object you're trying to freeze. If there's too much water, your subject will float to the top and the ice will be too thick to shoot through. **Image 5-134.** After putting the Pyrex dish in the freezer, I placed a slightly smaller-sized Tupperware plastic lid on top, weighted down the glass with custard cups, to stabilize the leaf and keep it near the bottom of the pan during the freezing process.

Frozen Maple Leaf

This technique involves freezing a leaf (or flower, or any other semi-transparent object) in a shallow glass baking pan and then photographing the leaf using a macro lens. When placing the leaf in the baking pan, you need enough water to barely cover the surface— about ¼ inch. If there's too much water, then the leaf will float to the top and the ice becomes too thick to shoot through. See **image 5-133**.

After placing the pan on a level surface in the freezer, you can place something like a slightly smaller-sized Tupperware plastic lid on top of the surface of the water, weighted down with something like glass custard cups to help stabilize the leaf and keep it near the bottom of the pan. (See **image 5-134**.) After a few hours when the ice becomes semi-solid, remove the glass custard cups and lid and leave in the freezer to further solidify. Once the leaf is frozen solid, remove it from the freezer.

Tip: If you want to achieve a more "cracked" look, then freeze the leaf for an hour or so, or until the surface has a good layer of ice over it. Then break the surface of the ice a little and re-freeze. This will give your ice a nice cracked texture.

There are a couple of ways you could photograph the leaf indoors: propping the pan up against a windowpane, or on a light table. Regardless of which method you choose, keep in mind the leaf looks best in strong backlight. In my case, I chose to take advantage of late-afternoon sunlight and shoot the maple leaf outdoors. As the ice began to melt, varying degrees of opacity appeared through my viewfinder, which added to the excitement.

As the ice began to melt, varying degrees of opacity appeared . . .

Notice in this illustration (**image 5-135**) that I placed the baking pan at a 45-degree angle

Image 5-135. By propping the baking pan up with a clear architectural block, I was able to catch sunlight shining through from behind the red maple leaf. Strong backlighting is particularly effective when shooting objects frozen in ice. In addition, I used my hand to avoid lens flare and was sure to keep the back of my camera as parallel as possible to the flat surface of the Pyrex dish as possible for maximum sharpness. **Image 5-136.** Nikon Micro-Nikkor 200mm f/4 lens. Exposure: f/13 at 1/60 second. **Image 5-137.** Nikon Micro-Nikkor 200mm f/4 lens. Exposure: f/40 at 1/13 second.

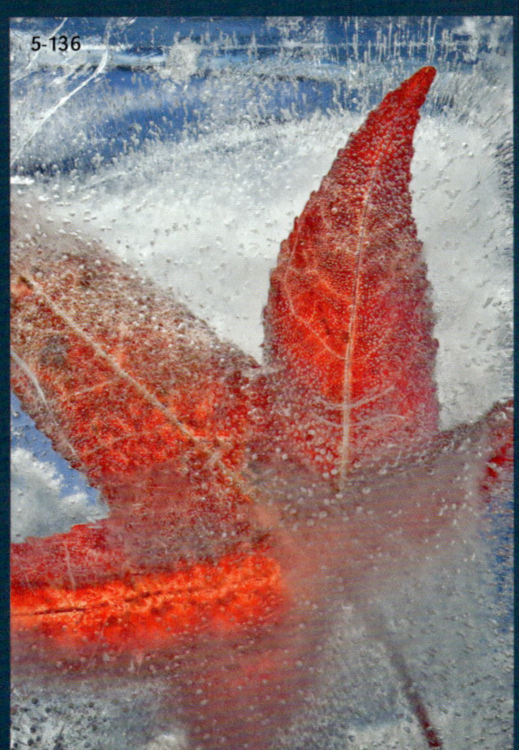

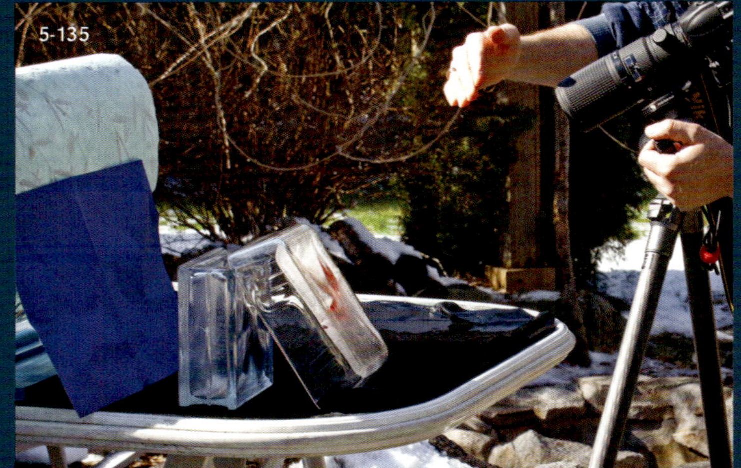

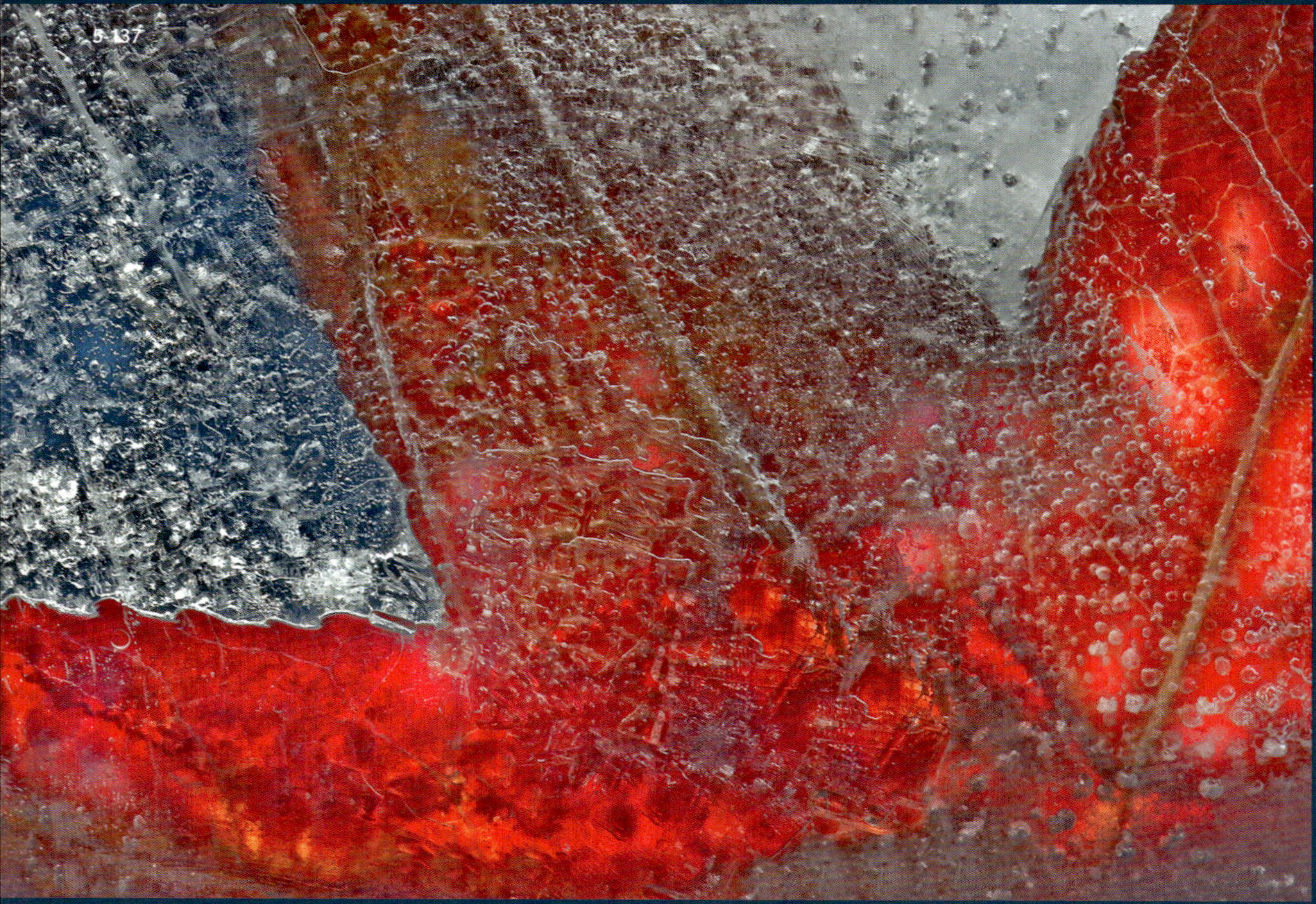

so the light would shine through from the backside. The background was created using a piece of blue construction paper. (I chose blue because it would complement the red leaf and simulate a blue sky.) It's important to remember to keep the camera back parallel to the bottom of the baking pan and stop the lens down to at least f/16 because of the thickness of the ice. (See **images 5-136** and **5-137**.)

If photographing this type of setup outdoors on a sunny day, you could also place a diffuser over the setup to create bright, overcast light.

My 42-inch diffuser worked well here because it covered the entire area and I could hold it in place during the exposure. (See **image 5-138**.) **Images 5-139** and **5-140** were made this way. Notice that the colors are a bit more saturated. Try various compositions, from medium range to super close. You'll need to work rather fast, since the ice is melting in the process!

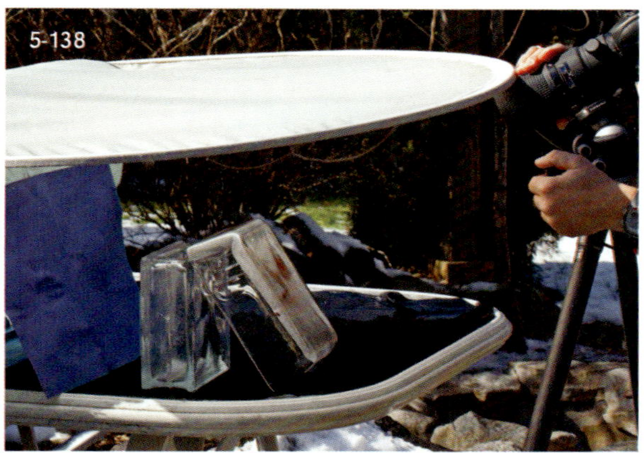

Image 5-138. Objects frozen in ice also work well when photographed under bright, overcast lighting conditions. Because I was working in my backyard on a sunny day, I was able to use my 42-inch diffuser to soften the light, as shown here. **Image 5-139.** Nikon Micro-Nikkor 200mm f/4 lens. Exposure: f/45 at 1/5 second. **Image 5-140.** Nikon Micro-Nikkor 200mm f/4 lens. Exposure: f/40 at 1/10 second.

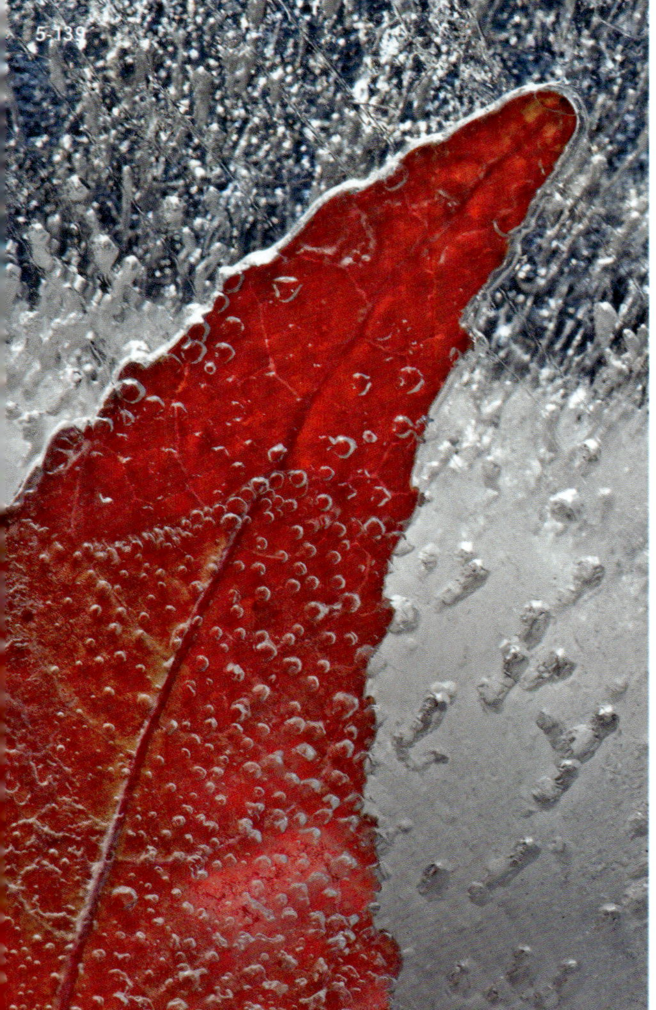

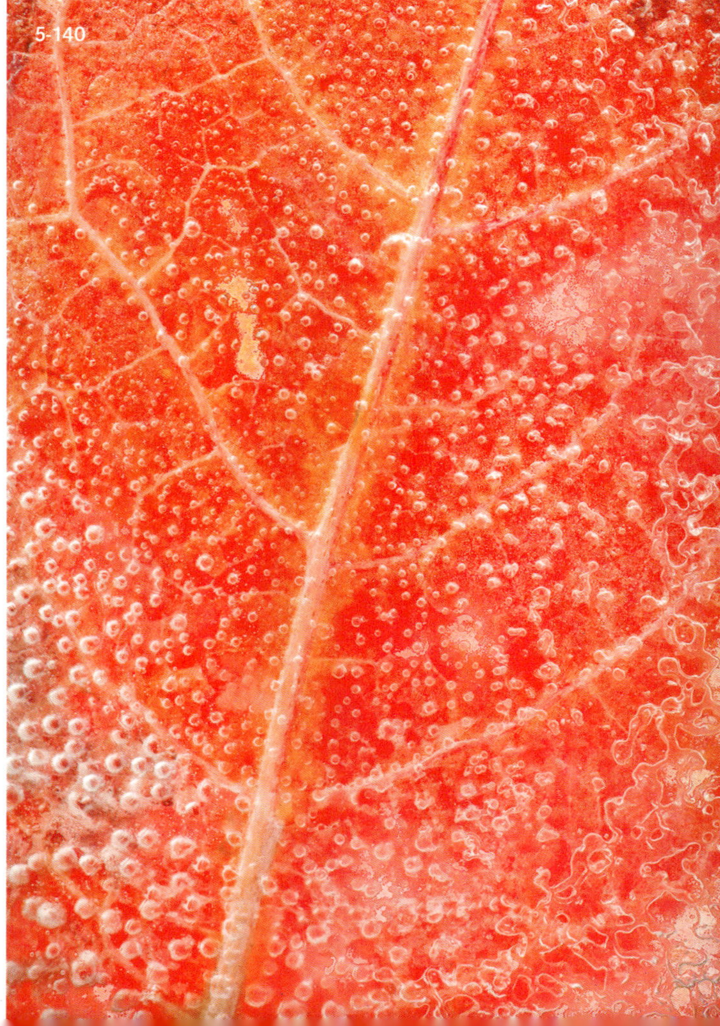

Garden Hose

This is a fun, creative close-up technique to try on a bright, sunny day in the early morning or late afternoon. You'll need an assistant (unless you want to put the camera on automatic timer and run back and forth—surely getting wet in the process), a small gold reflector, an ordinary garden hose with a spray-nozzle attachment (I recommend the "shower" nozzle setting), and lots of patience!

Position a flower (or group of flowers) on a deck railing or other stationary object you don't mind getting wet such that the flower is in front of a dark background in the shade, but the flower itself is backlit. Have your assistant aim the hose at a 45 to 75-degree angle just off to the side and behind the flower. (See **image 5-141**.) Because you're shooting at a low angle to the sun, you'll need to prevent lens flare by holding a gold reflector just above the lens and

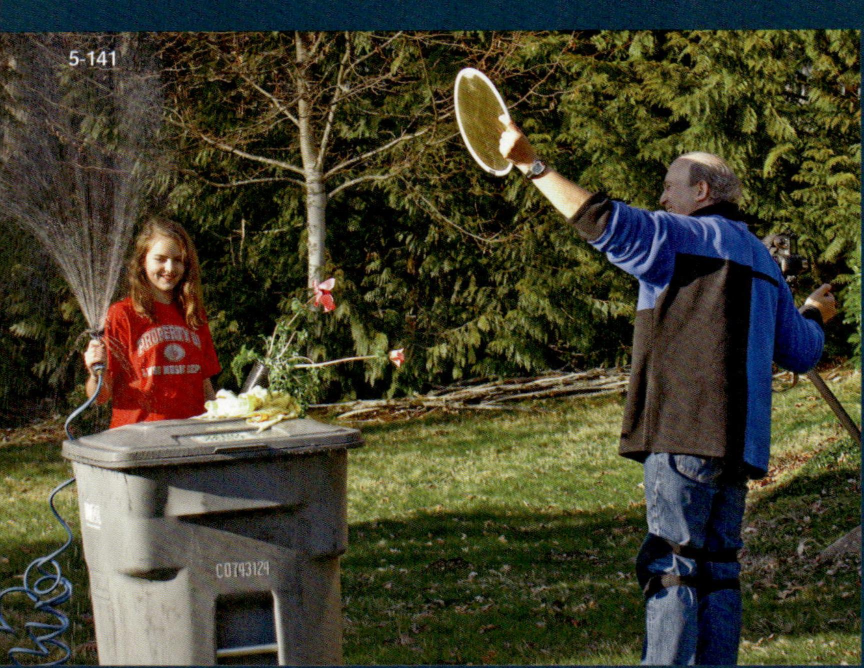

Image 5-141. Here's my setup for photographing a backlit flower with "rainfall" from behind. The key to success is positioning your backlit subject in front of a background in deep shade. Because the flower was backlit, I used my 12-inch gold reflector to bounce light into the flower and fill in the shadows. **Image 5-142.** Nikon Micro-Nikkor 200mm f/4 lens. Exposure: f/4.2 at 1/2000 second. **Image 5-143.** Nikon Micro-Nikkor 200mm f/4 lens. Exposure: f/8 at 1/1250 second. **Image 5-144.** Nikon Micro-Nikkor 200mm f/4 lens. Exposure: f/8 at 1/800 second.

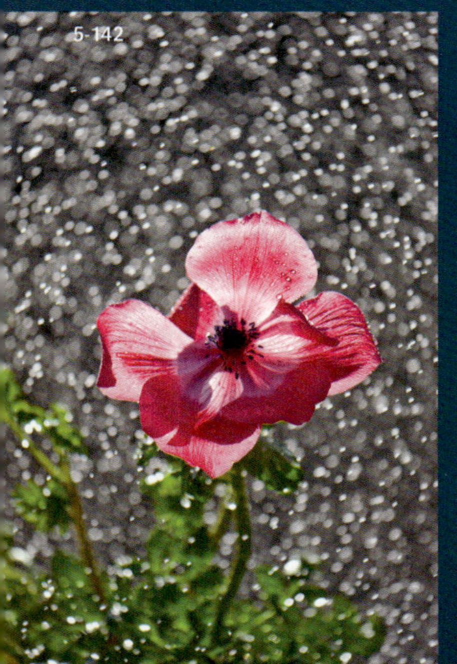

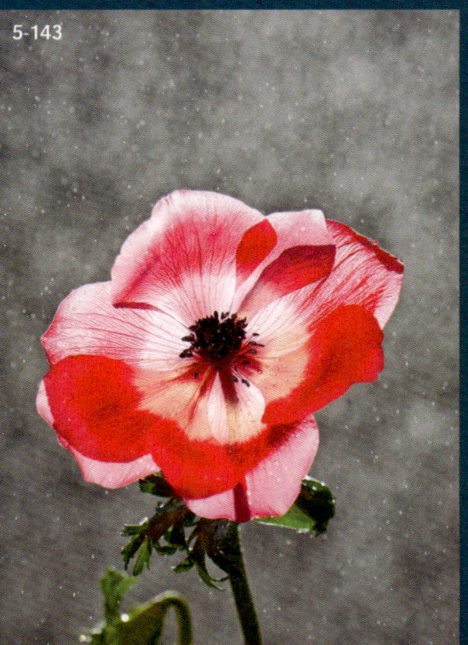

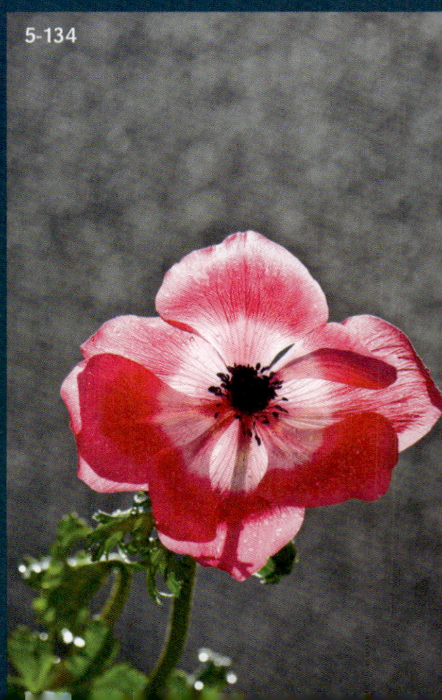

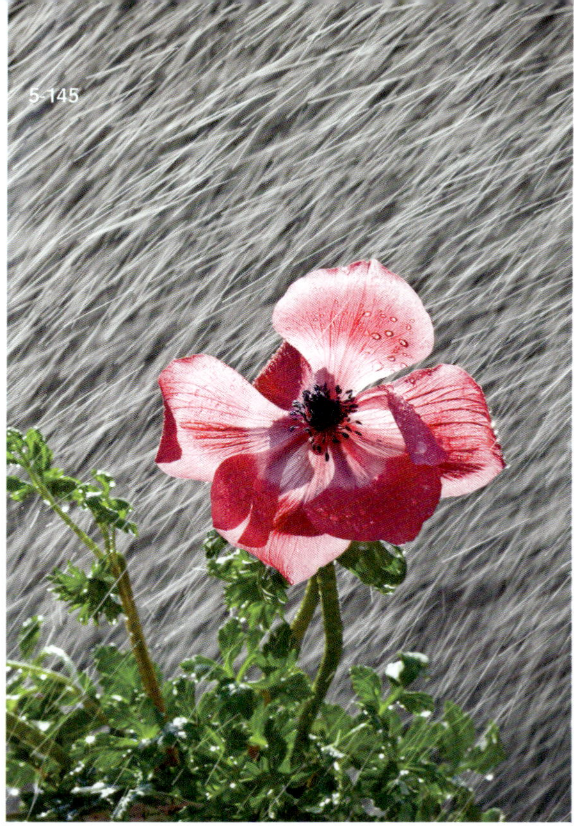

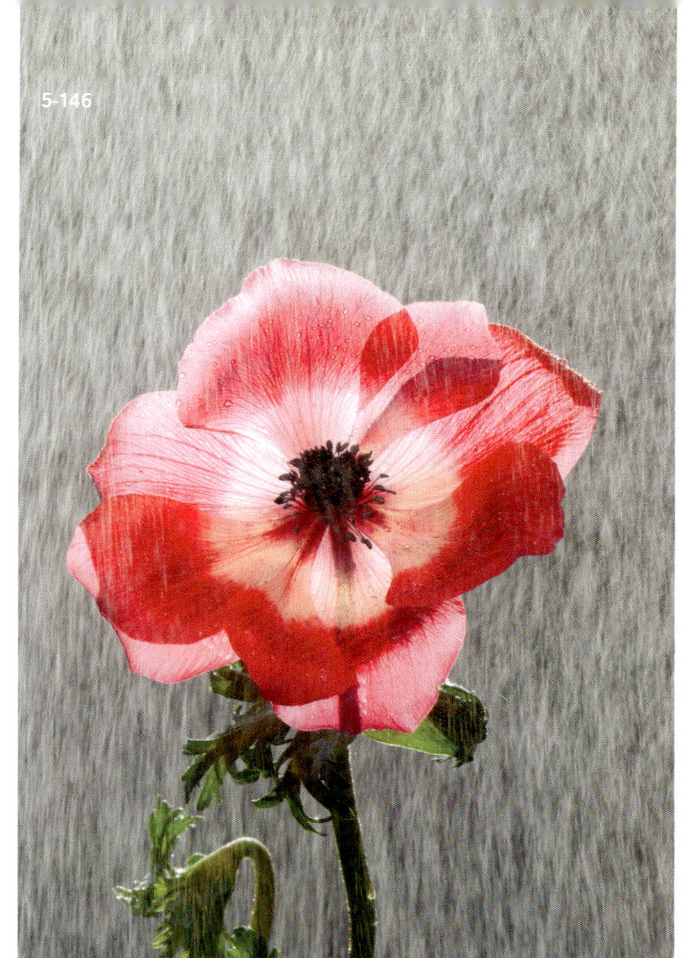

Image 5-145. Nikon Micro-Nikkor 200mm f/4 lens. Exposure: f/20 at 1/100 second. **Image 5-146.** Nikon Micro-Nikkor 200mm f/4 lens. Exposure: f/29 at 1/100 second. **Image 5-147.** Nikon Micro-Nikkor 200mm f/4 lens. Exposure: f/36 at 1/30 second.

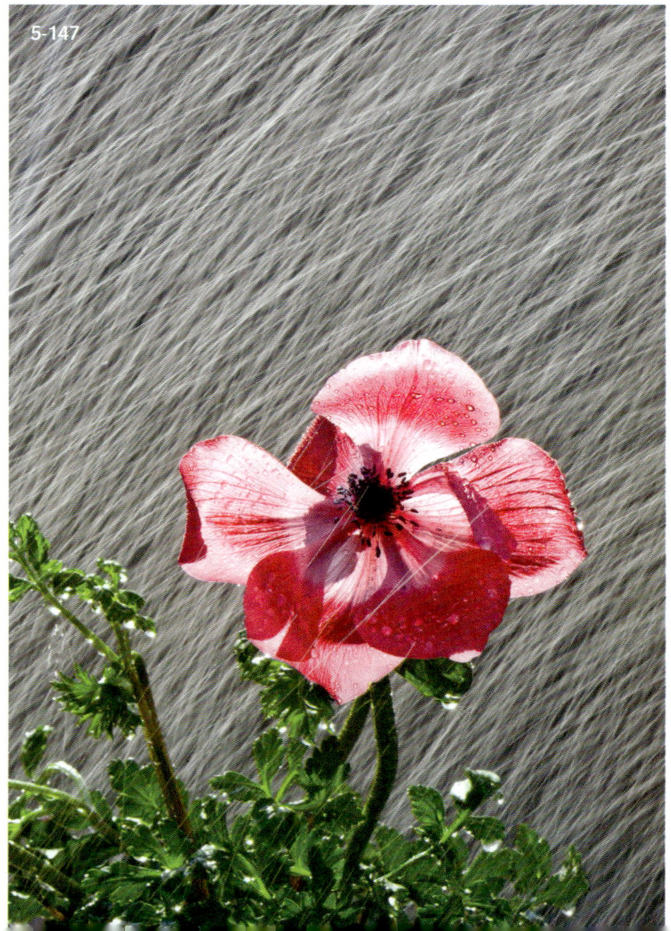

out of the shot. Using your cable release in the other hand, step to the side of your camera and keep your eye on the end of the lens to make sure you're shading the end of the lens. The advantage in using a gold reflector here is that it bounces some sunlight onto the front of the flower to fill in shadows, while it also serves as an effective lens shield.

Experiment with a wide range of shutter speeds, from $^1/_{30}$ to $^1/_{2000}$ second. You'll be amazed at how shutter speed can impact the way water is recorded in the background. (See **images 5-142** through **5-147**.)

You'll be amazed at how shutter speed can impact the way water is recorded in the background.

Resources

Inspiring Photographers

Sue Bishop—www.suebishop.com
Kathleen Clemons—www.kathleenclemonsphotography.com
Andre Gallant—www.andregallant.com
Frank Grisdale—www.frankgrisdale.com
Ernst Haas (deceased)
Denise Ippolito—www.deniseippolito.com
Mark S. Johnson—www.msjphotography.com
William Neill—www.williamneill.com
Freeman Patterson—www.freemanpatterson.com
Eva Polak—www.evapolak.com
Eliot Porter (deceased)
Nancy Rotenberg (deceased)
Les Saucier—www.appalachianjourney.com
John Shaw—www.johnshawphoto.com
Daniel Sroka—www.danielsroka.com
Tony Sweet—www.tonysweet.com
Minor White (deceased)

Equipment and Accessories

Nikon—www.nikonusa.com
Canon—www.usa.canon.com
Digital Photo Review—www.dpreview.com
LowePro (photo bags)—www.Lowepro.com
Kenko (extension tubes)—www.thkphoto.com
Joby (GorillaPod)—www.joby.com
Gitzo (tripods)—www.gitzo.com
Manfrotto (tripods)—www.manfrotto.com
Bogen Imaging (tripods)—www.bogenimaging.us
Kirk Enterprises (ballheads and lens plates)—
    www.kirkphoto.com
Really Right Stuff (ballheads and lens plates)—
    www.reallyrightstuff.com
Singh-Ray (filters)—www.singh-ray.com
Hoodman Corporation (LCD viewer and right-angle viewer)—
    www.hoodmanusa.com

Delkin Devices (sensor cleaning, memory cards)—
    www.delkin.com
Lensbaby—www.lensbaby.com
A. Laird Photo Accessories (macro ground cloth)—
    www.apogeephoto.com/laird_photo.htm
Lighthound (Fenix L1D flashlight)—www.lighthound.com
Optics Planet (flashlight accessories)—www.opticsplanet.com
Giottos (Rocket-Air blower for dust removal)—www.giottos.com
BorrowLenses.com (camera gear rental by mail)—
    www.borrowlenses.com
Pro Photo Rental (camera gear rental by mail)—
    www.prophotorental.com
Hunt's Photo & Video (family-run company with personalized
    customer service and competitive prices)—
    www.huntsphotoandvideo.com

Magazines and Newsletters

Outdoor Photographer—www.outdoorphotographer.com
Nature Photographer—www.naturephotographermag.com
Nature's Best—www.NaturesBestMagazine.com
Lenswork—www.lenswork.com
Digital Photo Pro—www.digitalphotopro.com
Photo Life—www.photolife.com
Photo District News—www.pdn-pix.com
Photograph America Newsletter—www.photographamerica.com
Photo Traveler Newsletter—www.phototravel.com
Shutterbug—www.shutterbug.net

Organizations

North American Nature Photography Association—
    www.nanpa.org
American Society of Media Photographers (ASMP)—www.asmp.org
National Association of Photoshop Professionals (NAPP)—
    www.photoshopuser.com
Professional Photographers of America (PPA)—www.ppa.com

Online Resources

Closer and closer (a huge macro photography group on Flickr)

MacroPhotography.org (articles, gallery, forum, and more)

Insect macro photography (very informative how-to on the subject)

Macro photography on a budget (get into macro photography without going broke)

Macro Photographers Flickr Pool

Macro Photos: No Limits

Water Macro Photography

Online nature photography forum— www.naturephotographer.net

Nikonians.org (Nikon community forum)—www.nikonians.org

Canon Digital Learning Center—www.usa.canon.com/dlc/

Digital Photo Review (digital equipment reviews)— www.dpreview.com

Digital SLR Gear (digital equipment reviews)—www.dslrgear.com

Fred Miranda (online photo community chock full of good info)— www.fredmiranda.com

Mac Rumors (all things Apple/Mac)—www.macrumors.com

Creative Techs (online photography classes)— www.creativetechs.com

Better Photo—(online photography classes) www.betterphoto.com

Note: Various photo accessories, specialized glass, and a glass stand are available ar www.charlesneedlephoto.com.

Miscellaneous

Glass stands—www.charlesneedlephoto.com

Iridescent glass (20x24-inch sheets)—www.charlesneedlephoto.com

Clear textured glass—www.charlesneedlephoto.com

Taleidoscopic lens— www.charlesneedlephoto.com

Multicolored LED flashlight— www.charlesneedlephoto.com

Shutter hat— www.charlesneedlephoto.com

Specialty papers—www.hyglossproducts.com or www.samflax.com

Copper leaf ornaments—www.naturesleaf.com

Plasticware for cross-polarization technique—www.partycity.com

Hammered copper pot—www.williams-sonoma.com

Michael's—www.michaels.com

JoAnn Fabric and Crafts Store—www.joann.com

Hobby Lobby—www.hobbylobby.com

Binders Art Supplies and Frames—www.bindersart.com

Pearl Fine Art Supplies—www.pearlpaint.com

Dick Blick Art Materials—www.dickblick.com

Dollar Tree Stores—www.dollartree.com

Antique stores

Inspiring Public Gardens

The Butchart Gardens (Victoria, B.C., Canada)— www.butchartgardens.com

Meadowlark Botanical Gardens (VA)— www.nvrpa.org/parks/meadowlark/

The Atlanta Botanical Garden (GA)— www.atlantabotanicalgarden.org

Callaway Gardens (GA)—www.callawaygardens.com

Bellevue Botanical Garden (WA)—www.bellevuebotanical.org

Monet's Garden (Giverny, France)—www.giverny.org/gardens

Keukenhof Gardens (Lisse, Holland)—www.keukenhof.nl/

Dunn Gardens (WA)—www.dunngardens.org

Stourhead Garden (England)— www.gardenvisit.com/garden/stourhead_garden

Sissinghurst Castle Garden (England)— www.nationaltrust.org.uk/sissinghurst/

Stowe Landscape Gardens (England)— www.nationaltrust.org.uk/main/w-stowegardens

Great Dixter Garden (England)—www.greatdixter.co.uk/

Royal Botanic Gardens, Kew (England)—www.kew.org

Pettifers Garden (England)—www.pettifers.com

Longwood Gardens (PA)—www.longwoodgardens.org

Biltmore Gardens (NC)—www.biltmore.com

Daniel Stowe Botanical Garden (NC)—www.dsbg.org

Kubota Garden (WA)—www.kubota.org

Bloedel Reserve (WA)—www.bloedelreserve.org

Portland Japanese Garden (OR)—www.japanesegarden.com

Bellingrath Gardens (AL)—www.bellingrath.org

Brookgreen Gardens (SC)—www.brookgreen.org

Magnolia Plantation Garden (SC)— www.magnoliaplantation.com

Middleton Place Garden (SC)—www.middletonplace.org

Shore Acres Gardens (OR)—www.shoreacres.net

Portland Classical Chinese Garden (OR)— www.portlandchinesegarden.org

New York Botanical Garden (NY)—www.nybg.org

Chicago Botanic Garden (IL)—www.chicagobotanic.org

Dallas Arboretum and Botanical Garden (TX)— www.dallasarboretum.org

Index